PEREGRINO

Peregrino

A Pilgrim Journey into Catholic Mexico

Ron Austin

WILLIAM B. EERDMANS PUBLISHING COMPANY

GRAND RAPIDS, MICHIGAN / CAMBRIDGE, U.K.

Wm. B. Eerdmans Publishing Co.

2140 Oak Industrial Drive N.E., Grand Rapids, Michigan 49505 /
P.O. Box 163, Cambridge CB3 9PU U.K.

Printed in the United States of America

16 15 14 13 12 11 10   7 6 5 4 3 2 1

Library of Congress Cataloging-in-Publication Data

Austin, Ron.

Peregrino: a pilgrim journey into Catholic Mexico / Ron Austin.

p.   cm.

Includes bibliographical references and index.

ISBN 978-0-8028-6584-7 (pbk.: alk. paper)

1. Catholic Church — Mexico — History.

2. Mexico — Church history.   I. Title.

BX1428.3.A97   2010

282′.72 — dc22

2010031091

www.eerdmans.com

Contents

Contents

Introduction

Peregrino means pilgrim, but it can also suggest someone who wanders purposefully. I first wandered purposefully in Mexico over fifty years ago when I made a documentary for American television about Mexican history.

The "new world" that the Spanish and others had discovered was pretty old by then, but it was new and wonderful to me. I traced Cortes's trail from Vera Cruz to the Valley of Mexico, filming historical and archeological sites, some of which had been only recently discovered. Over the many years since, I have wandered, not always purposefully, the length of Mexico from Sonora and the Sierra Madre Mountains to the *altos* of Chiapas and the ruins of Palenque. I subsequently lived in Mexico City for several years, working as a journalist. In that capacity, I conducted a series of interviews with various Mexican Catholic leaders and intellectuals. During the last decade, I have had the good fortune to reside in the *bajio,* the mountainous central area with its historic monuments and attractive colonial towns.

This book is meant to serve as a map for those open to wandering, spiritually and physically. I offer it as a sign along the trail for all *peregrinos,* and particularly for those who wish to venture into the Catholic culture of Mexico.

The term "pilgrim" isn't limited to those on a physical journey to holy places — though I'll describe and recommend such opportunities — but suggests our interior journey through life as well, and, in this case, our spiritual exploration of Mexico. I would hope that this journey would be for you what it was for me — a journey of body and soul.

When I first arrived in Mexico, I was a young man without religious faith; and now, after my own personal journey of many decades, I attend daily Mass at an eighteenth-century Mexican church. My view of Mexico and the Catholic faith is inseparable from my own personal experience. I don't write, then, as a neutral observer, nor as a scholar or tour guide, but as a *peregrino,* a pilgrim still on a journey — though now, perhaps, closer to the end of the trail. My viewpoint is not that of a Mexican, but of one whose personal faith and love of Mexico have become intertwined over many years.

I'm going to speak of "we" and "ours," but I want to be careful in doing so. I'm speaking as a Catholic, eager to share what the light of my faith reveals; but it is also my hope that this book might be of value to others making a similar journey, and of interest to anyone wishing to understand what I believe is the essential core of Mexican culture and history — that is, the beliefs and practices of Mexican Catholics.

The beliefs and teachings of the universal Church are contained in its Catechism, traditions, and the guiding interpretations of the Magisterium, and aren't altered by ethnicity or nationality. They are, nonetheless, often interpreted through a particular cultural lens. "Catholic" means "universal," but it also incorporates the particular. "Catholic Mexico" includes a unique historical experience, distinct cultural and spiritual practices, as well as symbols and words which are specific to the Mexican people.

Though the Gospels and the other writings in the Bible are revered as divinely inspired, the Catholic religion does not rest on a book, or even a particular reading of that book. The Catholic faith is about a Person and is based on the central Mysteries revealed by the person of Jesus Christ. For me, the *peregrino* experience offered, even forced, a paradigm shift, an exploration of a new relation with Christ, and in a manner that transcended my own culture and circumstances.

A paradigm shift produces surprise and sometimes discomfort. It is a radical change in perspective that can at times make the familiar seem new. What might we hope to learn from this experience as *peregrinos* in Mexico?

First, we must "open our eyes," and then remain open to the experience of Mystery. The central Mysteries of the Catholic faith — the Incarnation, Crucifixion, and Resurrection — are distinctive to Christianity; but the experience of Mystery — that is, a sense of something that is essential to our very being, yet transcends our full comprehension — is common to all traditional cultures. This universal experience has many variants, but is often described as "sacred" or "holy." Whatever the term, it persists throughout history as a basic, if not defining characteristic of human beings.

The experience of Catholic Mexico can not only open our eyes to the beauty and profundity of Mexican Catholic culture, but it can force us to view our own ideas in a different light. American popular culture is permeated with assumptions of superiority based on our advanced technology and the wealth and power it has produced. We have no reason to be ashamed of our accomplishments in industry and technology per se; but our use of this wealth and power has at times been inconsistent with our Christian values, and our extraordinary wealth tends to limit our vision. In any case, none of us can clearly see the world in which we live; and we sometimes take for granted a questionable "normality," or confuse the transitory with the everlasting. If we suffer from this kind of "blind eye," Mexico can help us to open it.

Mexican history reflects a quite different relationship, for instance, between Church and State, as well as the contrasting consequences of political revolutions, from its American counterpart. Mexican contemporary culture has also developed along quite different lines, dominated, as it has been, by an anti-clerical and even anti-religious elite, which looked to modern ideologies as alternatives to Catholicism. This secular "pretense of neutrality," as Octavio Paz, Mexico's great poet, described it, disguised many of the objectives of a political leadership divorced from its own religious tradition. To recognize this contradiction within Mexican history and culture may make us more aware of our American ones.

There are three threads of Mexican Catholic history that we will try to follow in our exploration. First and foremost is the "living history" of the lives and struggles of ordinary people. In this respect, we must remember that Mexicans, for all their appealing distinctiveness, are people like ourselves. They have many virtues; but in this life, none of us are angels.

The second historical strand is that of the Church as a sacramental and teaching institution, and, most especially, the role of the saints. The saints provide the true history of any Catholic people. They are the "red thread" of loving sacrifice that engenders the history of a nation and the light by which to understand that history.

The third thread is one still being woven; and that is the relationship between Mexicans and their often-dominant northern neighbors, the people of the United States. Beyond the familiar and often superficial comparisons, we need to see what we have in common as Christians, and how we can build a stronger bridge based on this shared faith.

However evaluated, the Catholic Church throughout the centuries has been the greatest experiment in human unity. This is primarily because it has not, in the long run of history, depended upon — indeed, could not depend upon — human power in terms of wealth or military might.

From the outset, St. Paul declared that within the Church there would be "neither Jew nor Greek" (that is, no test of race or ethnicity); "slave nor free" (no exclusion based on class, rich or poor); "male nor female" (no gender gap — many feel that we're still working on that one). The Church has persistently tried to be universal, rejecting distinctions that are fundamental to all other institutions, i.e., nationality, race, ethnicity, or class. It is a two-thousand-year-old "empire without an emperor or an army," and, as such, is historically unique.

Mexico and the United States are on the frontier of this experiment in spiritual unity. Both aspire to overcome barriers; and yet the very human impulse to unite as a people, a vision close to the heart of Christianity, can also create barriers of identity and even resentment. Our efforts to build a bridge between Americans and Mexicans do not arise, then, simply out of a desire to be good neighbors, but as a response to the demand that Christ placed upon all of us when He prayed to His Father: "Let them be one as you and I are One" (John 17:21).

The Paradigm Shift: Time, Identity, and Belief

I believe that if we are open to it, the paradigm shift of our Mexican journey will offer a different perspective regarding three concepts closely related to our Catholic beliefs: time, identity, and, perhaps, the nature of belief itself.

The Mexican experience of time, we will discover, is derived from their absorption of ancient indigenous cultures that existed long before the Spanish Conquest, the beliefs of which were based on a sense of cosmic time quite different than that derived from a European consciousness. The indigenous concepts of time related to their view of death as a natural part of the cosmic life cycle.

Mexican identity is itself radically new, the first new race, so to speak, to emerge from the New World. Our American identity, while also new, is more conceptual, based on a commitment to certain political ideals. How these two forms of identity relate to our Catholic faith might provoke some useful questions about the nature of a more fundamental and shared identity.

Religious belief among Mexican Catholics, as we shall see, is not so much based on abstract theories as it is on concrete relationships. Ideally, this should be true of all Christians. We Catholics should be, as the song says, "known by our love"; but, as we must admit, this is not always the case. The form the Catholic faith takes among common people, many still relatively uneducated, may provide some food for thought about the nature of religious commitment.

This change of perspective might also connect concepts of ritual, beauty, and memory in ways perhaps unfamiliar to our American perceptions. We must remember that some of the roots of Mexican Catholic culture are to be found in a syncretism, a mix of beliefs and practices, which was inescapable, given the historical circumstances.

As *peregrinos,* we are in a venerable Catholic tradition, found in the earliest desert experiences of the saints as well as those of the Spanish friars. We are seeking, as did they, constant renewal based on our understanding and experience of the Mysteries of our faith. Our journey to Mexico with open eyes and hearts can provide a rich opportunity to better understand all of our beliefs and teachings.

A Preface to History

In offering an interpretation of Mexican history, I make no pretense of neutrality nor will I hide my concerns behind a cloak of "objectivity." This is an effort to study events in Mexico and Spain from a religious point of view, and, most particularly, from a Catholic perspective. What does that mean? It does not mean a denial of the sins and errors of the Church — far from it. The mistakes that led to violence and the abuse of human rights in the name of Christ are painful to recount; but they provide the essential lessons of the past. *Where sin prevails, grace still more abounds,* St. Paul tells us (Rom 5:20); and where error is prevalent, the full and deepest truth must be vigorously sought.

Neither does this account attempt to present a Mexican or Spanish point of view. The task of telling the full story of their encounter must be left to those most formed by it. I seek a common denominator only in faith, compassion, and a hope for forgiveness.

From a Christian perspective, the true history of humanity is an inner history — that is, the ebb and flow of faith and belief as they interact with power. While we should respect secular scholarship, we must recognize that a religious view differs from most secular histories due to differing concepts of time. The sense of time as having meaning rooted in its ultimate end provokes different questions and offers a different context for judgment.

The question that Christ answers for us is not "why" but "how." *How* do we live our lives? *How* do we integrate death into life? Our pursuit of historical meaning is, therefore, a quest for redemption, requiring an assessment of time far beyond that of mere chronology. In that sense, our history is not one of powerful leaders, kings, generals, and presidents, or, for that matter, popes, but of the saints, known and anonymous. This "redemptive" approach will inescapably lead to different interpretations and conclusions than those proposed by mere chronology. So we proceed with great respect and indebtedness to the many historians and scholars who have chronicled the story of Mexico; but, in doing so, we must always try to address our own faith-based questions.

(We might note here, for our Mexican and other Spanish-speaking readers, that while we acknowledge that the term "American" applies to

Mexicans, and, for that matter, Canadians as well, there is no word equivalent to *estadounidense* — "citizen of the United States" — available to us in English.)

Beauty and Fear

An Introduction to the
Indigenous Period and Culture

D ue to the mistaken assumption that they had landed on the coast
of India, the European explorers originally called the indigenous
people they encountered "Indians." As do most commentators, including
Mexican, I will use the terms interchangeably; but the question remains:
If they weren't "Indians," who were these previously unknown people?

The dawn and the decline of the ancient Mesoamerican civilizations
remain mysterious; however, it is assumed that the prehistoric settlers in
the Americas most likely crossed the Bering Straits from Asia as early as
20,000 B.C. They were nomads and warriors who, then, over centuries,
developed highly advanced civilizations stretching from north of the Valley of Mexico to South America. It is estimated that the first agricultural
development in Mexico took place around 3500 B.C. One of the earliest
groups, the people later given the name Olmec, ruled the Gulf Coast
area from about 1200 to 900 B.C. The giant sculpted heads found in their
temple ruins, presumably figures of priest-rulers, have distinctly Asian
features, while the scale of the work suggests a historical parallel with ancient Egypt.

The civilization in the southern part of the continent, ranging from
below the Valley of Mexico to Central America, was primarily Mayan, a

group of city-states united by military alliances. These peoples built the elaborate pyramids, temples, and tombs that amaze visitors to this day. The Mayans created an advanced social and economic system comparable to Pharaonic Egypt or the Assyrian kingdoms, that is, around 1000 B.C. This was not a homogeneous people; but there was a shared common culture that lasted until about A.D. 900, a period longer than that of the Roman Empire.

There were actually several related cultures throughout the area of Mexico. There were the Totonecs on the coast; Tarascans centered in the middle, in what is now Michoacan; and Mixtec and Zapotec in the south, now Oaxaca. The more dominant and extensive civilizations that we commonly call Aztec and Mayan had conquered and absorbed many different tribes, most of which spoke different languages. Today, throughout Mexico, several indigenous languages are still spoken.

These ancient civilizations appeared before the time of Christ and then rather abruptly declined. By the ninth century A.D., they had collapsed. Their demise remains something of a puzzle, given the advanced state of their knowledge of mathematics and astronomy, and the vastness of their territory. It may have been, as anthropologists speculate, that a combination of civil wars and plagues or famines led to economic disintegration. At the time of the Spanish arrival, the initial explorers could not believe that the people they encountered, many of whom had regressed to the level of bare subsistence agriculture, had built the immense now-ruined temples and structures, such as Chichen Nitza or Palenque.

The later major civilization in the central area was located at Teotihuacan, the monumental ruins of which are near what is now Mexico City, and prospered from A.D. 250 to 600 when, perhaps due to internal strife and deforestation, it was apparently abandoned. The Toltecs followed the Teotihuacans. An aggressive northern tribe, usually called Aztecs, would eventually become rulers of the Valley of Mexico and create their own empire.

The Aztec empire was ruled by the Anahua or Nahua (Nahuatl-speakers), who assumed control of the remnant Toltec civilization. The Aztecs were, in this respect, similar to the Romans taking possession of Greek culture. To legitimize their predominance, these Aztec usurpers would "rewrite" the Toltec codices (pictograph histories) to promote their pre-eminence and then destroy the old ones. Sadly, the Spanish conquerors would subsequently also destroy almost all of these records, condemning them as demonic ciphers. The loss of this documentation made the later task of interpreting the shadowy indigenous history all the more difficult.

The Aztecs or Nahuas — a term now preferred by most scholars, as "Aztec" refers more to the empire than the culture — dominated the Valley of Mexico at the time of the Spanish Conquest. They were ruled by a royal line of warrior-priests who conducted frequent campaigns of conquest. The monarch that confronted the Spanish was Moctezuma II, who reigned over a vast empire of differing peoples and city-states. There were Aztec army garrisons in all of the large cities and increasingly burdensome taxes and tributes were collected from their subjugated neighbors. It was the defection of several of these vassal states that enabled the vastly outnumbered Spanish to eventually triumph. Most significantly, the Aztecs were rapidly increasing the number of human sacrifices in their temple rites. Contemporary anthropologists interpret this as indicative of a society in a state of precipitous decline.

Much of what we know, or presume to know, about the ancient civilizations of Mexico has been assembled in the twentieth century through archeological explorations and anthropological studies. There has also been an exhaustive academic study of source material, such as the records left by the early missionaries and colonists, as well as the comparatively fewer Nahua documents.

While we presume to have a more enlightened view than fifteenth- or sixteenth-century observers, we are looking at the fragmentary evidence of a distant past through our own filters, including our assumption of superior knowledge. A bit of humility might be in order as we undertake this part of the journey. The Spaniards of the *conquista* were far more familiar with the precepts of a warrior culture and, in many ways, closer to the indigenous spiritual sensibility than are present-day scholars. God's active presence in nature and human affairs would have been a shared assumption of both the conquerors and the conquered.

Our focus will go beyond the familiar and often tragic conflicts. We must probe what the indigenous and the Catholic intruders shared in common; for that was the ground on which Catholic Mexico was built. In doing so, we will not indulge in moral relativism nor romanticize the past, Spanish or indigenous. There was a profound clash between the beliefs of the Aztec or Mayan priests and the faith of the Catholic friars; and that prolonged conflict was as spiritually significant as the struggle between the tribes of Israel and the Canaanites.

We will first offer some generalizations about indigenous ancient religion, but with the customary caveat that there are always significant exceptions to generalizations.

The religious beliefs of the earliest Mesoamerican civilizations, such as the Toltec, cannot be separated from legend. However, scholars have noted contradictory aspects that suggest either deeply conflicting tendencies or devolution from a more pacific culture into a war-like one. On the one hand, there was an early belief in a singular creator God — "the God by whom we live" — even similar to that of the Hebrews, that is, invisible and benevolent. In time, however, gods of war became dominant, accompanied by numerous functional deities. There was also a remnant belief in a "golden age" of peace and prosperity ruled by a god or mythic figure, Quetzalcoatl, who, forced into exile, had vowed to return. Whatever the form, the indigenous were a deeply religious people with household gods in every home.

Some of the religious ceremonies and priestly practices also suggest at least the "seeds of Christianity." Marriage, funerals and the care of the dead, and naming ceremonies were conducted with careful reverence. Babies were sprinkled with water in a purification rite, and the priests heard a form of confession, particularly prior to death. There were a great many priests. According to the early historian Prescott, the Spanish counted five thousand in one large temple alone. Aztec clergy had varying ranks, though the priesthood, as such, was not related to noble birth. There is some evidence that the rulers and nobility, as with the Hebrews, were inclined to listen — at least at times — to the prophetic counsel and admonitions of the high priests. The life of the priest was one of prayer, fasting, and flagellation.

There was a fundamental dualism inherent in the religious concepts of these ancient cultures. Human life with its travails reflected a cosmic war among the gods. It was the human task to attempt to mediate or "balance" this celestial battle, primarily by appeasing the gods with the blood of human sacrifice. This practice was common for hundreds of years prior to the arrival of the Spanish; but during this era, the number of sacrificial victims had apparently grown considerably, estimated at not less than twenty thousand in a single year. The victims — men, women, and children — were often captives, the booty of the frequent wars, or unruly slaves. The sacrificial process, nonetheless, was clearly religious in nature. When the scarlet-clad high priest held the heart of the victim up to the sun, the crowds prostrated themselves in ritual adoration. It is not known how the authorities disposed of so many bodies, but a Spaniard reported counting over a hundred thousand human skulls in one temple.

Anthropologists have an increasingly clear view of the role of human sacrifice in social bonding and the subsequent need to rationalize this violence. The Aztec sacrificial ritual reflected their religion, but it was undoubtedly also inspired by a militarism stemming from nearly constant warfare. The Aztecs, as with many ancient peoples, could not conceive of a world without war and blood sacrifice.

The other aspect of this dualism was an inclination, perhaps echoing ancient Asian roots, to reject the present or "earthly" world as unreal. The indigenous religious language is highly poetic and speaks (or sings) of humans as only existing "to sleep, to dream," as "our bodies are but flowers."

The religion of the indigenous incorporated a rich mythology with primordial roots, which has been fruitfully explored by various scholars. Many of these myths suggest an underlying coherence, a systematic way of viewing the origins of life and seeking harmony with the cosmos. Myths of creation and destruction were thus related. There was an underworld, seen as both the place of human origin and a final destination, and there was a snake symbolizing primal sexuality. Among the myths was that of a place of repose for the souls of women who died in childbirth.

Rather than viewing these religious concepts of the Indians as utterly remote from those of the Europeans, we should note some important commonalities. As did many Greeks and Romans, the indigenous saw creation arising out of chaos. A series of catastrophes were anticipated that would end in destruction. We can recognize this as a kind of native Manichaeanism, a view that creation itself was hopelessly fallen and corrupt, and human life governed by relentless Fate — again, a view not uncommon to the ancient thinkers of the Mediterranean world.

We should also recognize that what the early Catholic missionaries confronted was a society far more vital than that depicted in the various reconstructions of twentieth-century anthropologists. These could only study what was left of a ceremonial and ritual life stemming from the beliefs of a long-vanished civilization. Nevertheless, contemporary researchers, to the best of their ability, have provided a fairly complete picture of a highly ritualized and communal nature religion.

The Aztec gods were deified aspects of the Sun, Earth, and, particularly, Lightning, which constituted a whole class of spirits, including those of war, death, fire, and rain. Their elaborate rituals included the preparation of food and items for the dead in their trip "below." This included forms of "speaking to the dead" and the ritual employment of animals as guardian spirits. Dogs were of particular importance, as they served to carry the dead across the rivers of the underworld. As did the people of the Bible, the indigenous incorporated dreams and visions as well as stories into their religion, such as those of ancestors turned to stone.

Many of these beliefs and rituals are similar to those of the ancient Egyptians and Greeks, reflecting the universal character of human needs, the various appeals to the gods, the meticulous care for the dead and concerns as to the nature of the afterlife.

Much of Aztec labor, including that of slaves, was devoted to temple building as well as communal field work and the maintenance of gardens that provided flowers and plants for religious purposes. The rich mix of ritual and decoration — *cantos y flores* (songs and flowers) — became, and remains, a characteristic of Mexican religious culture.

Significantly, a point emphasized by many historians, the Aztecs believed in a central god, Quetzalcoatl, represented by a plumed serpent, who had vowed to return at a propitious moment. There has been more speculation than consensus about the degree to which the appearance of the Spanish might have been related to this anticipated epiphany in the minds of the Aztecs.

A more notorious aspect of the Aztec religion involves their cult of human sacrifice to a sun god, practiced on an altar of skulls. Human sacrifice was clearly an essential part of the ritual process, and the source of the Spanish conviction that they were dealing with the demonic. There is evidence that child sacrifice, probably to a serpent god, was still part of the rituals at the time of the Spanish arrival. These practices, so shocking to the Spanish, correspond to the pre-Abrahamic period in the common history of Jews and Christians. One of the great turning points in human history was the Israelite conviction that God did not seek or desire human sacrifice. The Spaniards, however, did not have a modern developmental view of religion and culture. Human sacrifice was, for them, simply clear evidence of the presence of Satan and evil spirits at the heart of Aztec culture.

Again, we might wish to be cautious about quick judgments condemning elements of what we might now view as mere superstition. A personalized evil, such as a devil figure, for example, may strike us today as a crude medieval conception; but it may actually be closer to human experience than our abstract notions of sin and evil. Evil is not something out of a book.

While Aztec society has been compared by historians to that of the ancient Egyptians, or by some to "oriental" cultures marked by both elaborate decorum and cruel despotism, the more striking comparison, in many ways, is, as we shall see, with their conquerors, the Castilians from Spain. Both were warrior cultures, with religious beliefs that justified the conquest of others, including their closest neighbors. The highest public honor was reserved for warriors, including kings and priests who died in battle, who won the crown of martyrdom in a holy crusade.

Glory in Decline

Spain at the Time of the Conquest

To understand the nature of what was to be called *Nueva Espana* or the New Spain, which, in time, became Mexico, we must examine Spanish culture at the time of the Conquest and its aftermath — that is, during the fifteenth and sixteenth centuries. This seemingly glorious period of the Catholic kings of Spain was, in fact, marked by profound inner struggles and contradictions. It was a time of severe social conflicts and agonizing spiritual doubt played in counterpoint to great achievements.

To see the violent and often tragic encounter of Spanish Catholics with the primarily Aztec and Mayan indigenous peoples from only one perspective — either as the salvation of the Indian soul through the Christian faith, or as the imposition of foreign beliefs on a conquered people — distorts our understanding of the process. It is to miss the complex, miraculous nature of birth.

The Spanish Conquest of Mexico, the *conquista*, was completed by 1521 when Hernando Cortes established his headquarters in what is now Mexico City. In that the military conquest and incipient rule of Mexico by Cortes and his *conquistadores* is well chronicled, let us simply note some significant signpoints.

A dozen Franciscan friars, known as "the twelve apostles," were the first missionaries to arrive shortly after Cortes and, despite the language and cultural barriers, aggressively baptized thousands of Indians. The Franciscans, many of whom were uncompromising radicals called "spirituals," were followed by Dominicans, Augustinians, Salesians, Oratorians, Jesuits, and several other orders and congregations, all of whom played important roles in laying the foundation of Catholic belief.

In 1531, just a decade after the completion of the Conquest, a vision of the Virgin Mary, subsequently known as "the Virgin of Guadalupe," appeared to the indigenous Catholic convert Juan Diego. Three hundred years later, her image on banners and battle flags would unite all the people and create "Mexico." Four centuries after the miracle, Juan Diego would be recognized by the Church as a saint.

In response to the moral questions raised by the Conquest, Pope Paul III decreed in 1537 that the indigenous peoples were fully human and to be treated as such — an opinion in striking contrast to those of most of the "advanced" thinkers of that day. Most importantly, the decree meant that the Indians were to be instructed before baptism. This meant that, out of necessity, priests began to systematically study the indigenous languages and way of life.

By the 1700s, missionary priests such as Padres Kino and Serra had spread the faith and founded communities as far north as California and Arizona. These missionary efforts produced many disputes between the Church and the Spanish Crown over questions of control, as well as rivalry between and within the various religious orders. Many of the political and spiritual conflicts within Spain itself would have a lasting impact on colonial Mexico. For example, one of the consequences of the internal strife within the Catholic world was the expulsion of the Jesuits from Mexico in 1757, an event, given their extensive educational outreach, which would have far-reaching consequences for the development of Mexican culture.

The Golden Age of Spain

Given the military defeats and economic crises, much modern historical writing, especially in English, depicts sixteenth- and seventeenth-century

Spain primarily in terms of decline. Historical perspectives, however, shift over time. While it is true that during this period there was a growing climate of pessimism within Spain itself, there was simultaneously a flowering of high culture. One might even ask whether such turmoil wasn't a stimulus for great art; historians recognize the early seventeenth century as the "Golden Age" of Spanish art and literature.

The best-known artworks are the paintings of El Greco, Velasquez, Zurbaran, and Murillo, regarded as among the highest achievements in European art. The literary giant Miguel de Cervantes has been widely acknowledged as the creator of the first novel, in that his long tale of "the knight of the sad countenance," *Don Quixote de la Mancha,* published in two parts in 1605 and 1615, transcended the literary forms of the past. It is a story both contemporary and timeless, which merged the elite and popular cultures of that age.

The writings of Cervantes, Quevedo, and Gongora, and the plays of Lope de Vega, Calderon, and Tirso de Molina, constitute the canon of classic Spanish literature, much as does the work of their contemporaries, Shakespeare and Donne, in the English-speaking world.

The Cross and the Sword:
The Historical Background of Spanish Catholicism

The origins of the Spanish Catholicism practiced during the time of the Conquest lie as much in legend as in history. Is it historical fact or legend that St. James, rendered in Spanish as *Santiago,* came to Spain during the apostolic era? It is probably a mixture of both. Whether the saint himself came, or members of his community at some later date appeared as missionaries, can't be known. In any case, it is hard to reconcile the warrior-saint, *Santiago Matamoros,* "the killer of Moors," with Jesus' "brother" who, in his New Testament epistle, warns us not even to speak an evil word against others! During the sixteenth century, a relatively short time after her death, St. Teresa of Avila was made the co-patroness of Spain, an act that displeased some of the devotees of *Santiago.* His tomb at Compostela remains a major center of Catholic devotion.

The Catholic Church of Spain was, and remains, an organic part of the universal Church, and a larger sense of Church history is required to understand the Spanish circumstances.

What was called the Holy Roman Empire originated in the rule of Charlemagne, crowned in A.D. 800. Previously, the papacy in Rome had been weakened through clashes with the Byzantine East, rival bishops, and threats by Arabs, Vikings, and Magyars. After Charlemagne, the papacy began a long period of dependency on secular imperial power, and often suffered from the incessant rivalries and resulting instability. In the tenth century, there were more than thirty popes seated on the throne of Peter. Many were installed by powerful Roman families, and a full third of them were deposed or even murdered. Western Europe was beginning, virtually, a thousand years of internecine warfare.

The Church survived, as it always has, by strategically retreating from the world of power and corruption. Over time, it was revived at its farthest periphery by monasteries and ascetic communities, such as those in Ireland, Citeaux, and Monte Casino. In the year 910, William, prince of Aquitaine, founded the monastery at Cluny, which would become a major center of Catholic learning and culture. Cluniac monks would play a role in the early development of Spanish Catholicism, serving as guides on the "milky way," the road across the Pyrenees to Compostela and the devotion to *Santiago*.

The restoration of an effective papacy didn't occur until the eleventh century with the emergence of strong leaders, such as Leo IX and Gregory VII, who initiated the "Gregorian reforms" that established new procedures for papal elections and reaffirmed religious vows such as priestly celibacy. Most significantly, Gregory liberated the Church to some degree from imperial power, asserting not only the independence of the Church but papal authority to depose emperors! Later popes would be forced to compromise their political rights and authority, but the division of power between Church and empire was being formalized.

The empire and the Church were further linked together during the Crusades, the wars in and for the Holy Land. We lament the violent and sordid aspects of the Crusades; but they were initiated for understandable reasons, in particular, the attacks by armed Muslim forces on Christian pilgrims, the destruction of the Church of the Holy Sepulcher in Jerusalem, and the appeal of the Byzantine emperor for help. However legitimate these motives, the Crusades frequently degenerated into fanatical and mercenary campaigns. The Crusades would last for four hundred years and their effects are with us to this day.

The epoch A.D. 800 to 1300 marked the height of medieval Europe, a five-hundred-year period culminating in the Catholic high culture of the twelfth century. This was the time of the founding of great centers of learning, such as the University of Paris, and the height of Scholasticism. Saints appeared, such as Bernard of Clairvaux, Thomas Aquinas, Francis, Clare, King Louis of France, and the Spanish-born St. Dominic, founder of the Order of Preachers, the Dominicans.

This rich period remained, however, a time of theocratic kings, constant wars, and, again, instability in the Church. In the twelfth century alone, there were no fewer than seven "anti-popes," that is, rival claimants to the papacy endorsed by secular powers. In 1215, the Fourth Lateran Council, attended by kings and laity as well as clergy, attempted to spell out the duties of bishops and the religious requirements of the laity, such as the obligation of yearly confession. Conflicts, internal and external, nevertheless continued.

The most serious internal division in the Church, the so-called "Babylonian Captivity," was occasioned by a successful campaign on the part of the French monarch to gain control over the papacy. For more than seventy years, the popes, or claimants to the papacy, resided in Avignon, a state of affairs that did not end until 1415, at the Council of Constance. There were many attempts at reform during this period, but they came too late to prevent the decisive split in Christendom. In 1517, a German Augustinian monk, Martin Luther, initiated the Reformation, which led to the breakup of the universal Church.

The Rise of the Catholic Monarchs of Spain

During the long period that we've outlined, the Catholics of the Iberian Peninsula were ruled by Muslims. It can be argued that the Roman Catholic Church, that is, what was originally the western half of the universal Church, was itself, in many ways, formed out of a struggle with an aggressive and expanding Islam. In any case, this was certainly true of Spanish Catholicism.

It is not until the last half of the fifteenth century that we see the rise of the Spanish Catholic monarchs, beginning with Isabel and Ferdinand. At this time, the popes were functioning much as did secular princes ruling city-states, and were acting largely in self-defense, no longer able to command or control others. Thus, they turned for assistance to Spain, now emerging as the most powerful Catholic empire since Charlemagne.

Again, the broader context of Church history is necessary to understand developments in Spain.

During the early period of the Spanish Conquest, the pope was Leo X, a Medici, son of Lorenzo the Magnificent, but himself weak and indecisive. Confronted with Luther and the revolt of the German princes, he also looked to Spain for assistance. Later, Pope Adrian VI, who had played a decisive role in Spain, a development we'll examine later, faced even more numerous problems. There was a conflict with France as well as within Rome itself, and the Ottoman Turks, under Suleiman the Magnificent, were threatening Vienna.

Despite their vulnerability, this was the opulent era of the Renaissance popes, mostly educated, cultured men from elite Italian families. They sponsored great classical art, such as the works of Raphael and Michelangelo, but their concerns were often more worldly than spiritual. The growing wealth and luxury within the Church had a corrupting influence, even on popes such as Sixtus IV, once the superior of the Franciscans and known for his personal virtues. Ensnared in the intrigues over family power, Sixtus appointed numerous relatives to high Church positions; nepotism such as this would plague the papacy for decades. Paul III, a central figure in the post-conquest period, was a member of the powerful Farnese family. He was another great patron of the arts, but his rule was also marred by nepotism. Nonetheless, he proved to be an effective leader and, as we've seen, made the important proclamation on the full humanity of the Indians.

Perhaps the most notorious figure of the time was the Borgia pope, Alexander VI, who fathered several children and whose excesses led to the radical denunciations of the Florentine monk Savonarola. Yet, at a point when the Church seemed a prisoner of its own wealth and power, a renewal of spirit began. While Spain was consolidating its rule in the New World, over an eighteen-year period, 1545 to 1563, the historic Council of Trent took place. This was a turning point for the Church and the beginning of the Counter-Reformation, the historic response of the Catholic Church to Protestantism.

The Counter-Reformation undertook during this period many important reforms and clarified Catholic doctrines. It was also a time of strict — indeed, restrictive — morality, including the expulsion of prostitutes from the cities. The Index, established to censor books, appeared, and the Inquisition relentlessly probed heresies. Nonetheless, from 1572 to 1585, Pope Gregory XIII — influenced by the great reformer of the time, Cardinal Charles Borromeo, later canonized — established Rome as a center of clerical reform and education. Papal nuncios were created to represent the Vatican, and many of these innovations created lasting norms for the entire Church.

Secular and scientific education was encouraged; but devotions to saints, old and new, also flourished. Catholic religious practices, such as the devotion to the Sacred Heart, novenas, and the Angelus became universal. The Turkish defeat at the sea battle of Lepanto had led to the Feast of Our Lady of Victory, which, in turn, inspired devotion to Our Lady of the Rosary. The rosary, introduced by the Dominicans, became a normative feature of Catholic prayer life.

Beginning in 1493 with Pope Alexander VI, who granted Spain exclusive rights to evangelize the New World, political ties between the Spanish Crown and the papacy were long and deep. In 1508, Pope Julius II, desperate for Spanish military help in troubled Italy, extended the Spanish Crown's control over ecclesial affairs by decreeing the *Patronato*, the unique right of the king to have control over the Church in the New World, as well as access to its resources. No priest or friar could travel to New Spain without royal warrant.

The extent to which the Spanish Crown and the papacy became intertwined during this era is illustrated by the extraordinary role played by Adrian of Utrecht. When the Habsburg dynasty assumed the Spanish throne in the person of Carlos V, the foreign advisors to the king, primarily Flemish, soon dominated the Church as well. The Grand Chamberlain Chievres assumed control of Castile; made his sixteen-year-old nephew Archbishop of Toledo; and Adrian, the king's special agent to Spain prior to his ascendancy, Bishop of Tortosa. Adrian, the king's tutor, would also be appointed Inquisitor General of Aragon. He would then, with the king's assistance, go on to become Pope Adrian VI.

As pope, Adrian would reward the Spanish Crown richly, allowing it one-third of the Church tithes *(tercias reales)* as well as revenues derived from Church land and property. These holdings were then used by the Crown as security for bank loans to fund the growing military expenditures. For its part, the Crown allowed the Church to accumulate land with few restrictions, as Church property could be more easily taxed.

This alliance of power and wealth did not mean that the clergy were indifferent to the rights and needs of their common flock. Examples abound of churchmen and women "speaking to power," such as the Bishop of Gerona, who protected a rebellious town population from military reprisals by excommunicating all of the troops! The sincere though ultimately futile attempts at social reform made by King Felipe IV were aided by his spiritual advisor, known as the "remarkable nun," Sor Maria de Agreda.

No one familiar with the history will dispute that, in many ways, Spanish Catholicism is unique. Spanish religious sensibilities had been forged during several centuries of imposed rule, first by the Visigoths, who were Arians and thus heretics from the universal Church viewpoint, and then by Muslims. Undoubtedly, there were Jewish influences as well. We must remember that Spain was the center of a twelfth-century Jewish religious renaissance graced by innovative thinkers, such as Maimonides.

In some ways, the Spanish were a culturally colonized people who had become colonizers. The Spanish resistance to change is easier to understand when one realizes how inherently fragile their identity was, and how the conflict between power and faith became infused with a desperate desire for an elusive unity. There was, of course, strength and vibrancy in the heritage as well. As we shall see later in examining Mexico's religious culture, religious belief was expressed primarily in terms of images, rituals, and gestures. Spanish Catholicism also brought with it a vivid and concrete experience of suffering, identified with the crucified Christ, and sought the consolation of the Virgin Mary. This consolation would be sorely needed by both the peoples brought together in New Spain.

We might also note the role of Spanish and, later, Mexican women in maintaining the Catholic faith, and, indeed, orthodoxy. Spanish women such as the nun Egeria, also known as "Sylvia," who left a valuable diary of her pilgrimage to Jerusalem in A.D. 383, were significant figures. This feminine aspect of Catholicism has been carried over into Mexican culture. The qualities of humility and forgiveness were forged by the experience of God's love under extraordinary circumstances. The unique Christian experience of finding God's grace in profound suffering is thus part of the Spanish heritage, evident in the unrelenting, even extreme depiction of suffering in Spanish religious art.

The Spanish Religious Orders

The emergence of new spiritual movements — many of which exist to this day — is the most lasting feature of the Spanish Catholicism of this time. These movements not only served the most needy but, theologically and spiritually, led to a recognition of another level of reality. The Dominicans, the Carmelites, the Jesuits — these are Spain's lasting gift to the Church and humanity.

Among the first of the many inspiring leaders during the era we're examining was St. John of God (1485-1550), a Portuguese who founded the Hospitaller order (today known as the Hospitaller Brothers of St. John of God) to provide medical care for the poor, and was spurned in his time as a madman. The most prominent and influential saint of the era was Teresa of Avila, who inspired reforms within the Carmelite order. She began her work in 1562, and by the time she died twenty years later, she had established dozens of convents and priories, numbering over eighty by the 1590s. During that time, however, there was a revolt within her order, just as there had been dissent among the Franciscans immediately after Francis's death. Similarly, her friend and confessor, St. John of the Cross, who followed Teresa in urging reforms, was jailed by his fellow monks for his efforts. Saints are demanding, and sanctity is not created merely by reform.

It is said that St. Ignatius of Loyola, when a soldier at the court of Queen Isabel, was a member of the royal cortege accompanying her body back to the capital. The sight of the decomposition of the once-beautiful queen is reported to have initiated Ignatius's conversion. He was, in time, the founder of the Society of Jesus, the Jesuits. We will examine the influence of the Jesuits in New Spain in upcoming chapters.

As we shall see, these Spanish religious orders were to provide the foundations of the religious culture of Mexico. If there was one dominant figure in Spanish religious culture at the time, however, it was a woman, the *patrona* of Spain, St. Teresa of Avila.

St. Teresa of Avila

St. Teresa of Avila, known also by her religious name Teresa of Jesus, was born in Avila, Spain, on March 28, 1515. Her parents were Alfonso de Cepeda and his wife Beatriz. But there is already a story in the name.

Her paternal grandfather, Juan Sanchez of Toledo, was a *converso*, a Jew who had converted to Catholicism. He was accused in 1485 of heretical leanings, and did penance. The *conversos,* no matter how faithful (many became priests and even bishops), were always under suspicion in these troubled times of being "secret Jews," that is, covertly practicing their original faith. Following this, Juan Sanchez moved his family to Avila and, securing a higher position, took his wife's surname and became Don Juan de Cepeda. His son Alfonso was Teresa's father. The family prospered in Avila but, undoubtedly, their status as *conversos* would always mean an uncertain future. Teresa's brothers were thus among those who sought a future in the New World, and at least one, apparently, made his fortune there.

The details of her childhood and later life can be found in several biographies; but it is clear that Teresa was a lively young woman, high-spirited to the point of being willful. In fact, she defied her father by becoming a nun. This steely determination eventually transformed her life into one of sanctity, and would, indeed, transform many other lives as well. Her disciple St. John of the Cross followed in her steps as a reformer as well as becoming one of the first great poets in the Spanish language.

The forcefulness of Teresa's faith and personality is such that those writing about her occasionally strike a cautionary note: "Be careful that she doesn't overwhelm you!" Her writings are contemplative in the highest sense, but they are not placid. These are not always calm waters on which to drift. (One can only speculate, for instance, on the effects of St. Teresa's intense spirituality on the highly sensitive spirit of Sor Juana Ines de la Cruz, the great Mexican poet, who esteemed Teresa as her spiritual "mother." We will do so in a later chapter.)

St. Teresa's writings were extensive and among the most influential of her age. We will later examine the controversy regarding Sor Juana's cessation of her writing. She was encouraged by her religious superiors to cease writing at least secular works. Teresa's confessors did the opposite. Fortunately for the generations to come, they commanded her to write and she did so.

Undeterred by the occasional restraints of her superiors, Teresa's spiritual life became increasingly intense. Always charting a risky course, she experienced rapturous or ecstatic states, captured by the sculptor Bernini in his famous piece *Saint Teresa in Ecstasy.* That these states were akin to physical, even sexual experience was openly recognized even in those pre-Freudian times. Teresa herself admits that the comparison of the spiritual and the corporeal might at times be "coarse," but sexual union remains for many poets and artists an analogy of the divine union with God.

Like others throughout the ages, I have found her work to be inspiring and spiritually challenging. For me, she is "the mistress of the Present Moment" in that she sees, hears, tastes everything in the immediate moment. She lives in a way that unites her not only with God, but with nature and the human body. She persists in finding God in ordinary life, and, celebrating the "daily bread" of a meal, exulted that "God walks in the pots and pans." But she paid an enormous price — "everything" — for this relationship.

She was known as the most practical of the saints and scorned what she saw as the excessive spirituality of her day, writing, "God deliver me from people so spiritual that they want to turn everything into perfect contemplation, no matter what." Yet what she called her "Royal Road" was decidedly mystical, the experience of the miracle and mystery of the inner life.

St. Teresa's best known works include *The Interior Castle, The Way of Perfection,* and her spiritual biography; her writings also include numerous letters, poetry, and critiques. There are several excellent collections and translations of her writings included in the bibliography.

St. Teresa suffered serious illnesses throughout her life and died in 1582. She was canonized in 1622, and in 1970 Pope Paul VI declared her a Doctor of the Church, a recognition of the mystical-theological dimension of her work as well as its inspirational side. She was the second woman, with St. Catherine of Siena, to be so recognized.

Listening to St. Teresa

I have selected, and sometimes paraphrased, just a few of St. Teresa's thoughts. There are also several other citations in the chapter on Sor Juana.

> God gives us more than we ask — Himself!
> He gives beyond what we ask, which is for the wrong thing. We ask for too little!
> Don't be frightened by your spiritual thirst. We cannot put water into the well.
> Be patient with your wandering mind. He will understand us. God doesn't want us to be breaking our heads trying to speak a great deal to Him. It isn't necessary to shout.
> Pray with longing, not words.
> Don't worry about "thinking" about humility — God will provide!
> Don't think that a spiritual life will spare you from desire and fear.
> To desire to be an angel when we are on earth is foolishness.
> It is wonderful to see how the Lord mixes sorrows and joys.
> Praise the Lord for the desire you have to pray.
> A soul must not only walk, but fly!

Power and Dread: The Spanish Inquisition

The Inquisition is a bloody thread that runs throughout most histories of Spain and Mexico, and in many Mexican cities there remains a "house of the Inquisition," an historic building preserved as a museum. As fearsome as the Inquisition undoubtedly was, many misconceptions remain. Some of these misconceptions are related to what is called "the Black Legend," propaganda promoted by Spain's political rivals, which spread the idea of a presumably unique "Spanish" cruelty. Portrayed usually as a kind of institutional torture chamber, the Inquisition was, in fact, an official tribunal that investigated charges of heresy and disloyalty. There is no question that the standards of evidence were appalling from a rational, humane point of view, and often did involve torture and threats of death.

The Inquisition originated in Italy as a means of investigating the heretical views of the Cathars, a sect in France in the twelfth and thirteenth centuries. As an official "Holy Office" of the Church, the Inquisition eventually exercised its jurisdiction throughout Europe, but is most often associated with Spain, although it did not come to Castile until the 1480s. Once in Spain, the Inquisition took on a uniquely invasive character, primarily aimed at the great number of Jewish converts, the *conversos,* and was a potent weapon used by those who resented their success and influence. A heresy allegation was a convenient means of extortion and revenge. It also at times provided a form of political coercion used by Castile against other rival powers.

While led by a clerical Grand Inquisitor, the Inquisition was often more the punitive arm of the Crown than of the Church. It functioned primarily to preserve the existing order by attempting to arrest change. That it was primarily the instrument of the Spanish Crown was illustrated by Felipe II's decree that all final decisions of the Inquisition were in the hands of his appointed Grand Inquisitor, and not the pope.

Among the new ideas that seemed dangerous, if not heretical, to the established order at one time included concepts of "interior prayer" as practiced by St. Teresa, and the apocalyptic notions of the Franciscans under the influence of the charismatic visionary monk Joachim of Fiore. These radical friars, often in tension with their own order, were the earliest missionaries in New Spain. The rational humanism of Erasmus, influenced by Greco-Roman philosophy, also became a target of the Inquisition. These disputes, seemingly over doctrine and even rather obscure theological questions, were as much about politics as religion, and emanated from tensions between the Crown and the Church. Carlos's heir, Felipe II, was eager to increase his royal power at the expense of the papacy. Spain's unsurpassed military might provided the pope, ever vulnerable to secular foes, with protection while the king was always in need of Church revenues. The Inquisition, frequently employed as a weapon in these endless conflicts, had a long arm that could reach even to high positions in the Church. Cardinal Carranza, the highly respected Archbishop of Toledo, was arrested in 1559 under suspicion of heresy, unproven charges based on his foreign travel and contacts. Despite his prestigious position — he had been a delegate at the Council of Trent and spiritual advisor to Mary Tudor — he spent most of the rest of his life in prison.

The Inquisition, a sign of the growing insecurity of the Spanish empire, came to Mexico as early as 1571 and, though diminishing in power, would operate until 1820. Its many abuses in Mexico included a form of blackmail and legalized robbery. If a person was convicted of heresy, his or her entire family was at risk of losing their property. The temptation to gain wealth or revenge through anonymous, contrived, and false charges was obvious.

The evils of the Inquisition were many, including its use of fear and ignorance as propaganda against the enemies of the Church. The greatest abuse of the Inquisition was not, however, the one most commonly assumed. The means of torture at its disposal, such as fire or "the rack," however horrific, were neither original nor unusual for the time, and, as historians have noted, the numbers of executions were relatively few. The French Revolution, in the name of justice and equality, killed more innocent people in one week than the Inquisition did in all the centuries of its existence.

The worst crimes of the Inquisition were spiritual. By accepting anonymous accusations and testimony as part of its legal arsenal, it set neighbor against neighbor and spread a climate of fear and suspicion that was subversive not only to any notion of Christian community, but to civilization itself. What is extraordinary is that many otherwise thoughtful and pious clerics approved of it. The concept that "error has no rights" was used as a weapon against the freedom of conscience for some time to come; but this fear of free thought, in that it ultimately denies the freely chosen love of God, is itself, ironically, profoundly "heretical."

If there is a lasting lesson for us as Catholics, however, it is to recognize that the Church's indisputable culpability in the often cruel excesses of the Inquisition is rooted in its allowing itself to become an instrument of unlimited earthly power.

Spanish Religious Ritual

An examination of Spanish religious rituals of this era reveals a fragile human dimension that can be found, to varying degrees, in all cultures. Religious ceremony is not simply a matter of shared faith, belief, and inspiration, but is inseparable from social bonds and purposes. Religion as a social institution is as sacred — and as imperfect — as we who are part of it. It can bind or separate, even preserve our innocence, but, more often than not, includes an attempt to alleviate our guilt.

Cervantes, in *Don Quixote,* lamented how wealth had gradually replaced virtue as a goal and ideal. It is as if the flow of silver from the New World was as lethal to the Spanish soul as the epidemics carried by the Europeans were to indigenous bodies. The corruption of wealth brought, among other anxieties, a fear of rebellion as the gap between social classes grew.

The festivals — the *fiestas* — were not simply religious observances, but served to unify the Spanish as they would, later, Mexicans. The major festival — particularly the elaborate processions of *Corpus Christi,* still a tourist attraction in cities such as Seville — produced a kind of religious frenzy of collective expiation and, thus, a ritual of social unity. As the social tensions grew within Spain, including an increasing distance between the Habsburg kings and the Spanish people, the *fiestas* grew more elaborate. The long processions established social rank and with ornate costumes, masks, statues, and symbols, offered a kind of visual sacred history.

As with the earliest ceremonies of Eastern Christianity, what was of vital importance was for the king or emperor to be legitimized as God's representative by the blessings of the high clergy. The medieval world, with its fixed social positions, was meant to reflect, indeed, represent, an equally fixed divine order. As the spiritual dimension diminished and the social order weakened, the riotous carnival replaced the intensity of the religious festival — still offering catharsis, but of a more Dionysian variety. We must remember that ritual is not a lesser language, merely a different one.

The "other side" of the *fiesta,* and of religion itself, was the purging of a sense of collective sin through the ritual sacrifice of a victim, a scapegoat. This scapegoating process is at the root of all prejudice because the element of judgment is spurious. A judicial proceeding can disguise the real purpose, which is a ritual purging and catharsis for which a victim, someone to be blamed, is essential. The culpability of the victim is irrelevant to the process. Actual guilt serves only as a convenience.

The quasi-judicial ceremony in Spain was provided by the Inquisition, which employed a ceremony called an *auto-da-fe* ("act of faith"). This was a mass gathering, presumably for the judging and condemnation of a heretic. Its central feature was a sermon preached by an inquisitor. The *auto-da-fe* was a highly participatory event, but not to be confused with a mock trial or a lynching. The victim, the presumed heretic, was often an active participant, and the crowd wept and tore their hair as the sins of the victim were recited. It was, in a sense, a perverse form of compassion as the purpose was not punishment but, again, collective expiation. The *auto-da-fe* of the Inquisition was, in reality, a rendition of the ancient sacrificial rituals out of which the earliest forms of religion emerged. Its most striking, if not horrific, aspect was its unconscious imitation of the Crucifixion.

If condemned to death, the victim was taken outside the city gates to be executed by civil authorities, as an inquisitor could not shed blood. The death by asphyxiation, the *garrote,* was seen in those times as a merciful form of death. Some of the crowd would gather to watch the burning of the body and the scattering of the ashes; but the mood was repentant, not celebratory.

While some of the victims were defiant, therefore automatically condemning themselves to death, others openly confessed their sins. Again, this demonstrates that this was not a judicial process, but an ancient expiation ritual in which the condemned, even if innocent, could find collective affirmation, if not meaning in their deaths. However distorted, redemption was the purpose, not justice.

We should avoid any dubious moral relativism; but it is hard not to see some parallels between these ritual proceedings that unified the in-

creasingly unstable medieval Spanish society and the human sacrifices offered to their quarrelsome gods by the anxious Aztecs. The *conquistidores*
were naturally appalled at the Aztec practices, but would have been even
more disturbed, one imagines, had they noticed even this slight similarity
with their own public rituals.

The highly theatrical nature of events such as the *Corpus Christi* festival should not surprise us for, as Rene Girard has noted, the sacrificial
process was not only the origin of primitive religion, but of drama and
theater as well.

(The pioneering studies of religion and culture by Rene Girard, a
classical scholar with a Catholic understanding, provide much of the
foundation of this far more limited analysis.)

The "Strangers Within":
The Expulsion of the Spanish Jews and Muslims

The Spain of the Middle Ages could be called multi-ethnic, if not multi-
cultural, in that the Iberian Peninsula was originally divided among many
kingdoms and cultures. This, however, changed throughout the fifteenth
and sixteenth centuries when the long-established Jewish and Muslim
communities were expelled or forced to convert to Catholicism. This expulsion signaled a transformation of the Iberian culture from one that was
multi-religious and inclusive to what historian Teofilo Ruiz characterized
as "a mentality of exclusion." He relates this not only to religious passions
but to the end of feudalism and the growing desire for private property.
This was the era of the rise of commerce and what would eventually become the bourgeois society of landowners and merchants. In this newly
developing social order, one's identity and status were increasingly related
to ownership and wealth, which is another way of saying "insecure."

Muslims had ruled the Spanish lands for over three hundred years,
from 711 when they came from North Africa and conquered the Visigoth
kingdom, until their reversals, beginning in 1085 with the fall of Toledo.
During much of this period there was a tolerance of diversity, but there
were also times of harsh repression. Christian martyrdom sustained a
deep resentment that finally took the form of armed resistance. There is

a pattern here: The triumph of one group, when seen as a catastrophe for the other, results in permanent hostility. The fall of Toledo in 1085 was the beginning of the inevitable end of Muslim rule, though the struggle would persist for another three hundred years.

During this long bellicose period, there was simultaneously a new sense of identity for the increasingly dominant Castilians, and a growing antagonism against anyone perceived as "foreign." Fears of "pollution" through sexual contact planted the seeds of the later xenophobia and racism. This need to segregate and exclude was not limited to Spain. What has been called the "crisis of the Middle Ages," in effect, the end of feudalism, saw a growth of anti-Jewish sentiment as well as fears of heresy throughout Europe.

Anti-Jewish sentiments had been present in Visigothic Spain following the fall of Rome and resurfaced during the eleventh century at the time of the First Crusade. There were renewed attacks on Jews in Spain as early as the year 1300, particularly during religious festivals, and then a violent explosion in 1391. In that year, a forcible mass conversion of Jews took place. This led, despite the duress, to many Jews becoming authentically Catholic and integrating successfully into Christian society. This integration, however, would not save many *conversos* a century later. The intermarriage of *conversos* and Catholics was sufficiently widespread that many of the most celebrated Spaniards of the time were known to have Jewish ancestry — including St. Teresa of Avila, and, possibly, King Ferdinand himself.

Sadly, most of the Jews who were attacked and ultimately expelled in 1492 were *conversos,* either compelled or compliant converts to Christianity. In this atmosphere of fear and suspicion, any *converso* might be accused of secretly practicing the Jewish faith, and, indeed, some, perhaps many, did. It is inherent in human nature, but equally sad to note, that many of the Inquisition's most fervent persecutors of the Jews, such as the notorious Torquemada, were themselves *conversos.*

Interpreting the Expulsions

The expulsion of the Jews and Muslims from Spain illustrates the point of Rene Girard's analysis of the role of "sacred" or "ritual violence." Girard's anthropological insights shed light, not just on Spanish history, but on how human society evolves through rivalry and violence. The intensified civil strife in Spain was eased only by redirecting the divisive force of these animosities on "outsiders," the "strangers in our midst." Whether Muslim resistance or *converso* dissimulation contributed to this, Girard would point out, is irrelevant to the scapegoating process. What was required to achieve social order was the creation of "the Other," someone, in other words, who could be blamed. The religious aspect, the "sacred" violence, provides the ultimate rationalization.

No country has suffered more from internal strife than Spain. Their civil wars, including the twentieth-century fratricide, have left deep and lasting scars. Yet a legacy emerged from these bitter conflicts; and it is one that, I believe, has shaped Mexican consciousness as well.

The true history of any people, unlike the schoolbook versions compiled by conquerors and victors, is a history of human suffering far more than it is of human triumph. This perception, derived from Spain's own history, is the profound legacy articulated by one of the most influential Spanish writers of the twentieth century, Miguel de Unamuno. In his classic study *The Tragic Sense of Life*, Unamuno recognizes the centrality of suffering ("it is suffering that makes us human") and thus offers a more perceptive assessment of human nature than that found in the shallow progressivism of the modern age, religious or secular. Unamuno's sensibility, in this respect, is very similar to that of Octavio Paz; and, as does the Mexican poet, he opens a door to a spiritual dialogue. We will examine this affinity further in a later chapter.

Unamuno was essentially an existential philosopher in the tradition of Pascal and Kierkegaard, and spoke in philosophical more than religious terms. He affirmed the necessity of faith, but resisted systematic thought. "A faith without doubt is a dead faith," was his credo; yet his work is replete with references to the saints, almost as if in dialogue with them. Above all, Unamuno sought truth; yet he knew, and openly affirmed, that it can never be fully grasped in this life.

A Meeting of Strangers

The Conquest of Mexico

The Spanish who conquered Mexico might well be called "Christian warriors." They were, for the most part, natives of Castile, the largest and richest of the Iberian Peninsula kingdoms. Castilians were a resourceful and deeply Catholic people who had nonetheless forged their Christian faith into a militant warrior mentality. They had endured and at times resisted seven centuries of Moorish rule. The Moors of North Africa, equally militant converts to Islam, weren't expelled from Spain until the rise of the Spanish monarchy at the end of the momentous fifteenth century.

During this period, the marriage of Isabel of Castile at age seventeen with Ferdinand, actually a Catalan but heir to the rival throne of Aragon, and a year younger, created a united kingdom of Spain. This royal alliance laid the foundation of what was to become the most powerful empire of its time. During the reign of Isabel, so devout that she is still known as *Isabel la catolica,* not only were the Moors finally expelled from their last stronghold of Granada, but, starting in 1492, Columbus, sponsored by the Spanish Crown, made his voyages to the New World. Spanish history, in fact, shaped world history for two hundred years. (Please note that as we are exploring Spanish-speaking Mexico, I will primarily use Spanish names and titles, followed by English translations.)

When Hernando Cortes completed his conquest of the Valley of Mexico, the Spanish empire was at its height in terms of wealth and political supremacy. From the time of Isabel and Ferdinand, through the proud reign of their successor, Carlos (Charles — note his two simultaneous titles: Carlos I of Spain, and Carlos V, Holy Roman Emperor), and into the even longer reign of his son, Felipe II (Philip II), Spanish economic and military power had become increasingly centralized. The relatively new kingdom of Spain was now an aggregate of what had been separate monarchies and medieval city-states. It was also transforming itself into a society with large and prosperous cities. Seville, with a population of over a hundred thousand by the 1580s, was surpassed in size and prestige only by Paris. There was a prosperous trade in goods, such as wool, supported by a powerful naval fleet; yet the economy remained based on a medieval agricultural system with an impoverished and sometimes rebellious peasantry.

What makes the chronology of the Spanish monarchs difficult to follow is that Spain was, for the most part, ruled by Austrian royalty, the Habsburgs. These were heirs to the Holy Roman Empire founded by Charlemagne in A.D. 800 and fought over by various European rulers for centuries thereafter. The heir to the throne of Isabel and Ferdinand was their grandson Carlos (Charles of Ghent), a Habsburg, but born in what is now the Netherlands. He was to become Holy Roman emperor after the death of his grandfather. When he came to power this "Carlos," king of Spain, couldn't speak Spanish!

The Spanish empire at the time of his succession included not only all the once-separate territories of Spain, including Portugal, but what is now the Netherlands, Austria, border areas of France, and parts of Italy, as well as its colonies. The Spanish kingdom has been compared to Rome in that it ruled over such widely diverse and even previously unknown peoples. Spain itself, after centuries of Moorish domination, could be called "Afro-European" in that it retained many aspects of North African Muslim culture, including the rich splendor of their décor and the benefits of their then-advanced scientific knowledge.

As historians such as J. H. Elliott have pointed out, perhaps the most remarkable accomplishment of the Spanish Catholic kings was the establishment of order at a time of frequent revolts. Yet within Spain itself there were serious and persistent internal conflicts. In the very years of the Conquest of Mexico, there was a violent uprising, that of the so-called *Communeros* within Castile. This was a revolt of native Castilians against the Habsburg dynasty, the Austrian royal family, and was suppressed by German soldiers. It was, however, in some respects, a civil war involving many different factions, leaving scars that did not heal for generations.

The Spanish ruling class had initially felt that the success of their new imperial regime pointed to divine election and purpose. In 1571, the sea battle at Lepanto, in which the combined Catholic forces defeated the Turks, also seemed a providential sign. But increasing instability and later failures, political, financial, and military — especially the British defeat of Spain's "invincible armada" in 1588 — were interpreted by many as a punishment from God. A profound sense of disquiet and even fatalism took hold, paradoxically, at the very height of Spanish power.

The insights of historian Teofilo Ruiz can help us to understand how this came about. Ruiz argues that Spain clung to a unifying historical myth, which was that of the *reconquista,* the protracted struggle to liberate Christian territory from Muslim rule. This struggle for independence, while genuine, has been cast as a religious war; but the process was more than a struggle for liberation or a clash of religions. Ruiz maintains that political and economic changes were at least as fundamental. From 1260 to 1474, the Spanish kingdoms, not yet united, suffered an economic crisis aggravated by civil strife and a power struggle between the monarchs and the feudal lords known as "magnates." There was also a gradual process of bringing a new population from the north of the peninsula to the south, which was suffering from a labor shortage. Only later, as a new "Spanish" identity emerged, did these essentially internal conflicts take on a purely religious and ideological character.

The end of feudal Spain, and, indeed, the Europe of the Middle Ages, had a profound effect on the individual's sense of relationship to God. It was during this time that the concept of purgatory was formulated, which, for some, degenerated into a kind of bargaining with God about the afterlife. Christian doctrine, based on Jesus' own admonitions, warned against the accumulation of wealth, especially at the cost of the needs of others. As early as 1250, however, there was an increase in the number of landless and impoverished peasants, and legislation became necessary to control the discontent. The concept of charity became less communal and, in many ways, stigmatized the poor. One might recognize much of the modern world in this description; but we must remember that Spain was a devout, self-consciously Catholic kingdom with no acknowledged separation between faith, power, and daily life.

The Catholic kings had themselves been desacralized by not being crowned but "dubbed," and this not by a prelate but by a mechanical statue of St. James! The king, thus, was not anointed. Possessing no "divine rights" or attributes presumably freed him to govern with fewer moral scruples. Kings were either self-proclaimed or took power through consensus or so-called "popular demand."

Another inherent contradiction within Spanish society by the seventeenth century was that it remained, in most respects, a medieval social order at a time when technological developments had vastly accelerated the pace of change. The perfection of navigation through the improvement of the compass and the invention of the printing press were taking place at a time when Spanish ideals were still that of the absolute monarch and the courtly knights. Miguel de Cervantes's Don Quixote is a soul lost in time, who, pursuing "honor," is actually fighting the windmills of his imagination. Cervantes, it should be noted, had himself fought in the victorious battle at Lepanto.

The political and economic troubles in Spain remained acute until 1476 when Isabel became queen, and stability was finally achieved. The kingdom of Spain was then eventually transformed into one of the first truly centralized governments. The Crown's legitimacy was recognized, but was based on a monopoly of power and what Ruiz terms "legalized" or "rationalized violence." Perhaps this thirst for power had more to do with the influence of Machiavelli than the devout Isabel. In fact, it has been suggested that Machiavelli's model for his unscrupulous "Prince" may have been Ferdinand of Spain rather than Cesare Borgia or one of the Medicis. In any case, in some ways, the new monarchy prefigured the modern state with its layers of bureaucracy and sea of commissioned reports. Yet this new rule was at the same time an attempt to restore a medieval order. There was trade but little industry, and landowners remained a privileged elite. Sincere and often effective measures were taken to reform the Church; but this also was part of an attempt to conserve an outmoded feudal order — history's last vital medieval society. Spain's absolute monarchy, unified by Isabel and Ferdinand, lasted for two hundred years, but it was the last of its kind.

A profound struggle was also taking place within the Catholic world between the new humanism of the Renaissance and the long-established medieval theologies. The king himself, Carlos, was influenced by the "new thinking," such as Dante's humanism, and intrigued by concepts of a "Christian republic." This concept contradicted traditional autocratic rule, and if anyone less exalted than King Carlos had brought such "foreign ideas" to Spain at that time, they would have been in grave peril from the Inquisition.

The first encounter with the unknown and exotic peoples of the New World thus came at a time of growing insecurity about moral legitimacy within Spain itself. Spanish Catholicism, despite fear and resistance, was merging with Renaissance thought and seeking an integrity of faith that would be consistent with the existing order. A deep Christian faith, however, always eventually challenges the exploitive practices of conquering powers and temporal rulers. Spain was no exception. It should be recognized, however, that the most courageous voices mounting this faith-based challenge were themselves Spanish. Despite the stereotypes promulgated by later historians, extensive Church documentation in Spain and Mexico indicates that a debate within the Church as to the nature of what we would now call "human rights" began during the earliest days of the Conquest — and it was a conflict that never ended.

Spain was, indeed, facing serious external problems throughout this era. The Protestant Reformation was a source of fear for any Catholic monarch and not without reason, as the bloody religious wars in France demonstrated. There were periodic wars with France, and in 1568, Calvinist riots in the Spanish Netherlands. English pirates boldly raided Spanish sea lanes, and there remained a constant concern about revolt at home. And always, there were the Muslim threats, either from the Ottomans or the resurgent Moors.

The vast Spanish empire, despite the wealth in silver and spices pouring in from New Spain, was over-extended, and royal ambitions frequently outstripped any realistic means. The Spanish Crown was bankrupt in 1557, only the first of its several financial debacles.

Spiritual Conflict and Contradiction

The fighting inherent in the Spanish Conquest was not just military. During this period there were several prolonged theological disputes as well. There were ongoing disagreements between the Jesuits and Dominicans that involved perennial questions, such as the nature of grace and free will. Given the power and wealth of the Church, and its compromised political position, these ecclesial conflicts were inevitably caught up in secular power struggles. The cardinals and bishops of Spain were often brave and, indeed, some were genuinely holy; yet their general outlook was seldom different from that of the upper class from which they came, and their appointments made as much on the basis of privilege and ambition as any other royal entitlement. A seventeenth-century archbishop of Toledo, the primate of Spain, was given his title at the age of four!

Sixteenth-century thought within the Church had become increasingly Aristotelian, that is, rational and categorical, at a time when Spanish society maintained a highly legalistic and hierarchical faith, which seldom questioned any authority, and certainly not on the basis of mere Reason. This was the conflicted form of Christianity that confronted the paganism of Aztec and Mayan Mexico. To look back through the lens of contemporary universalism or anthropological relativism will lead to a distorted understanding of Spanish objectives and attitudes. The inescapable moral question of self-interest disguised as altruism was, of course, as central to the Spaniards of that time as it is to our own.

Moral philosophy during this difficult period in Spain, by contrast, was creative and innovative, particularly at the University of Salamanca where distinguished figures, such as the Dominican rector Francisco de Vitoria, were making lasting contributions to Catholic thought. The struggle to reconcile faith with empire was, moreover, not limited to ecclesial circles. Following the Conquest, questions of the nature of evil, for example, were widely discussed in the light of the encounter with the unfamiliar behaviors of the newly discovered peoples across the sea. Much of this discussion anticipates the issue of "cultural relativism" that has confronted Western societies to the present day.

The Aftermath

The historical depictions of Hernando Cortes and his military achievements, his march from Vera Cruz to the Valley of Mexico in 1519, the battles, the narrow escapes, and the intrigues, are too familiar to need much elaboration. What we are seeking is an understanding of these events insofar as they contributed to the creation of Catholic Mexico. It is therefore the immediate aftermath of the Conquest that we will examine at some length. (For those unfamiliar with or having a greater interest in the Conquest, there are several historical studies suggested in the bibliography.)

From the very beginning, the Conquest was viewed by the Spanish themselves from contrasting, indeed, opposing, points of view. Here are two representative perspectives:

Bernal Diaz del Castillo — a first-hand account by a
conquistador **of a visit to the temple at Tenochtitlan in 1519:**

"The blackened hearts of three Indians sacrificed that day lay smoldering before the altar. The floor was bathed in blood and encrusted layers of blood blackened the walls of the shrine. The stench was overwhelming. The idol on the opposite side of the shrine was Tescatepuca, the god of the infernal regions. This idol had the face of a bear and its mirrored eyes seemed to glow with a light from some inner evil source. The waist was girdled with figures that resembled tiny devils with tails like serpents. That day they had offered the idol the hearts of five Indians, and the stench that rose from the floor, still slippery with blood, was more sickening than that of any slaughter house in Castile."

Bishop Bartolome de Las Casas — a denunciation of the
Conquest is found in the conclusion of Las Casas's book
The Devastation of the Indies **(1552):**

". . . [T]he tyrants in other parts of the New World have disregarded the new laws and are behaving in the same way. For they cannot bring themselves to relinquish the estates and properties they have usurped or let go their hold on the Indians, whom they maintain in perpetual subjection. And wherever killing with the sword has come to an end, they are killing the Indians little by little by subjecting them to servitude. And until now the King has been powerless to check them, for all the Spaniards, young and old, in the Indies, are occupied in pillage, some openly, others secretly and stealthily. And with the pretense of serving the King they are dishonoring God and robbing and destroying the King."

What is perhaps disquieting to the critics of the Church as well as its defenders is the clearly religious motivation of the Spanish conquerors — this despite the often grave consequences of their actions. From the outset, their banners and emblems bore the image of the Virgin and Child. Masses and religious devotions were held regularly and Cortes himself had to be restrained from an impetuous urge to proclaim the "one true God" to the Indians, even when this would have been clearly misunderstood or provocative. His spiritual advisor, Father Olmedo, who accompanied Cortes throughout the expedition, was apparently more prudent and personally questioned the value of coerced conversions. He doubted that intimidation could remove the "idol that remained in the heart," and advised patient instruction.

The Rebel Bishop: Bartolome de Las Casas

The inner conflicts that permeated New Spain and the mother country itself during the aftermath of the Conquest were embodied in the person of the most influential and controversial Catholic prelate of the time, Bishop Bartolome de Las Casas.

Born in Seville in 1484, Bartolome was the son of a merchant who sailed with Columbus on his second voyage, and who brought back to his son the gift of a slave. Bartolome, prophetically signaling the cause to which he would later devote his life, freed the young slave and had him returned to the Indies.

In 1502, at the age of eighteen, Las Casas himself went to the Indies as a soldier. His spiritual transformation began during that time and around 1507 he traveled to Rome to be ordained in the diaconate. He then returned to become the first Catholic priest ordained in New Spain. Almost immediately, he began to denounce the *encomienda* system in which the Indians worked the land for Spanish owners virtually as slaves.

During his time in the Indies, Las Casas began to learn the indigenous languages. He met the celebrated conquerors, Cortes and Alvarado, and participated as a chaplain in the occupation of Cuba. His moral consciousness only grew, however; a turning point came in 1514 when, in a homily given on Pentecost, Las Casas categorically condemned the exploitation in terms that suggested that the Conquest itself was inherently unjust. This began his lifelong campaign to end the mistreatment of the Indians that would bring him fame, occasional success, many powerful enemies, and frequent defeats.

For the next thirty years, Las Casas would relentlessly argue the case that the Indians should be treated as equal human beings, and — his most important insight — that genuine conversions could only be brought about by peaceful means. In 1520, he gained a hearing before King Carlos V. To the monarch's credit, Carlos listened sympathetically and, based on the interview, subsequently initiated several reforms. He permitted Las Casas to employ a non-coercive approach to conversion in Venezuela and later Guatemala. The failure of the Venezuelan experiment, which ended in an Indian uprising instigated by his enemies, discouraged Las Casas and undoubtedly led to his decision to become a Dominican friar.

These years ushered in another period of spiritual growth for Las Casas. He contributed his theological insights during the controversies over baptism, arguing that indigenous acts of repentance within their own culture were potentially compatible with Catholic practices.

In 1537, Pope Paul III's declaration that the Indians were to be treated as fully human was a great victory for Las Casas and his supporters. In 1542, there was another gain when King Carlos authorized new laws, the *Leyes Nuevas,* which, while weakened a few years later, struck a serious blow to the *encomienda* system.

At the height of his reputation, Las Casas was offered the bishopric of Lima in Peru, then the highest Church position in New Spain. He turned it down, preferring to become the Bishop of Chiapas, one of the poorest regions. This new position only intensified his efforts to gain rights for the Indians, and he became even more outspoken. When he preached that Spaniards should seek absolution for the spoils of the Conquest, his position became more precarious. His powerful opponents were finally able to have him recalled to Spain in 1547.

During this time, recognizing that the royal proclamations on Indian rights were not substantially improving conditions, Las Casas turned to the pen as a weapon and began writing his major works, which included valuable anthropological data based on the early accounts of the explorations of Columbus.

In April 1550, King Carlos, troubled by the many indictments of Spanish rule, insisted on a "debate" between Las Casas and a formidable opponent, the humanist philosopher Juan Gines de Sepulveda. This was actually less a debate than a kind of court hearing. The two men never met face-to-face, but made presentations similar to legal briefs and at great length. In fact, it took several days for Las Casas to complete the argument in his "brief." Again, it is one of those ironies of intellectual history that the new "enlightened" humanist philosophy would be used to justify both slavery and war. Sepulveda offered a natural law argument, based on Aristotle, that the "naturally inferior" Indians required military conquest and subjugation for their own good. Las Casas elaborated on the reality of the abuses and degradation. In the end, Las Casas won a pyrrhic victory. The majority of the court favored him, but no real action was taken to improve the situation.

In any case, Las Casas's greatest and most lasting achievement lay ahead. Without the permission of the Inquisition, or perhaps anyone else, in 1552 he published his detailed account of the cruelties inflicted on the indigenous, the now-classic *The Devastation of the Indies*. The book became a sensation in Europe and was published in several languages. It also inadvertently aided the Protestant powers in their struggle with Spain for control of the Americas.

Las Casas won one last battle, shrewdly using legal maneuvers to protect the rights of the exploited Peruvian Indians; but he was now increasingly isolated and unpopular. He died in July 1566 and is buried on the grounds of the Our Lady of Atocha convent in Madrid.

While recognizing the moral courage and contributions of Bartolome de Las Casas, contemporary scholars, such as historian Bill

Donovan, have noted that his descriptions of the post-conquest period are best recognized as propaganda for a just cause rather than scrupulously accurate history. For understandable reasons, Las Casas exaggerated the numbers of indigenous deaths at the hands of the Spanish, ignoring the effects of the pandemics. He also exaggerates, again for good purposes, the virtue of the Indians, invariably depicting them as innocent, humble, and, most inaccurately, as always peaceable. This blatantly ignores the role the many Indian allies played in the Conquest, who supported the Spanish and served as their mercenaries.

Most grievously, Las Casas ignored the many others among his countrymen, including the friars and other bishops, who faithfully served the Indians and had also protested their exploitation. As early as 1511, the Dominican friar Antonio de Montesinos had outraged his Spanish congregation in Hispanola by condemning their exploitation of the natives. However, as Donovan points out, Las Casas was desperately struggling against a firmly entrenched hierarchy, and at a time when the Church's ordered world was coming apart. His opponents were defensive and insecure, and Las Casas, in his own way, was hardly less rigid. This imbalance, nonetheless, distorts the history of the period. The Spanish, for all their sins, made an unprecedented effort to try to understand the people that they had conquered; and, though often subverted, many efforts at reform were made, some of which had lasting effects. It should be noted that this did not happen among the other conquering powers in the Americas — England, France, Netherlands, or, for that matter, the new American colonies.

Las Casas was deeply concerned that the Spanish would be condemned by God for their sins in the New World. He was not an Enlightenment figure, a Voltaire or a Tom Paine. For him, human rights weren't based on conceptions of personal liberty, but on the Christian belief that all human beings are made in the image of God as manifested in Christ. His legacy has been misused at times, even evoked to justify violence as a means of change, contradicting Las Casas's most fundamental principle; but the legacy remains a noble and lasting one.

The lovely city that bears his name in Chiapas is called San Cristobal de las Casas. San Cristobal (St. Christopher) is said to have carried Jesus across a river on his back. The city's name rightly recognizes the great faith and strength of this brave priest.

The "Black Legend"

While it was certainly never his intention, Las Casas's writings, as we have noted, contributed to a misrepresentation of Spanish history later known as "the Black Legend," *La Leyenda Negra*, a term coined by historian Julian Juderias in his 1914 study. All human history is open to conflicting interpretations; however, the period following the Conquest has been particularly subject to distortion. Historians such as Juderias and Charles Gibson have helped to explain the origins and persistence of the "myth" of a unique Spanish cruelty and the subsequent Indian desolation. The "Legend" stems from a deliberately distorted account of the Spanish Conquest promulgated by the Spanish empire's rivals, especially the English and Dutch. For example, one can find what became the standard stereotypes in a popular nineteenth-century novel published in England, in which the Spanish are depicted as cruel monsters, and the Indians as helpless innocents. The only recourse of the utterly crushed Indians, in this version, is to place a curse on the Spanish, which is ultimately fulfilled by — can you guess? — the defeat of the Spanish Armada by the English!

The debunking of this "Black Legend" hardly exonerates the Spanish conquerors. Indeed, the major sources of the "Legend" came from the Spaniards themselves, including courageous figures such as Bishop Las Casas, whose detailed report of the cruel exploitation of the Indians by his fellow Spaniards was presented to the Spanish court, and then published throughout Europe. The "Legend" was further embellished by Mexican nationalists in the nineteenth century, reflecting their strong bias against the Spanish as exploiters; then, by the Mexican revolutionaries of the twentieth century, who also promoted nativist myths of the Conquest for their own political ends.

It is ironic that the still-widespread prejudice displayed by Mexicans against Spaniards would be the basis of a bias toward them by Anglo-Americans. Historian Joseph P. Sanchez, in his 1990 monograph, persuasively relates the "Black Legend" to persistent anti-Hispanic attitudes. From the time of the Battle of the Alamo in 1836 to the Mexican-American War and the Gold Rush, the negative portrayal of Mexicans employed the same stereotypes. Early ballads depicted Mexicans as a "swarthy horde" and the "spawn of hell" who "knife and lie and cheat."

Mexican men were "ignorant, dishonest, treacherous" and their women were without virtue.

A second historical irony is that the Anglo-American propagandists — echoing the *conquistidores* centuries before — were now arguing that Mexicans were incapable of self-government; hence, any conquest would be justified.

During the Spanish-American War of 1898, the slogan "Remember the Maine" replaced "Remember the Alamo." For Protestant Anglo-Americans of that era, who viewed the pope as the "anti-Christ," it was not Mexico but Spain that remained the "ruthless foe," as it had been since the defeat of the Armada more than three hundred years before. Bishop Las Casas's book was reprinted in America as a *True Account of the Massacre and Slaughter of 20,000,000 People in the West Indies by the Spaniards* with vivid illustrations showing Spaniards torturing helpless Indians. The result of the war, whatever the provocations, was the emergence of the United States as an imperial power in its own right, as it wrested both Cuba and the Philippines from Spain.

The most lasting and damaging effect of the "Black Legend," however, was the distortion of history. The most influential nineteenth-century American historians — Francis Parkman, George Bancroft, and William H. Prescott — perpetuated not just self-serving misrepresentations, but an ugly prejudice. In his study *Tree of Hate* (1971), historian Philip Wayne Powell noted that these scholars were uniformly anti-Catholic. This is no exaggeration. Parkman, writing in 1881, informed his readers that the Spanish "monks and Jesuits" had the "dark and narrow mind of [the] tyrannical recluse," which had formed a Spanish character "quenched in blood." He cited the chief characteristics of the Spaniard as "bigotry blind" and pride. Spain, he concluded, was the "citadel of darkness" and "a scourge as dire as ever fell on man." Apparently, "bigotry blind" was also contagious.

By the twentieth century, the "Black Legend" had metastasized into overt racism. In the 1930s, a history of the Texas Rangers attributed what the author considered the inherent cruelty of Mexicans not just to their Spanish inheritance but to their "Indian blood."

The crude depiction of the Spanish as despoilers led also to the inadvertent misrepresentation of the Indians as either vainly heroic or passive and helpless. What is frequently, if not persistently, missing are the accounts of personal interactions. The transformation of the indigenous cultures into a synthesis with the Spanish produced, in time, a new people. This is the story worth telling. A more accurate depiction of this history is no less fascinating than the "mythic" ones.

It is tempting to attribute the cruelty of war and conquest to the character of other people. However, there is not a single European power, Catholic or Protestant, that did not inflict suffering on others or engage in religious persecution. The American colonists, many fleeing such intolerance, burned people as witches, and, most sadly, attempted at times to virtually exterminate the native population.

No one should be casting stones.

Blessed Voyagers: The Spanish Friars

Undoubtedly one of the most fascinating "meeting of strangers" in history took place when the Spanish priests and friars encountered the equally religious but entirely unknown peoples of Mesoamerica. The first Spanish clerics to arrive were the Franciscan friars known as "the twelve apostles." Led by Friar Martin de Valencia, they landed in Vera Cruz in 1524. Valencia was a strict-observance friar who, earlier, had a vision of the end of the world. He and some of the others, such as Friar Benavente, the chronicler of much of this early history, whom the Indians called "Motolinia," were among the Franciscans known as "spirituals." As early as the twelfth century, the apocalyptic visionary teachings of a monk, Joachim de Fiore, had influenced many Franciscans. These "spirituals" had little interest in maintaining earthly kingdoms, including the Spanish. They saw the New World as a place to begin again rather than as a colony of an existing power. This attitude naturally placed them in conflict with the established authorities, royal and ecclesiastical.

These Franciscans were not alone in their utopian visions. Throughout Europe, there was a growing distaste for the wealth and power of the Church, and a desire to return to an original apostolic purity. The peasant revolts in Germany and Puritan dissent in England, each in its own way and despite different beliefs, wanted to "go back."

These radical friars were inspired to baptize the indigenous peoples immediately and often did so through mass baptisms with little or no prior spiritual preparation on the part of the indigenous. To some extent, their missionary efforts were supported by the teaching of the Council of Trent, which had given considerable latitude to priests to hear the confessions of people with an imperfect understanding of doctrine or, for that matter, the nature of sin.

Father Juan de Tecto, formerly a professor at the University of Paris and confessor to Carlos V, had arrived in New Spain shortly before the friars. Tecto was a distinguished *letrado,* or "man of letters," who played a role in determining the proper use of ritual under these new circumstances; but disputes between the "spirituals" and Church intellectuals were often bitter. There had long been quarrels within the Franciscan movement between those who saw St. Francis's spirituality as something deeper than the abstractions of Scholastic theology and canon law, and the more educated clergy who tried to conform Francis's teaching to that of the contemporary Church. Other early figures, such as Father Geronimo de Mendieta, also tried to establish a balance between the sometimes-extreme efforts of the Franciscans and established norms of conversion and the proper use of the sacraments.

A group of Dominicans, led by Father Tomas Ortiz, then arrived in 1527; but several early deaths restrained their activities among the Indians for some time. In 1533, the Franciscans and Dominicans were joined by a small group of Augustinians and these three orders would constitute the initial missionary wave.

In many ways, the conflicts within and between the orders and the hierarchy, and that between the missionaries in the field, so to speak, and the theologians, reflect a never-ending struggle within the Church, no matter where it brings the message of salvation, or to whom. The central questions remain with us: To what extent is a missionary priest allowed to adapt the teachings and the rituals to the best understanding of those he seeks to convert? And, more importantly, doesn't the imposition of authority kill the spirit rather than kindle it?

The Council of Trent had given priests increased latitude in such matters and theologians such as the Jesuit Father Jose de Acosta tried to offer further guidance. In 1539, the distinguished theologian Francisco de

Vitoria of the University of Salamanca persuaded the king that the Indians had the right to proper instruction prior to baptism, and that the Church had the obligation to provide it. In time, the more unorthodox methods of some of the early Franciscans, such as mass baptisms, would be regulated; but during this first period of global exploration, from the New World to China, Japan, and the Pacific islands, Catholic missionaries were struggling with these questions. Much of the Church's later missionary practice was developed from an understanding of the accomplishments — and the errors — of these early pioneers.

There are other priestly figures from this early era who should be mentioned, if for no other reason than that their extensive writings not only provide much of the historical data but became the foundation of what we now consider ethnography or the study of cultures.

Two Franciscans, Friars Bernardino de Sahagun and Alfonso de Molina, are perhaps the most notable of these early ethnographers and often cited in scholarly texts. Sahagun (1499-1590?) is in a class by himself for transcending the limited understanding of his times. His *General History of the Things of New Spain* is an exhaustive examination of every aspect of Aztec society and customs from birth to death. Friar Molina was the first to create what was in effect a dictionary of the Nahuatl language. Other priests who were classically educated, such as Acosta and Duran, contributed an important historical perspective, seeing indigenous civilization in a stage of development rather than arrested in time.

Naturally, language was a major challenge. Franciscans and Dominicans debated, for example, how to translate the word "God" into Nahuatl. Should they use an earlier Nahuatl term for a nature god or an idiom stressing the difference, in a specifically Christian concept? They also deliberated as to whether a Nahuatl term for "ritual" could be properly used for "sacrament." These were not merely linguistic problems. The priests had increasingly noted similarities between indigenous beliefs and practices and those of the Church, and, thus, language could be used as a bridge as well as a corrective.

The millenarian visions of the radical Franciscans undoubtedly encouraged Hernando Cortes to think of himself as not just the "elect of God" but as possibly the creator of a new empire. In contrast to the later portrayals of Cortes as crude and brutal, as in the murals of Diego

Rivera, Cortes, in fact, was admired in his own day, indeed, lionized, as one of the new humanists. His friends included the great humanist Erasmus himself. One of Cortes's admirers even dedicated a book to him on the theme of the Dignity of Man! Cortes's view of himself as a visionary and liberator, however self-serving, was quite consistent with the liberal humanism of the period.

Perhaps these differences in perception are instructive. If we are inclined to look for the "heroes" and "villains" of history, we are apt to be frustrated. As this encounter between Europeans and the natives of the New World shows us, the most advanced ideas of the Renaissance, derived from Plato and Aristotle, could produce results that the present-day progressive might find unpalatable. Aristotle's categorizing of physical traits, for example, later combined with evolutionary theory, laid the basis for modern racism, and Plato's concept of the State has been used to support despotic authoritarianism. These Spanish Church intellectuals, in a way, anticipated our own age, in that we have all suffered grievously from the unintended consequences of our ideas — even the best of them.

Troubled Vision: The Spanish View of the Indigenous

It is extraordinary, if not miraculous, that these "strangers," the conquerors and the conquered, would eventually be integrated into one people; for it is clear that many of the Spanish viewed the indigenous, at least initially, as possibly an entirely different species.

From the outset of the *conquista,* the Castilians considered themselves "soldiers of Christ" pledged to fight and conquer the enemies of their Catholic faith, such as they had the Moors and Turks. This merging of a warrior caste with religious faith, however sincere, led the Spanish soldiers to treat their adversaries as inherently evil. This obsession with evil and sin was the bitter fruit that grew from the centuries of religious oppression and the never-ending fear and suspicion of apostasy and betrayal.

Significantly for the coming encounter, the Aztecs were also a vulnerable empire and similarly preoccupied with their own sense of evil and fate. They were making a desperate attempt to placate the gods through a mountain of human sacrifices. These horrendous rites led many of the Spanish invaders to view the Aztecs as hopeless "slaves of the Prince of darkness." The condemnation of Aztec paganism, however, wasn't based merely on the bloody sacrificial system, or the horrific figures adorning the temples, but on more subtle observations that have relevance today.

The futile efforts to control nature and human fate that led to ritual violence were, in part, rooted in the Aztec obsession with calculation. As the British author Graham Greene noted centuries later, human fortunes, even the right to live, were dependent upon systems of intricate and "endless numbering," whether of rows of terraced stone steps or astronomical signs. Greene, viewing the vast temple ruins, reacted to what he termed this "stony mathematical discipline" and described the Aztec "artifice of counting" not so much as an inhuman aberration of feeling, but as a kind of metaphysical error, a system of precise but futile calculations. This wasn't so much barbarism as it was an all-too-human, and very contemporary, desire to control life and nature through computation.

We have come a long way in recognizing the inherent grace and beauty in much of indigenous culture as well as acknowledging elements of spiritual compatibility; but we stop short if we refuse to see the common human frailty at the root of collective violence. If we look with unblinking eyes at the imagery of the fierce and demanding gods, the snakes and threatening half-human visages, we can see that there was not merely fear at the heart of these rites, but a deep well of collective terror.

It is easy to see why the Spanish, however narrow their perceptions, reacted to the native religions with revulsion rather than appreciation or in a spirit of "objectivity." Much of contemporary scholarship seems indifferent, if not oblivious to the notion of evil, a naiveté for which we've paid dearly. The Spaniards, by contrast, were primed to see evil all around them, and so they did. Yet this Spanish preoccupation with the forces of evil pulled them in opposite directions. On the one hand, the Aztecs were seen as prisoners of the devil; but, on the other hand, therefore, not as devils themselves. The Indians were viewed by the Catholic missionaries as deluded men who could and must be enlightened, but still as human beings. The writings of Friars Sahagun and Acosta, to cite but two, reveal their determination to liberate rather than to condemn.

This would not be the tolerant view of all or even most of the conquerors. The military adventurers were more concerned with their own gains in wealth and power than with the condition of Indian souls. The more common assumption, hardly limited to the Spanish, was that any deviation from their own religious and social norms was simply the result of deficiency, degeneracy, or damnation.

The Franciscan friars had differing perspectives. Quite common was Friar Acosta's conclusion that the Indians, in their present state, were "half-men," that is, comparable to children, but fully human and thus capable of being raised, through Christian education, to maturity. Some of the Franciscan friars were far more radical. They feared the "contamination" of corrupt European values, which they associated with the "end-time," and thus sought to create a "new man" in the "new world." Other Spaniards, such as Juan de Cardenas, writing in 1591, concluded that the more fierce Indians, such as the Chichimecas of the north, lived lives so fundamentally incompatible with anything "civilized" that, for these people, change could only bring death. Sadly, considering the vulnerability of these people to new diseases, in many cases, he was proved all-too-correct.

The typically harsh depiction of the Spanish conquerors ignores the depth and even sophistication of these early expressions of concern. One of Friar Sahagun's insights, for example, was that the attempt to impose Spanish culture had failed because it disregarded the natural temperament of the indigenous people, which had been shaped by a unique physical environment. The Indians, in this early environmentalist view, were simply living in an earlier stage of history, limited by their natural geographic setting. The Aztec form of government, he noted, for all of its pagan brutality, had been sober if not just, and, to a great degree, restrained vice and excess. The effect of Spanish rule, on the other hand, had reduced many of the Indians to a broken and despondent condition.

These initial observations by the friars and their theologians marked, in effect, the beginning of anthropology, the systematic study of the human species in all its forms. The Spanish of this era were thus the first Europeans to recognize the remarkable diversity of the human race, and were morally perplexed by this revelation. To what extent, they asked, are people determined by nature? To what degree are they adaptable or malleable? What are the responsibilities of more "advanced" people toward others living in what seem "primitive" conditions? From a religious point of view, these studies raised the even more fundamental questions of who or what is human?

"Saving the Indian Soul": The Indigenous and the Sacraments

For Catholics everywhere, the sacraments of the Church — Baptism, Confirmation, Eucharist, Marriage, Ordination, the rites of Reconciliation (Confession), and the Anointing of the Sick — are the core of the practice of the faith. They can be viewed conceptually, but they are also profound and lasting experiences of our "life in Christ," or are meant to be. They are, so to speak, essential to our souls.

This was certainly the view of the Spanish clergy; but the problems they faced in administering the sacraments to the indigenous people raised universal and timeless questions about the very nature of the sacraments and the sacramental life.

The friars had an understandable dependence on ritual, but knew that there was a danger of ritual becoming simply imitative. Nahua custom featured a ritual "baptism" with water and a "naming" ceremony related to time, place, and circumstance. Could a bridge be built between these vastly different cultures? Can there be a baptism without a common language, in effect, without words?

Other difficulties were soon apparent. What is the proper ritual use of objects and song? Is conversion primarily a matter of intellectual understanding? Can one confess through an interpreter? What are the authentic signs of contrition? These are some of the questions debated at that time, and, for that matter, ever since.

The first controversy, and one that would last for decades, concerned baptism. In 1536, Bishops Zumarraga of Mexico City, Vasco de Quiroga of Michoacan, and Juan de Zarate of Oaxaca debated the issue at length, with few concrete conclusions. There was agreement, however, as to the need for at least some instruction (including, if necessary, exorcism) before baptism.

The central question posed at the time was: who to baptize and when? How could a priest assess the sincerity and understanding of an adult candidate, much less that of a child? What constituted a "necessity" for baptism, such as impending death? The Mexican Church, unable to resolve these disputes itself, appealed to the pope for an authoritative solution. Two representatives — a Franciscan and a Dominican — were sent to a Church council held in Mantua in 1537. The Franciscans tended to spurn the university-trained theologians or *letrados* as inexperienced in pastoral matters, and the Franciscan spirituality of poverty and simplicity aroused a resistance to the highly intellectualized Scholastic doctrines dominant at the time.

Given the shortage of priests in New Spain, the Franciscans had often performed mass baptisms by using an aspergillum to sprinkle holy water over an assembly in lieu of the normative rituals. The friars would attempt to determine the family and marital status before the baptisms, but relatively little else might be known about the newly baptized. The papal bull that was forthcoming, *Altitudo Divini Consilii,* ended this practice by declaring that baptism required prior religious instruction. This papal decree, as we've noted, was of great significance. Disallowing mass baptisms meant that, however superficial or transitory, a personal relationship had to be established between the priest, representing the Church, and the indigenous catechumen.

Beyond the matter of norms and customs, the primary problem the friars faced was how to make the sacraments integral to the life of the indigenous peoples. Their theologians at the University of Salamanca were also stressing the necessity of integrating belief and ritual.

There was, then, the troubling issue of forced baptisms.

Baptisms in this era were viewed, by some at least, as more of an "inoculation" against evil than an affirmation of grace. The love of God and neighbor took second place to the survival of the soul. In this context, it isn't entirely clear whether a "forced baptism" was seen as an act of compassion or simply coercion. As early as 633, the fourth Council of Toledo had authorized the removal of Jewish children from their parents to be baptized as a form of "rescue." This decree provided the basis for the coercive baptism of Indians in Mexico. The question for the friars, then, was not "should we do it?" but whether baptism would be valid if not truly consensual. These questions first pertained to the Jewish converts in Spain, the *conversos,* who had been compelled to convert or face exile or worse. There had also been forced mass baptisms of Spanish Muslims, sometimes by mobs of lay religious fanatics. The Church rarely, if ever, rejected these baptisms as invalid, but insisted on further formation and education.

Other questions faced by the friars concerned the Eucharist and communion. Communion seemed to the early friars to be less important than religious instruction. In 1555, there was a ruling that confessors themselves should determine who could receive communion, and that the primary reasons for denying it would be adherence to superstitions, drunkenness, or concubinage. The Indians, however, for whatever reasons, were frequently denied communion and this became, in time, a scandal.

The Franciscans, in particular, felt that many aspects of the Nahua culture had prepared the Indians for a Christian sacramental life. On special religious occasions, the Nahua nobles and children ate edible figures of their gods called *Ixiptlas.* This was seen as a merging of nature and the divine, though, at times, also part of an attempt to assume a supernatural identity or that of an animal. In any case, given these affinities, the Feast of *Corpus Christi* (the Body of Christ) was fervently celebrated by the indigenous with dramatizations written in their own language under the supervision of the friars.

The indigenous, not surprisingly, viewed the receiving of communion as a privilege and a mark of status. Among the first Indian communicants were "Juan" and his wife, natives of Michoacan but related to Moctezuma's royal line. The Indians were also drawn to take communion due to stories about its healing properties. One such tale is particularly poignant. An Indian convert named "Diego" received communion but only through divine intervention when two "mysterious strangers" appeared to him as he was dying. He identified these divine figures as Franciscans, though it had been "cowardly" Franciscans who had initially denied him the sacrament even though he had been to confession.

The friars, limited by language barriers, looked for "visible signs of contrition" among Indian penitents who came to confession. Particularly important was the "water of tears that comes from grace." The sense of sorrow, *dolores,* and regret could come from personal contrition or as the result of divine intervention — a view fully within the tradition and understanding of the times. Church teaching specified that proper confession should be "tearful" *(lachrimabilis),* and it was accepted that "only tears reveal the true state of the heart." Friar Molina, when compiling his *dicionario* of Nahua, had looked for such signs of contrition, and affirmed that the Indians tended to "be solely moved by the love of God" rather than simply fear or conformity.

In a 1533 letter to the king, the Franciscans defended their practices in administering the sacraments, and, according to the scholar Osvaldo Pardo, somewhat exaggerated their successes in bringing about conversions. Friar Motolinia claimed more than fifteen million converts by 1537, and two priests alone claimed more than two hundred thousand. Whatever the actual figures, the Franciscans saw the basis of their success in the natural receptivity of the Indians. They argued that the Nahua culture had reached a stage in which it was predisposed toward Christianity. They cited the indigenous customs of law and courtesy, in which the social elite displayed elaborate signs of deference and even tears of regret should they fail to adequately respond to their equals.

A serious, if not excessive, concern about the demonic characterized the period, particularly fear of the use of *execramentos,* that is, the deliberate, and diabolical distortion of rituals and sacraments. The Reformers in Europe were largely opposed to exorcism; yet Aquinas, following established Catholic belief, saw it as essential to religious formation. Evil spirits or demonic forces had to be expelled before baptism, a practice mandated since the third century. The Indians, it was felt, must be "delivered from the devil." Yet this same period saw an increased awareness of the role of Reason, which, once perfected by faith, served as the road to salvation and immortality.

Again, as contemporary Catholics, we might be inclined to view demonic forces as a remnant of ancient belief and even superstition; however, psychological studies suggest the importance of non-rational and unconscious forces. Given the unprecedented violence of the twentieth century, we might want to reconsider whether rational analysis alone is the most efficacious means of dealing with such forces.

The Origins of a New People

The Melding of Indigenous and Spanish Cultures

W hat creates a new people and a new culture is not primarily an exchange of concepts or the altering of institutions, but personal interactions over time. How did this "melding" of peoples occur? We need to look more closely at both Spanish and indigenous cultures.

As we have seen, the so-called "Indians" were not homogeneous, but a varied group of ethnically and linguistically different peoples, many of whom had long histories of enmity and conflict with each other.

At the time of the Spanish invasion, in the north of what is now Mexico, resided the fearsome nomadic tribes — Chichimecas, Tarahumara, and Apache. In the south, the Tzotzil, Olmec, and Zapotec peoples occupied the remains of a once-great Mayan culture. The central valleys, the sites of the extensive sedentary civilizations — Mixtec, Toltec, Huaxtec, and Totenac — were now occupied by their descendents, including the Mexica, Tarascans, and Tlaxcalans. As would become apparent during the Conquest, many of these peoples were unhappy under the domination of an empire ruled by another once-alien intruder, the Aztecs.

There seems to be a consensus among scholars that a particularly high degree of anxiety, even a form of despair, prevailed throughout the Aztec empire at this time, as the people, and particularly the priests, anticipated an ominous "return of the gods." That there was an underlying sense of dread in the culture is evident in some of the statuary and masks. It is impossible to "see through their eyes"; but one can imagine the fear and shock they felt at the sight of light-skinned men, some with red beards, dressed in metal, carrying weapons that shot fire, riding huge animals, and shouting in an incomprehensible tongue.

Historian James Lockhart of Stanford University, who has scrutinized many of the early accounts written in Nahuatl, the language of the dominant group in central Mexico, has written an impressive study of the immediate post-conquest period. Lockhart has used these early sources to correct the assumptions, indeed the "myths," promulgated by previous historians. (Following Lockhart, we will use the term *Nahua* in this survey rather than *Aztec*.)

In contrast to previous assumptions, Lockhart concluded that the response of the Nahuas to the imposition of Spanish religion and culture was more a process of adaptation than resistance or rejection. Lockhart observes: "The indigenous priests instead of casting doubt on the new doctrines, insist on retaining the core of their own traditions, while the friars, rather than employing persuasive arts, immediately undertake detailed instruction on the basic tenets of Christianity."

This overview of a prolonged process of adaptation in many ways contradicts the interpretations of the nineteenth- and early twentieth-century historians, such as William Prescott, who emphasized the military aspect, and Robert Ricard, who depicted the Indians as utterly displaced and despoiled. As Lockhart points out, this view, which prevailed for so long, neglected the continuity of important Indian social structures. Rather than being frozen in time or paralyzed by fear, the indigenous peoples were resourceful in merging their own institutions and beliefs with those of the Spaniards. Most of these indigenous groups were not only familiar with armed conflict, but accustomed to the many consequences of losing wars.

By the late eighteenth century, Lockhart attests, the Spanish and Indian institutional merger had established a social system of relatively "stable composites," all of which were rooted in the Indian cultures.

Let's take a closer look at this process.

The "Spaniards" who spearheaded the Conquest were actually

Castilians, also a group who dominated a territory composed of previously diverse populations. They included warriors, of course, but also clergy, some laity, a few nobles, but usually artisans, and, most important, an invaluable group of Indian allies and translators.

The rulers of the various indigenous groups, living in distinct territories known as *Atapetl,* were those of noble families and a priesthood related to military conquest. As with the Castilians, these were highly stratified societies, though with no distinctions between religion, power, and wealth. For all the many differences, these similarities made a future adaptation possible.

As we have noted, the early friars were Franciscans, many of whom were religious radicals known as "spirituals" who shared an apocalyptic view of the imminent end of the world and a concomitant utopian vision of a New World without sin or corruption. Many were barely literate, though a few were highly educated. Some were probably militant fanatics; others were extraordinarily humane and idealistic. In any case, they were disinclined to simply replicate Spanish society.

It is the process by which the indigenous people came to accept the Catholic faith that most interests us, and has been perhaps the aspect of the Conquest most subject to distortion.

Contemporary historians, such as Lockhart, tend to agree on the following correctives: First, the most serious conflicts in the post-conquest period were internal fights among the Spanish and among the indigenous — not with each other. If it had not been for their numerous Indian allies, ethnic groups with their own self-interests, the Spanish could not have conquered the vast Aztec empire.

Secondly, both the Spanish and the Aztecs were imperialists who considered themselves inherently superior to those they dominated. The wealthy and aggressive Castilians of the sixteenth century represented a world power and viewed themselves as superior not only to other Iberians but to most other Europeans. Nahuas saw all strangers who "babbled" in another language as inferior. It was only natural that, following the military conquest, the Spanish would then employ the previously dominant Nahuas as their auxiliaries in conquering and ruling the many other groups in Mesoamerica.

Similarly, some of the earlier myths of the Conquest concern the nature of the religious conversion imposed by the Spanish friars. There is no doubt that it was imposed, and at times harshly; but the full reality of the process is more complex than mere forceful imposition. While a dispute among Spaniards about the human nature of the Indians, and thus their abilities and rights, would rage for decades, many missionaries perceived what Lockhart terms some "special affinities" with the Nahuas.

Being conquered and occupied was hardly a new experience for most indigenous peoples. What's even more significant, the acceptance of the "gods" of the conquering group was an inherent part of the nature of conquest. The deities of the victorious were considered more efficacious by virtue of the victory itself. It was not, therefore, unprecedented that the Nahua authorities accepted Christianity and then immediately began to integrate their old ways, particularly cures and incantations, into the new beliefs. This acceptance of "new gods" was a natural and thoroughly traditional development.

The early friars, while deploring what they perceived as "the work of the devil" in the pagan Nahua rites, were thus able to instruct and mold more than challenge previous beliefs. The indigenous translators became crucial agents in guiding this assimilation, and undoubtedly the strong faith of much of the Spanish laity also reinforced Indian beliefs in the supernatural and in miracles.

In time, religious beliefs coincided and the assimilation was reinforced by the adaptation of rituals. The Catholicism of the Castilians was, as Lockhart points out, as "ritualistic, propitiatory and corporate" as the indigenous religion. We will see later evidence of this assimilation in examining the remnants of indigenous rites in twentieth-century Mexico.

Needless to say, serious discrepancies remained. The indigenous concepts of morality were communal and tied to social obligations rather than personal ones; and, therefore, the concept of individual redemption, or the necessity of the forgiveness of sin, remained foreign.

This is not to suggest that the original indigenous culture was without its own morality. In some respects, Aztec society had been as morally strict as the Spanish. Many transgressions, including adultery, were punishable by death; and while the moral code was enforced by fear, there was recognition of the need of spiritual discipline as well. Similar to the Christian admonition to avoid "lust in the heart," the Aztecs warned against "adultery of the eyes." The early friars admired many facets of the Aztec life, especially their love and care of children, but deplored conduct such as frequent inebriation.

The most important aspect of the religious assimilation, which affects Mexican Catholic life to this day, was the role of the saints. The devotion of the Spanish to the saints of their native regions and families formed a vital part of their inheritance. The Indians recognized in these devotions a pattern in their own culture, and quickly adopted the Spanish saints, or at least their names, as their own patrimony. The indigenous elders would often make the selection of a saint based on dreams, or propitious dates or signs, or sometimes inspired by Spanish iconography. What had been a pantheon of gods became intertwined with the lives of the Catholic saints. In time, not only the saints but miracles and religious images became cross-cultural. Contradicting earlier assumptions, the early friars did not encourage the cult of the saints for their own purposes. They were quite aware of the dangers of pagan appropriation. But devotion to the saints became a unifying factor in what was to become "Mexican" culture. In Mexico City in 1593, for instance, there was a large procession honoring St. Francis in which both Spaniards and indigenous participated. The saint was depicted as astride the symbolic eagle of the *Mexicas,* much to the acclaim of all.

The ability of the indigenous to incorporate the saints into their daily life was remarkable. The Tlxacalan term for what would later be called a *barrio* or neighborhood was *santopan,* that is, "the place of the saint." To simply maintain a residence was "to serve the saint" at that place; and, adapting an earlier indigenous communal concept of land, to bequeath a piece of land meant willing it to the saint — literally, an image of some kind — and then willing the image to a relative. Separate dwellings called "saint-houses" were maintained for altars and images, and I have seen elaborate home altars in present-day Chiapas that are the heart of the dwelling.

The centrality of the devotion to the saints remains to this day in Mexico. The festival or *fiesta* of a particularly important saint is often the most elaborate of the year.

Miracles, including their depictions in artworks, or in effigies of cures attached to the statues of saints, also played an important role in as-

similating the indigenous into the Catholic faith. An Indian chronicler of
the sixteenth century named Chimalpahim, writing in Nahuatl, tells of
"great miracles" *(huey tlamahuicalli)* celebrated in Mexico City in 1583,
featuring a procession of the image of Our Lady of Remedios with Spanish and indigenous, again, jointly participating. In the year 1600, a miracle
was attributed to the intervention of San Diego, who reportedly resusci-
tated two drowned children. In 1611 and again in 1615, miracles were attributed to St. Nicholas for preserving the life of a Spanish woman in an
earthquake and then rescuing a child from a well.

What became the Nahua form of Catholic Christianity was communal and corporate. It was not primarily a system of propositions or ideas
derived from the catechism. It was based on a series of rituals concerning
death, birth, and marriage — and in that order of importance.

Death and burial rites were related to social and family standing, including inheritance. These religious rites amounted to protocols that
preserved one's status and kinship. Indigenous culture was based upon
fixed household relationships rooted in gender, age, and seniority. Family
members employed an extraordinarily formal language with a persistent
religious character, including references to *"the Lord and creator, giver of
life."* It is easy to see, then, how the cults of saints could be incorporated
into a daily existence so conscious of cycles of time and with such a dependency upon the supernatural.

Change was, of course, inevitable. As happened in Spain a century
earlier, much of what had been communal gradually became private
property. Property rights were increasingly disputed and rivalries broke
out. For example, many Indians wanted to hold onto the churches they
had built and would occasionally reject the presence of a new religious
order. There was also discord within monastery churches shared by different ethnic groups. Mexican-born priests sometimes left religious orders to become "secular" clergy in order to better protect family and local interests. Even in religious processions, such as those on a saint's day,
rivalries developed over the prominence of a group's place, or over the
right to hold an independent procession.

It is only natural that as the process of assimilation developed, so did
new forms of status and distinction. The community leaders became
known as *Teopantlaca,* or literally the "church people." Their leaders,

called *fiscals,* were often from noble Indian origins, but not from the line of high priests whom the Catholic clergy had deposed. The "church people" were an elite second only to the community's chief leader, hyphenated as the *Tlatoani-Gobernador.* Characteristic of a ritualistic society, the cantors and musicians had considerable status and derived income from their participation in important events such as funerals. Everyone paid a form of dues to the Church, either in money or in staples such as cacao beans, a custom that carried into modern times.

Another important feature of community life was active participation in the *cofradias,* sodalities or fraternal orders. These were local organizations, often competitive with those in other districts, which arranged the rituals. There were rivalries concerning places in processions, the size of images to be carried, and those permitted to carry them. Membership included funeral benefits.

Significantly, women not only made up the majority of active participants in the *cofradias* but occasionally served as leaders — surprising, given their otherwise low status in the culture. Nahuatl documents list several older women ("mothers") as *deputadas* as early as 1632, their task described as keeping "order and respect for sacraments." One wonders how many of the active men were simply obliging husbands.

Social status in these communities was largely based on the number of masses paid for after one's death. Unfortunately, this often led to considerable indebtedness to the Church; and, as land would be exchanged to settle the debt, led to the problem known as "land for masses." The indebtedness to the community or to its leaders based on high expenditures for obligatory rituals was, and still remains, a characteristic of indigenous societies; but, in time, the Church's accumulation of land in this manner would be perceived as an injustice, and, thus, resented.

The primary significance of the emergence of the "church people" and the *cofradias* was that, as indigenous life became less localized, due in part to the development of the larger *hacienda* economy, these social structures began to include different ethnic groups, and even occasionally the Spanish and Creoles (Mexican-born Spanish).

Eventually, as we will examine later, the devotion to, and the image of, the Virgin of Guadalupe would begin to augment, if not replace, local and "rival" saints.

While we will want to consider this most important of all Mexican religious figures and symbols in more detail, let's note here that the Virgin of Guadalupe was a potentially unifying figure at the outset. While identified with Tepeyac, a site then near but not in Mexico City, she was never primarily a localized figure of devotion. As we shall see, the devotion was linked to a growing sense of Creole and later *mestizo* (mixed Spanish and Indian) identities, but she also united the many Indian groups. The Guadalupe devotion facilitated what Lockhart calls an "expanding consciousness" among the Indians, due to the more diverse economy, migration, and their increasing use of the Spanish language.

This linguistic development had some significant spiritual implications. The expanded use of Spanish included the increasing adoption of Spanish names, particularly among the Indian noble families where it became common to join Spanish and indigenous surnames. It is hard to underestimate the profound psychological effect of one aspect of this new "naming," and that was the giving of proper personal names to women. Previously designated by order of birth and kinship (daughter "one" or eldest girl or youngest girl), a practice not limited to Mesoamericans, these young women often became "Lupe" or "Juanita" and, of course, "Maria."

During the seventeenth century, following the publication in 1649 of Father Laso de la Vega's account of her miraculous appearance, the Virgin of Guadalupe, *La Morena* ("the dark one"), became unrivaled in her ability to unite Mexicans across all lines of class and ethnicity. This was, however, a process that took place over time and was controversial from the outset, as many within the Church saw the devotion as dangerously syncretic. We shall deal with these controversies in a later chapter.

By the nineteenth century, as we shall see, the Virgin of Guadalupe formed the core of a national identity. And even before that, as James Lockhart remarks, she "changes the center of gravity" in New Spain.

Living Vestiges: Twentieth-Century Indigenous Adaptations

The number of Mexican indigenous peoples who still do not speak Spanish, most living in isolated areas, continues to diminish; but there remains in Mexico ample evidence of a persistent, even resilient, religious syncretism. The documentary sources scholars have used to reconstruct the process of assimilation following the Conquest is limited; so the existing remnants of indigenous life are vitally important in that they provide a glimpse of the character of the original religious practices.

The pioneering anthropological studies of the first half of the twentieth century suggest that, despite four hundred years of Catholic dominance, a high degree of syncretism was widespread in rural areas. Many of the Catholic rituals with parallels in the Indian culture had been incorporated into indigenous religious life, including the use of candles, flowers, processions, incense, vows, and pilgrimages (which were called "going to see the saint").

In 1936, the anthropologist Elsie Clews Parsons completed her extensive and often-cited study of the Zapoteca village of Mitla in Oaxaca, near the monumental ruins of Monte Alban and the site of ancient stone mosaics. Mitla had been an important Zapoteca religious center, but Parsons found the local religion to be a sometimes strange mixture of native and Catholic rites and beliefs. For example, the Church's holy water was used in customary ways, but also to induce speech in babies. Concepts of sin were a blend of medieval Catholic and pagan ideas. The presence of the mentally-ill or deaf mutes, for instance, was seen as a sign of parental sin or neglect, or even a punishment for the abuse of neighbors.

This syncretism was most apparent at the time of a person's death. Distinctly Catholic funerals were held in twentieth-century Mitla, but local attitudes toward death, Parsons reported, remained largely indigenous. The dead were placed on a cross of lime (possibly derived from native sand paintings), with flowers, candles, a cross in hand, and a picture of a saint placed on the body. It was believed, however, that no one afflicted with a sickness should be in proximity to the dead as "death spirits" might attack any form of weakness. Traditional black-and-white kerchiefs and head scarves were a sign of mourning.

As in the post-conquest era, funerals in Mitla were costly, as the priest and the formal "prayer-givers," as well as the obligatory band, all charged fees. There were no real last rites in a Catholic sense because of the lack of a sense of personal sin and responsibility. The last journey required food, but "going down" to the "better place" was possible despite having lived a sinful life. As Parsons put it: The "Indians pray not for, but *to* the dead."

Catholic beliefs and ceremonies were, nonetheless, dominant through-out the year. Children were confirmed and received first communion, and at age seven they were no longer considered innocent *angelitos* (little angels) free from sin if they were to die.

All of the major Catholic feast days and numerous saints' days were observed. However, most of the twenty-one saints celebrated in Mitla were also related to ancient local gods. The indigenous year had con-sisted of twenty months of thirteen days, and included auspicious or "lucky" days that had been incorporated into the Catholic calendar. Other remnants of numerology persisted as well as a belief in auguries and astrology.

Catholic priests were employed primarily for marriage, funerals, and "naming" ceremonies. Surnames still weren't commonly used as a per-son's name was customarily derived from animals, dates, or related to the number of siblings. Among the sacraments, baptism was most readily ac-cepted because it was considered as either "good medicine" or as a form of exorcism.

The indigenous priestly hierarchy had been inseparable from the rul-ers of the society and the later Catholic priests and friars, largely *mestizo*, who replaced them often became the *de facto* local rulers, particularly of small rural towns. Whatever their influence might have been, by the 1930s, social life retained most of the native customs. This was particu-larly true regarding family life and gender roles. Mitla women were re-stricted to domestic labor and still had limited roles in religious rituals. Wives were sometimes sought from other groups, and male promiscuity was common, as was drunkenness. As in other ancient societies, the use of herbs for abortions, despite Catholic teaching, was not uncommon.

Indigenous culture had discouraged individualism, signs of wealth, and even competition for leadership as behaviors endangering social cohe-sion. Sexual interest and attraction were never even acknowledged, and there was little overt expression of personal affection except between women and children. Despite this elaborate system for avoiding social conflict, rivalries between towns and even neighborhoods were common.

Some analysts have suggested that this lack of individualism contrib-uted to the persistent poverty of the indigenous peoples. The traditional barter system prevented an accumulation of wealth, which, while it maintained some degree of social equilibrium, also hampered the accrual of capital that could have provided irrigation and fertilizers. But in such a highly communal system, there was also no real motivation to "improve" one's self. Personal advancement would only increase the danger of envy, which created enemies who might harm you, perhaps through witchcraft, in this life or in the next.

In this highly static and communal culture, it is not surprising, then, that the concept of personal virtues or vices remained foreign. Sins were still viewed as individual acts that lacked any real significance outside a social context. As a result, the people of Mitla did not re-enact the Passion of Christ at Easter because it simply made no sense to them.

The object and basis of moral obligation was to avoid shame and ridicule. Misfortunes such as drought, however, might be seen as a punishment for "waste" or a neglect of nature. The traditional miniature food offerings, small items of food and drink in small cups, reflected the belief that "much comes from little." This was a kind of early ecological awareness, celebrating the inexhaustible wealth of nature as well as a practice of conservation.

The price for this stress on impersonal and collective behavior, from a Christian point of view, was a loss of many aspects of what we would see as love or charity. Personal commitments were made among the indigenous, but were seen as obligations established by tribal custom. One can only speculate about what inner conflicts may have existed.

The indigenous integrated the outward aspects of Catholicism, but rejected many aspects of the Spanish culture, significantly, the preoccupation with romance and courtship. The concepts of honor and the need for sexual conquest, though not incorporated into the indigenous culture, did however assume a role in the emergent Mexican culture.

Two long-term studies of Tepoztlan, a village sixty miles from Mexico City, by Robert Redfield and Oscar Lewis, both renowned anthropologists, chart the notable changes modernity brought to indigenous life during the first decades of the twentieth century.

Much of the reality of daily village life was seemingly little altered at the time of Redfield's observations in the 1920s. Once a center of Aztec culture — in fact, the legendary birthplace of their major god, Quetzalcoatl — by the early twentieth century Tepoztlan, like Mitla, was a syncretic Catholic village. Many of the homes had their own altars and no less than fifty-three *fiestas,* including those of the saints, in a year. There was still a prevalent fear of the "evil eye" arising from social envy.

Oscar Lewis, in the later study, also saw the Tepoztlan as still a "natural man," fearful of God, strangers, and evil spirits, whose goal in life was not the future, but maintaining a balance in the present moment. Yet Lewis recorded some significant changes as well. By the 1940s, Mexico's economic development was beginning to create a middle class, or at least class differences in the village. American styles and attitudes were now apparent. The young were less provincial, more open to interaction with others, more ambitious and individualistic. They were also displaying increased signs of anxiety.

It was, however, the changes in the status of women and marriage that were most striking. Parsons had observed that women had retained more of their original indigenous attitudes than the men due to less exposure to outside pressures, but some changes were now evident. A girl was still considered a *nina,* a child, only until the age of twelve; so, clearly, any concept of adolescent development was lacking. But by the 1940s, a young girl having a *novio,* a boyfriend, was increasingly acceptable. Fifty percent of the marriages took the obligatory Mexican form following the Revolution, that is, requisite civil as well as Church ceremonies. Fifteen percent of marriages were *union libre* or common-law, and only ten percent were strictly civil and that primarily because of the costs of the additional Church ceremonies. The average age at marriage was nineteen for males, sixteen for females.

Changes were also noted in the behavior of children, who now seemed, according to Lewis, more expressive and less repressed. Nonetheless, traditional attitudes persisted. Many of the village women saw childbirth and sexual intercourse as inherently cruel and abusive. The women, on the other hand, almost never alone, seemed better socialized than the men, and older women, especially, seemed to gain increased freedom and status with age.

Clearly, with changes in child rearing and the status of women, however incremental, some fundamental transformations seemed inevitable in Tepoztlan. In 1956, Oscar Lewis questioned whether the Tepoztlans would survive culturally. Could they maintain their language and customs?

By the end of the twentieth century, the community had certainly changed. Some Nahuatl speakers remained and children were learning it now as a second language in school; but the town had become a somewhat fashionable tourist attraction and a retreat for Mexico City urbanites not more than a day's drive away.

Something of the spiritual atmosphere had also inspired an influx of American "seekers," including "New Age" devotees. The town had even been described as a "hippy haven." Nevertheless, the Dominican monastery has been preserved as a museum and on September 8, a *Fiesta del Templo* (Church festival) is held featuring Catholic-themed plays given in Nahuatl.

Oscar Lewis's noted colleague, Elsie Parsons, was perhaps prescient when she predicted that within fifty years of her study, that is, by the 1980s, free-market capitalism, with its relentless individualism, would accomplish what the Church had failed to do — that is, finally eliminate the old ways. The end of the story is yet to be written.

The "Natural Man": Interpreting the Indigenous Culture

There have been numerous, indeed, seemingly endless, attempts to interpret the legacy of Mexico's indigenous culture and its significance for us in the modern era.

Octavio Paz, Mexico's most prominent modern intellectual, perceived in the Mexican embrace of the indigenous inheritance a persistent desire for "the Eternal Return," that is, a desire to either return to nature or to a mythified unspoiled past. Paz saw a symbolic commonality in such historic figures as the Aztec martyr Cuahtemoc and the revolutionaries Morelos and Zapata — all as appealing "natural men." Emiliano Zapata, now romanticized more than ever, came from the south and, as Paz noted, remained an isolated and opaque stranger amidst his contemporaries.

Perhaps due to his disappointment in aspects of modern Mexico, Paz himself tended to idealize the indigenous legacy as "the most stable and lasting heritage" in Mexico. This seems to be in tension with Paz's own liberal precepts. When Paz stated that "man is a being who can realize himself" and "man is a possibility frustrated by injustice," he was expressing liberal ideals that would be incomprehensible to the traditional indigenous mind.

This "desire to return" is not unique to Mexicans, but seems to have emerged concurrently with the rise of modernity. Rousseau's "natural man" in pre-revolutionary France was anticipated by an idealization of the primitive among European thinkers as early as the sixteenth century, and was the basis for Shakespeare's deflating depiction of "Caliban," a pathetic half-human creature in *The Tempest*. Perhaps the return to some pure origin is a natural desire, a longing common to all human beings.

More perceptively, Paz asked why animosity toward the Spanish has been so durable in Mexico. He concluded that it stemmed from the deepest internal contradiction in Mexico. He described the Mexicans as "adopted children" of their one true mother, Guadalupe; but, as they were neither purely Spanish nor *Indios,* sadly, they rejected both.

In reflecting upon what the indigenous heritage means to us, all of us, we should perhaps be cautious of contemporary evaluations, including our own. We have seen a growing inclination in late or "post" modernity to attempt to "escape from history" and, thus, to evade contemporary problems of power and responsibility.

In this respect, there is a cautionary tale from the past: In the 1930s, Antonin Artaud, the French creator of the ultramodern "Theater of Cruelty" came to Mexico looking for his own imagined magical kingdom, a desire not unlike that of some of the early Spaniards.

Artaud clearly desired to glorify the primitive past, wherever it could be found; but, not speaking Spanish, much less any indigenous language, he discovered his "magic" in museums and books. He then projected onto Mexicans his own "surrealist" views. What does he find in Mexico? "Death, doubt, ambiguity, destruction" — in other words, the nihilism of his own time and place. He didn't need to leave Europe in 1936 to find despair and chaos.

The danger for us is that as our once strenuously rational culture declines in intellectual vigor, we will want to romanticize the past out of our own disillusionment. We might fantasize that, somehow, the indigenous in their primitive purity had the key to solving the inherent life-death contradictions in human existence. Perhaps we would do better to simply respect their doubts and fears — that is, the humanity they share with us.

Crown, Court, and Church

The Colonial Period in New Spain

For all of its successes, including the discovery of the New World and the exploitation of its resources, imperial Spain was suffering internal dissensions and growing self-doubt. This condition, following the defeat of the Armada in 1588, worsened to the degree that, by 1640, the Spanish empire was nearly bankrupt and tottering. By 1700, French royalty, the Bourbons, replaced the old Habsburg regime. "Spanish" rule would continue for more than another hundred years; but by then, as we shall see, New Spain was increasingly independent and self-conscious of what would become its separate "Mexican" identity.

The contradictory character of Spanish culture stemmed from a never-resolved struggle between the Church and the Crown. Octavio Paz contended that this was the source of what became an increasingly authoritarian rule. The search for universality, ironically if not paradoxically, led to the regime's paranoid "inquisitional tone." Yet, Paz observes, medieval Spanish Catholicism had been a "living faith" and a "fountain of life" that bonded the saints and ordinary people. In this spirit, Paz concludes, the Church gave the Indians of New Spain a "place in the cosmos" as well as in society, though it was clearly a Spanish cosmos and society.

The transition from the last stages of the Conquest, from roughly the end of the sixteenth century into the eighteenth century, was also a time of tumultuous changes in the European Christian world. This is the incipient period of what has been called the "crisis of modernity," during which sacred texts were gradually replaced by the authority of Reason.

The result of this "new thinking" was a growing anxiety throughout the European world. It was not just that sacred texts and traditions were being questioned, but that the social order based on previously unquestioned assumptions was at risk.

As the colonial period in Mexico began, the prevailing sense in Spain was that of the risk of irretrievable loss. This was the result of the end of a way of life, the breakup of the last coherent attributes of medieval communality.

The colonial period of New Spain, roughly the seventeenth and eighteenth centuries, constitutes the era of the *vicereignal* (vice-royalty), the rule of a viceroy or vice-regent appointed by the Spanish king. This was the time of the first flourishing of a "Mexican," that is, at that time, Creole culture in music, literature, and architecture. The most significant and revealing figure of this era was not, however, a royal personage, but a religious Sister and distinguished poet, Sor Juana Ines de la Cruz, who will be the subject of a following chapter.

The look of colonial New Spain is still evident in Mexican cities and towns today. There is usually a central plaza with a government building such as a city hall *(presidencia)* on one side and a church or cathedral opposite. On the other sides of the plaza stood the palaces or palatial homes of the leading families, and, in time, businesses. The other civic institutions were schools, universities, and military garrisons as well as many churches, convents, and monasteries. At the end of the colonial period, there were more than forty convents and monasteries in Mexico City alone.

The plaza mirrored a social unity in colonial times based on the unique alliance of power and faith. The viceroy, always from a noble Spanish family, had several titles, including Governor and Captain General of the Army; but the king limited his power by balancing it with that of the Church hierarchy, particularly the archbishops of the two largest cities, Mexico City and Puebla. At times, an archbishop, also a noble, might serve simultaneously as viceroy and hierarch. In case there might be any tendency toward independence, the viceroy's family was required to remain in Spain.

The economy was based on mercantilism, particularly trade with Spain, and an embryonic middle class of entrepreneurs, speculators, and shop owners was emerging. The upper class, however, still based its wealth and prestige on the *latifundista* system of huge land ownings, and on their control of the people who worked the land. Significant for the future, the control of land and trade was increasingly in the hands of Creoles. The wealth of the Church was considerable, as it collected, at least theoretically, a ten-percent tithe, the *diezmo,* from all earnings.

New Spain was not in any sense a modern society. It might even be termed an "anti-modern society." The state was based on the absolute power of the monarch, and the viceregal court consciously imitated the manners and customs of Spain and aped the elegant extravagances of the Versailles of Louis XIV. This was a society of patronage, courtesies, and courtesans. The aesthetics were elaborate and decorative, and the morals often hypocritical. Appearances mattered more than substance or behavior. In the elegance of the provincial court, the gracious life of the landed elite, the splendor of its Baroque churches, and the obedience of the impoverished Indians, colonial New Spain reached its cultural height in the early seventeenth century when Spanish imperial rule was relatively stable and firmly regimented.

There was in all this, however, an ongoing unifying process. Peninsulars, Creoles, and *mestizos* were beginning to mix, racially and culturally. A new consciousness was being created. New Spain was not a colony of dissenters as in New England; but, like the Americans to the north, a strong sense of competition with and resentment toward the mother country was growing.

The colonial period was a time of a gradual transformation that ended in an implosion of conflicting visions. The dream of a New World in New Spain had been shared by Cortes and many *conquistidores* as well as the Franciscan friars. Those who stayed eventually considered themselves "new," that is, "Mexicans." It was the Creoles and the *mestizos* who were developing a new nation. Mexico was born out of a utopian vision from the beginning. For the *conquistidores,* the search for *El Dorado,* the city of gold, and similar fantasies, had inspired dreams of a land of un-limited wealth. The early Franciscans, on the other hand, sought to initi-ate a primitive Christianity in a land unspoiled by imperial greed and Church corruption. Later, the nineteenth-century liberal idealists em-braced a new vision of a society governed by reason, law, and science. Needless to say, none of these visions was fulfilled.

The Enlightenment or "the Age of Reason" brought profound changes in European thought as brilliant figures, such as Francis Bacon and Isaac Newton, sought a deeper understanding of the natural world and the cosmos. Radical philosophers, such as Spinoza, Descartes, and Voltaire, challenged religious dogma in the name of liberty and reason. It was an artistically fertile period as well, in which the greatest music of the Western world was created, from Monteverdi and Vivaldi to Bach and Mozart. Artists of stature, such as Rembrandt and Rubens appeared, as well as lesser-known but extraordinary painters in New Spain, includ-ing Miguel Cabrera, Cristobal de Villalpando, and Juan Correa.

The Catholic Church of Spain resolutely resisted these changes, and was often rigid and defensive in the face of them. Yet the intellectual and spiritual challenges that most threatened the stability of the Church did not come from Protestants or dissident humanists, but from within the Church itself. The most controversial agents of change were the Jesuits, the members of the Society of Jesus, who became the dominant educa-tional force in New Spain — the "teachers of the new nation." It was the Jesuit concept of universalism, particularly the recognition of other cul-tures as prefigurations of Christ and Christianity, that inspired the new consciousness of the Creoles. The impulses creating this new identity, however, were in tension with the desire to maintain stability. As Paz states, "New Spain was made not to change but to endure." Lamentably, it would do neither.

During this time, a growing sense of independence and importance — Mexico City was soon to be larger than Madrid — increased the antag-onism of the Creole elite toward Spain. The origins of a popular Aztec mythology — that is, the notion that the achievements of the indigenous civilizations were comparable to Rome or Athens — was born during this period. It met the need of the Creoles for an autonomous lineage, that is, a distinctly "American" heritage fully equal to that of Europe.

It was not until the mid-seventeenth century that the Virgin of Guadalupe was first widely celebrated as a miraculous sign of divine favor, if not election. We will discuss this pivotal event in more detail, but here we simply note its importance in the context of Creole aspirations. It is not the first time in which a spiritual figure became fused with national identity. In 1648, a hundred years after the miracle, Manuel Sanchez, a Creole priest, declared that the Virgin of Guadalupe should be recognized as "the first Creole woman" — this despite her clearly *mestiza* features. The Virgin would, in time, become the Mother of all Mexicans, and, indeed, of the Western Hemisphere; but one of her first maternal blessings was to legitimize the Creole ascendancy in New Spain. In the same spirit, there were other efforts to incorporate religious beliefs into a new identity, such as the claim that the Aztec god Quetzalcoatl was actually St. Thomas the Apostle, who brought the faith to the New World long before it appeared in Spain.

A prominent advocate of this *criollismo* was Carlos Siguenza y Gongora, a remarkable figure, comparable in his gifts to a late Renaissance man. Expelled from the Jesuit seminary for unknown reasons, Siguenza y Gongora, an adventuresome intellectual, unsuccessfully sought readmission to the Society, but remained close to the Jesuits his whole life. He was a priest, scholar, and writer who claimed to have verified that the original account of the Guadalupe miracle had been written in Nahuatl. This substantiated its significance for the indigenous as well as promoted the Creole sense of equality with Spain. Siguenza y Gongora and others wrote idealized portraits of Aztec rulers such as Moctezuma, Cuahtemoc, and Iztcoatl. Siguenza y Gongora was also a confidant of Sor Juana, whose play *Lord of the Seeds* affirmed a degree of congruence between indigenous spirituality and Catholic beliefs.

The aspirations of the Creoles were frustrated when Napoleon deposed the Spanish king. Though the relationship had become increasingly tense and rivalrous, Spain had still provided stability, support, and a societal model. From the Creole viewpoint, a covenant had been broken. New Spain was on its own. Genuine independence was now simply a matter of time.

The revolution in 1810 brought the colonial period to an end. The viceregal reign came to be viewed by Mexicans much as Americans viewed the England of George III, a prelude to mature national identity; yet, for more than a hundred years, the colonial era was a time of relative civil order and a flourishing culture.

Preachers and Teachers: The Jesuits in New Spain

The history of the Mexican Church, especially in the colonial period, is inseparable from that of the Society of Jesus, the religious order known as the Jesuits. The role of the Jesuits themselves must then be viewed in the context of the Counter-Reformation and Latin Catholicism after the Renaissance, roughly a two-hundred-year period.

The Society of Jesus was formed by St. Ignatius of Loyola, a former Spanish soldier. Their first assemblies were held in 1558 and then in 1565, with Ignatius himself present. St. Ignatius, in his original writings, spoke simply of the new Society as "coming together in honesty" to perform "pious deeds."

The Jesuits emerged as a strong force at the Council of Trent in 1563, and, as vigorous defenders of the faith against Protestants and other dissenters, they became known as "the pope's men."

The rise of the Jesuits took place during the early period of the Enlightenment, when new concepts in philosophy, science, and the arts were emerging. It is understandable, then, that the Jesuits would respond to these new ideas, and, in some cases, develop them further, even while defending the Catholic tradition. Some of this "new thinking" would prove controversial and provoke the resentment of the established order. The reputation of the Jesuits as casuists, that is, logical analysts of cause and effect, and the use of the term "Jesuitical" as a pejorative, indicating a deceptive use of reasoning, came out of their many disputes, primarily within the Church.

The original mission of the Society of Jesus was to preach and teach, especially the ignorant and children. They were enormously successful in this effort. Logical reasoning wasn't going to reach the illiterate poor, so they developed a pedagogy based on an *aptum* (adaptation) that was more emotional than conceptual or rhetorical.

During the last decades of the sixteenth century, Jesuit missionaries were sent around the world — to China, the Philippines, and, of course, to New Spain. Among their accomplishments was the conversion of isolated tribes, such as the fierce Yaqui Indians, who, hitherto, had resisted Spanish intrusions. Missions were established in some of the most desolate parts of Mexico and the renowned Father Kino labored as far north as present-day Arizona.

The Jesuits also introduced various Spanish devotions to the New World, emphasizing images, relics, and miracles. However, their greatest accomplishments were in the field of education. Their historic innovations created what came to be known as the "classical education." Faith and knowledge were linked, as was theory and practice. The Jesuits, in effect, brought about a revolution in education, bringing an order to the curriculum that had been previously lacking. Corporal punishment, fundamental to medieval schooling, was now balanced with praise, rewards, and honors. The primary goal of education was the development of moral character, self-discipline, virtue, and faith; but the further objective was to "educate the mind as well as the will." The Jesuits also incorporated the laity into their work, particularly the newly developing elites in New Spain. In time, they created a religious intelligentsia beyond the clergy. This largely Creole elite was Mexico's first educated class.

After only thirty years in New Spain, the Jesuits had established eleven colleges, and by 1767, the year of their expulsion, there were more than twenty, as well as boarding schools, and public schools for Indians. Their Royal Pontifical University was the only institution in Mexico that granted university degrees.

Literally, for centuries, Jesuits educated the leaders of the Western world, including, ironically, some who became their bitterest critics, including Descartes, Moliere, and Voltaire. The Jesuits were, in fact, the most controversial and, hence, the most criticized of all the Catholic religious orders.

Moreover, the Jesuits were spreading a Spanish Catholicism related to the Crown and earthly power at a time, as we have seen, of profound change and spiritual crisis. A new elite was emerging, a merchant class preoccupied with wealth and honors. A new consciousness of identity, a nascent nationalism, was awakening in Europe. In places such as Ghent and Naples, "patria" was being emblazoned on banners as a battle cry. In

England, the philosopher Hobbes, an early advocate of unlimited state power, praised members of parliament for being "good patriots." These were signs of the dissolution of central authority, both imperial and religious. The Jesuits, in their loyal support of the papacy, were defending a dying universalism.

In 1600, when Maria de Medici became queen of France, Spain's chief rival, the Jesuits aligned themselves with the French monarchy. This entanglement would prove costly. King Felipe II of Spain was no friend of the Jesuits. The order's independence and resistance to Spanish royal authority only aggravated religious disputes in Spain. In 1588, a book by the Jesuit Luis de Molina provoked a bitter dispute with the Dominicans. The issue was a venerable one, the relationship between grace and free will. Molina's emphasis on free will would lead to accusations of heresy, but there was clearly more than theology involved.

The Jesuit embrace of notions of liberty and justice was inevitably viewed as subversive by the existing powers. Jesuit thinkers, such as Francisco Suarez and Molina, were expounding notions of an inherent equality and right to be free, and Juan de Mariana, a hundred years prior to the American or French revolutions, proclaimed the right to resist tyranny even to the point of regicide.

There was much criticism of the Jesuits as being prone to promote themselves in the "wealthy countries" of the East, such as China. In New Spain, their conflict with the powerful Bishop Polifax of Puebla involved funds from tithes and raised further questions. The financial foundation of Jesuit work in New Spain had come in large part from a wealthy silver-mine owner who advised them to invest in land and haciendas. This proved very profitable, especially in that they paid few taxes. In 1766, King Carlos, whose advisors were often anti-Jesuit Franciscans, ordered an inquiry into Jesuit finances. Their situation then worsened when the riots that broke out in Madrid at that time were blamed, fairly or not, on the influence of overly independent Jesuits.

All the animosity, fear, and criticism of the Jesuits coalesced in the eighteenth century and led to the order of their expulsion from New Spain in 1767. In 1773, Pope Clement suppressed the Society itself. The reasons for the expulsion, suppression, and later restoration were all primarily political, and had little to do with New Spain. However, a whole generation of Creoles was thus deprived of the remarkable educational system that had nurtured them.

Other noted Jesuits in New Spain included Father Jose Vidal, whose missionary efforts were enormously effective. Vidal also bravely challenged Spanish medieval attitudes by preaching against "the fanatical idol of honor" which caused "discord and envy." Another was Francisco de Florencia, a prolific writer who promoted devotions to the saints in his iconographic "Marian Zodiac" of 1755, which offered more than a hundred sacred images. Yet another was Juan Antonio de Olviedo, rector of the Jesuit college, who was known for his gentle and reconciling manner. It was said that in his labors he always "brought peace, not bitterness."

A more controversial figure was Father Antonio Nunez de Miranda (1618-1675), who has been criticized by some historians for his harsh treatment of Sor Juana. We will explore this further in a later chapter; but even his critics acknowledged that Father Antonio was a pious priest who gave special attention to the poor and indigenous. To this list should be added the many Jesuit martyrs who died often torturous and obscure deaths in remote places throughout the Americas.

The Ordered Imagination: Jesuit Spirituality and the Arts

The role of the Jesuits in relationship to the arts, seen in historical perspective, was a vital and heroic one.

One of the most extreme aspects of the Protestant upheaval was the return of iconoclasm, the opposition to figurative religious imagery. This led in 1527 to the sack of Rome and the desecration of sacred images, including the *Vera Icon,* an ancient image of Christ. Other treasured artworks, including some of the frescoes of Raphael, were destroyed as well. The French civil war then led to an even more widespread destruction of religious images. It was just three years later, in 1540, that Pope Paul III recognized the Jesuits. It was, in this context, a call to battle. In the decades that followed, one might say that, while there perhaps was as yet no real "Jesuit style," it was the efforts of the Society of Jesus that effectively rescued religious art.

The Jesuits provided a new and fresh perspective by resuming the inquiry into the nature of human vision begun by the Oxford Franciscans in the thirteenth century, pursuing the question of perspective from a scientific viewpoint. We might remember that it wasn't until the seventeenth century that the scientist Kepler determined the role of the retina. The Jesuit Andrea Pozzo, a remarkable artist, architect, and theoretician, then began to integrate ideas about art, theology, and science. Optics, the science of vision, was seen as related to an "inner vision" which revealed the inner order of the Creation.

Is God a painter, or a writer? The question behind this rhetorical quip has to do with the relationship between word and image. The Word, capitalized or not, was fundamental to Christianity and Judaism, but the image was often suspect as a form of idolatry. The Jesuits played a major role in this debate. Richeome, a French Jesuit, wrote *Saints and Images* in 1598, a defense of sacred images consistent with the eighth-century *iconophilia* decree of the Seventh Ecumenical Council. Richeome argued that sacred images were an essential part of salvation history. The discovery of first-century symbolic images in the catacomb of St. Priscilla in Rome gave weight to the Jesuit argument. The legitimate devotion to sacred images, what was then called the *devotio moderna,* the "modern devotion," was a renewal of not just "the love of images," but a full integration of the senses into faith and belief.

The Jesuits argued that the Scriptures, in a sense, were "talking paintings" in that they evoked images. The Cross is therefore the master image, the primary visual sign. On the other hand, sacred art could be seen as a form of "mute poetry." Giambattista Marino, a poet, wrote a "prose poem" in 1613 that defended "sacred images" as coming from Christ himself. There were at that time three sacred images particularly revered: the *Mandylion* of King Agar, "Veronica's Veil," and the "Shroud of Turin" *(Santo Sindone),* a copy of which was displayed in Mexico in the sixteenth century. In 1636, the artist Poussin used the visage on the shroud as the basis of his painting of Jesus wearing the Crown of Thorns. This became, in time, the prototypical Christ representation. As we shall see, the *tilma,* the cloak of Juan Diego bearing the miraculous figure of the Virgin of Guadalupe, is firmly within this tradition.

The Jesuits were able defenders of the tradition of sacred images, but their influence on the arts was to grow even more significant.

The Age of the Baroque

A two-hundred-year period in the history of European art — from the Renaissance and Vasari to the Enlightenment and Goethe — coincides with the rise of what has been called a Jesuit art movement, that is, the age of the Baroque. This era saw the flowering of the dynamic and elaborate work of artists such as Rubens and Bernini.

The aesthetic foundation of this movement was provided by St. Ignatius Loyola's mystical experiences and a theology that linked the "visible to the invisible." This Jesuit spirituality formed the basis of a whole Catholic culture — art, literature, education, science. It was part of a political imperium that ended in collapse, but left a lasting legacy.

The earliest origins of the Baroque aesthetic are to be found in the otherworldly Byzantine iconic tradition; but artists such as Giotto, influenced by St. Francis, began to move toward the figurative in the twelfth century. Renaissance humanism then contributed its idealized and heroic human figures. It was, however, the Jesuits' recognition of the incarnational dimension of the Eucharist that grounded this new art work in Catholic spirituality.

The Ignatian Exercises, the basis of Jesuit spiritual discipline, have the goal of a total integration of reason, emotion, imagination, and all of the senses. This provides a method by which one can then move from reflection to contemplation. Called "discernment of spirits," this process has the goal of developing an "ordered imagination."

The imagination of the Baroque artist was thus freed to explore new forms. Painters could leave the safety of the circle of the Byzantine icon — that is, the symbol of the ancient world with its cyclical sense of time. These artists would embrace the spiral — endlessly weaving, ascending figures reaching toward heaven.

A technique of radical vertical perspective, derived from Michelangelo and Correggio, was developed by Rubens, giving the viewer the sense of being "lifted up." In time, this art went from the celebration of God's plentitude to an incredibly ornate style, and, then, yet further to the spiritual "gift of ecstasy," a kind of rapture. Bernini's sculptures and even his elaborate fountains provide an example of this magnificence in stone, water, and light.

A distinctly ornate Baroque style further developed in Mexico during the colonial era is referred to as *churrigueresque,* a term derived from the name of a family of Spanish architects. It is most manifest in the architectural style of many churches, facades, and interiors, some listed in the appendix. During the eighteenth century, the Baroque style culminated also in the paintings of remarkable Mexican artists, such as Cabrera, Correa, and Villalpando.

In time, this direction had to play itself out in excess. The glory of God, after all, is beyond images. Perhaps the limitations reached by the Baroque are themselves instructive, reminding us that "eye has not seen, nor the ear heard, nor the heart of man conceived what God has prepared for those who love Him" (1 Cor. 2:9).

The Coded Silence

Rediscovering Sor Juana Ines de la Cruz

One of the most significant figures of the colonial period — indeed, in all of Mexican history — wasn't a conqueror or a ruler, but a seventeenth-century nun. You might say she was an "explorer," but her explorations were spiritual and artistic. Examining her life not only sheds light on her era, but illuminates some continuing cross-currents of Mexican culture. We will not be trying to resolve the many controversies she has provoked, but attempting to relate her life and work to Catholic Mexico, including the Spanish tradition which she inherited and passed on with such eloquence.

Sor (that is, Sister) Juana Ines de la Cruz, as she came to be called, is such an important historical figure in Mexico that you will find her lovely dignified visage on the two hundred peso bill. While she is far more valuable than any denomination of currency, I suspect that for most contemporary Mexicans she is now little more than an illustrious name. She was a poor girl who achieved great acclaim, and as late as the nineteenth century, she was an idealized religious figure. She was later romanticized as a proto-feminist; but, as a national symbol, it is increasingly unclear what she symbolizes.

She was, above all, a poet, and so we will draw upon a major study of her life and work by another great Mexican poet, Octavio Paz. Paz's insights, however, tend to be more relevant to the aesthetics of her poetry than to the meaning of her life. A later study, that of the theologian George Tavard, offers, in our judgment, a more integrated view of her spiritual life as reflected in her writings. Tavard declares Sor Juana to be not only Mexico's first great poet, but the nation's first distinctive theologian. We shall further examine these differing viewpoints, along with others, for what they reveal about Sor Juana as a Mexican icon.

She was born Inez Ramirez de Asbaje near Mexico City, probably in 1648. She died in 1695 at the age of forty-seven, in a convent, attending to her sick sisters during a plague, eventually succumbing to the same disease. She was illegitimate; her father, whom she apparently never knew, was a Spanish soldier, and her mother a *Criolla*. She had therefore no paternal benefits, such as a dowry, a distinct disadvantage at that time. These are among the few facts about her life that are seldom disputed. There is endless conjecture about the rest. It is universally agreed, however, that she was beautiful, charming, witty, and a genius.

For the last three hundred years, highly imaginative speculation has been the dominant mode in Sor Juana studies, so let us join in. It seems apparent from her life, death, and writings that Sor Juana was a devout Catholic Religious whose personal expressions, particularly in her poetry, were original, but whose faith was deep and traditional. She initially joined the Carmelites, but left after a short while to join the Hieronymite order founded on the spirituality and teachings of St. Jerome, the great fourth-century biblical scholar.

Her decision to live a vowed religious life was possibly, at least at first, given her circumstances, simply a prudent choice. Sor Juana herself referred to her calling as the "least unsuitable and most honorable," that is, for a young woman without a dowry or even a proper family name. But, again, this is only speculation. Her life at the time of this crucial turning point was complicated, but not without opportunities. She was already an acclaimed poet, and was enjoying, if not the pleasures, at the least the privileges and protection of life at the viceregal court.

A largely self-educated prodigy, Juana had been sent to live with an aunt in Mexico City. Around 1668, at perhaps age twenty, her exceptional charm and abilities had come to the attention of members of the court.

Juana then became a "lady in waiting" to the wife of the viceroy, and a member of a court known for its frivolities and dalliances. Juana at this early age was recognized not for her piety or scholarship, but for her wit and beauty.

She was influenced in her decision, five years later, to enter the convent by one of the most respected priests of the day, a brilliant Jesuit scholar, who, given her already illustrious reputation, undoubtedly viewed her decision with a degree of personal triumph. Of course, we cannot know Juana's inner struggle or all of her motives, or, for that matter, the motives of others around her. Was she seeking a life of purity and dedication, or escape? Some ambiguous lines in her poetry suggest a possible frustrated romance. We must remember, however, that, as Tavard points out, love and marriage were far from synonymous in this era. As an attractive young woman living at the court and lacking family connections, she was clearly vulnerable, if not susceptible, to intrigue and gossip.

Juana had attracted in succession three *vicereines,* wives of the most powerful men in New Spain, as her *patronas,* all of whom offered her at least some degree of protection. She dedicated a great deal of her poetry to these women, all from the highest rank of Spanish nobility. The first was the Marchioness de Mancera, whom Juana referred to as "Laura" in her poetic tributes. The last was the Countess de Galve. The most important of the three, however, in terms of friendship and advantages was Maria Luisa Manrique de Lara y Gonzaga (the name suggests her pedigree), the Countess de Paredes, whom Juana immortalized in her verses as "The Divine Lysi." There is an atmosphere of intimacy, including praise of the countess's physical beauty in Juana's adulatory poems, which has raised questions — inescapable given our present-day preoccupations — as to the nature of their relationship. We will examine this further when we consider poetic style; but we might note that the Countess de Paredes was known in her time not only for her physical beauty but for her piety. In our day, a woman deemed beautiful, sophisticated, and pious might seem incongruous, but perhaps this should make us more aware of the tenor of our times than of Sor Juana's. In any case, the extravagance of Sor Juana's poetic diction was thoroughly consistent with the style of the court and with that of Baroque Spanish literature, filled as it was with mythological references. The "Divine Lysi" is merely a lovely woman, not a goddess, and her husband, the viceroy, despite Sor Juana's lavish praise in her verses for his birthday, isn't a god, merely an aristocratic ruler.

In that much of Sor Juana's poetry is about love and romance, the most typical theme of that era, let us address the first of the many controversies, that of the nature of her own sexuality. Again, we do not know, nor can we know her private desires, nor is there any clear record of her intimate relationships. All we have is her writings and our perceptions.

During the Baroque period, the languages of romance and spirituality were utterly intertwined, particularly in Spain, and in ways that might shock contemporary sensibilities. Sexual metaphors were frequently employed in the religious poetry of St. John of the Cross and St. Teresa herself speaks of a "divine intimacy" that incorporates a "kiss of your mouth" and "breasts better than wine." These are expressions noticeably free of naiveté or repression. So when either St. Teresa or Sor Juana refers to Christ as "entering into me," they are unabashedly using carnal metaphors.

Not only is there a considerable gap between Baroque sensibilities and those of our day, but there are philosophical divergences as well. It is a contemporary assumption that sexuality can be best understood in terms of personal psychology, or even simple physical desire and sensation. These are not, needless to say, seventeenth-century assumptions. The Baroque era had a serious concern about virginity and chastity from both a spiritual and social viewpoint; but there was also less inhibition, compared to the Victorian sublimation of the physical, or the modern repression of the spiritual.

While we know nothing of the range of her sexual experiences, Sor Juana's best-known writings testify to her strength as a woman. Mexico's two-hundred-peso representation of Sor Juana in her habit contains her famous quote in tiny print deploring the stupidity of men who question the intellectual capacity of women. As we noted, she is now perhaps best known as a proto-feminist based on her eloquent defense of the right and ability of women to study and learn. A scholar and musician as well as a poet, she was certainly well qualified to put the male supremacists of her day in their place, a brave act given the relentless masculinity of Spanish culture. While Sor Juana is justly celebrated for this defense of her sex, it is too limiting to see her in a secular feminist mode. She was, in fact, far more radical. She was pursuing and articulating a radical feminine, not "feminist," view of God. Furthermore, in this pursuit, she was in an established tradition.

If we are to fully appreciate Sor Juana's defiance of a male authority that would subjugate women, then we need to be aware not only of her personal valor but of the many female figures that she undoubtedly studied and admired. In addition to Teresa, Sor Juana cites and, in some cases, writes extensively about Sts. Catherine of Alexandria and Paula. She might also have found inspiration in such exemplars as Sts. Clare, Elizabeth of Portugal, Bridget of Sweden, Catherine of Siena, and Rose of Lima.

Further, among her seventeenth-century contemporaries were Sts. Margaret Mary Alacoque, who established the Sacred Heart devotion, Marie de l'Incarnation, an Ursuline Sister who wrote mystical treaties, as well as Jane Francis de Chantal and Louise de Marillac, both of whom founded religious orders.

But it is the saint whom Sor Juana referred to as her spiritual "mother," Teresa of Avila, who is her most likely model. This seems clear not only from Juana's references but on the basis of the similarities of their experiences. Teresa was the most influential saint in the Spanish-speaking world, indeed, the co-patron saint of Spain, and she prefigures Sor Juana's ideals and, perhaps, her actions.

In her youth, Teresa was also known as brilliant and witty. She later disavowed her earlier social attainments, but remained intellectually open and inquiring. She asked with eager curiosity: "What would happen if we knew the property of every created thing? It is very beneficial for us to busy ourselves thinking of these grandeurs!"

Teresa, too, had been tempted by romance, and she had defied her father to become a nun. She was challenged by male authority many times yet encouraged women to simply pursue their work diligently, assuring them that "you will astonish men!"

As with Sor Juana, Teresa was devoted to study and intellectual pursuits, and wrote: "My fondness for good books was my salvation," for without a book, "my thoughts went wild." She preferred, however, the simplicity of the Gospels to "cleverly written works."

"How is it," she asks, "that you want to please God only with words?" — a question which may have had special resonance for the poet Juana.

In her voluminous writings, Teresa reveals the many struggles in her own life. She writes of trying to overcome "a thousand vanities" and having endured "unbearable trials," many inflicted by Church authorities and rivals in her own order. Much has been made of Sor Juana's conflict and eventual break with her Jesuit confessor. Regarding a clash with her own confessor, Teresa wrote: "What he said grieved me more than everything else put together. This made me so extremely distressed I was thrown into complete confusion and severely afflicted." She concludes: "If I might have had someone to make me fly I would have turned desire into deeds more quickly!"

The Bishop of Puebla in his appeal to Sor Juana to renew her spiritual life and refrain from secular themes in her writing, urged her to "imitate Saint Teresa." During her last years, when Juana chose to "enter into silence," there were sentiments of St. Teresa that must have spoken directly to her. Regarding what she saw as the goal of "ego annihilation," Teresa described the quest as a gradual process, yet requiring at some point a momentous leap.

Sor Juana must have also found strength in Teresa's recognition of the challenges of the life she had chosen. Teresa uses the word "fight," meaning struggle, which she sees as "our only purpose" in life. Therefore, there is always a need for "courage and determination." "More courage is needed for the path to perfection," she wrote, "than a quick martyrdom."

"God is a friend of courageous souls," she concludes, "if they walk in humility without trusting in the self." Teresa's mantra was: "Have a bold daring!"

Sor Juana's life in her convent was not what we might picture. She had her own quarters — which she later actually purchased from the order — an extensive library and collection of musical instruments, and a "girl slave," common at the time, whom she later "sold" to a relative. The convent was in many respects a social center where a famous poet, albeit a nun, could receive equally distinguished intellectuals, clerics, and members of the royal entourage.

It is easy to see that this comfortable lifestyle could produce deep contradictions in Juana's spiritual life. If St. Teresa was her "mother" and Sor Juana's confessors (often portrayed as insensitive or self-serving) were urging a radical examination of conscience, a crisis was inevitable.

This presents us with the most controversial aspect of Sor Juana's life. In 1693, this remarkable poet, the most distinguished of her time, renewed her religious vows, disposed of her library, and "entered into silence," never to write again. Why?

Speculations, particularly those of Octavio Paz, about Sor Juana's silence and the motives behind it often suggest the concerns of our own age rather than those of the colonial period in New Spain. Paz's views reveal the contrasting perspectives of the modern secular intellectual and a religious, particularly Catholic sensibility. These differences, as we will see, have shaped modern Mexican culture.

The religious understanding of "silence," the recognition of the limits of language, is hardly new in Catholic thought. One of the early Church fathers, St. Hilary, fearful of the effects of theological disputes, wrote: "We are forced to imprison indescribable things within the weakness of our language . . . and in expressing it, to surrender to the dangers of the human word what should have been kept and worshipped in our hearts."

A similar insight was expressed by the twentieth-century French mystic Simone Weil who wrote that "a mind enclosed in language is in prison."

Was Sor Juana, in effect, "silenced" by her religious superiors? Was she intimidated or "worn down," as some suggest, to the point of intellectual suicide, or wanting to escape from life itself? Or was her choice of silence in her last years a free choice, a determination to pursue what she would have seen, following St. Teresa, as "spiritual perfection"? In the end, was she defeated, or triumphant?

We don't know. There may have been more personal and even prosaic factors involved than coercion by powerful men or the pursuit of a deeper spirituality. Sor Juana refers in her writing to petty jealousies and malicious rumors both within the convent and at the court. Also, the years prior to Sor Juana's withdrawal, as Tavard notes, were particularly discouraging, even terrifying for the people of New Spain. Numerous disasters struck Mexico City, such as floods, riots, and finally the plague

The original banner of Hernan Cortes, c. 16th century.
The Granger Collection, New York

The meeting of Cortes and Montezuma II at Tenochtitlan, 8 November 1519. Oil on canvas.
The Granger Collection, New York

The Aztec Stone of the Sun, discovered in 1790 in Mexico City. It was first misidentified as a calendar but actually served as an altar for human sacrifice. Diameter: 12 feet.
The Granger Collection, New York

Friar Bartolome de Las Casas (1474-1566), by Felix Parra. Oil on canvas.
Museo Nacional de Arte, Mexico / The Bridgeman Art Library

Crucifixion of Christ, by Sebastian Lopez de Arteaga, 18th century. Oil on wood.
The Granger Collection, New York

The Virgin of Guadalupe, banner at the Atotonilco Sanctuary.
Miguel Hidalgo carried this banner in his call to revolt.
The Granger Collection, New York

The Virgin of Guadalupe appearing to Juan Diego in 1531,
fresco at the Church of San Francisco Javier, Tepotzotlan, Mexico, 1756.

St. Francis in Meditation, by Francisco de Zurbaran, 1639,
depicting St. Francis of Assisi (1181-1226). Oil on canvas.
The Granger Collection, New York

St. Teresa of Avila (1515-1582), by Juan de la Miseria, 1562. Oil on canvas.
The Granger Collection, New York

St. Ignatius Loyola (1491-1556), by Juan de Roelas, c. 1600. Oil on canvas.
The Granger Collection, New York

Sor Juana Ines de la Cruz (1651–1695), by Juan de Miranda, 18th century. Oil on canvas.

Detail from *A Popular History of Mexico,* by Diego Rivera, 1953, depicting Fr. Jose Maria Morelos, Fr. Miguel Hidalgo, and Benito Juarez. Mosaic on the Teatro de los Insurgentes, Mexico City.

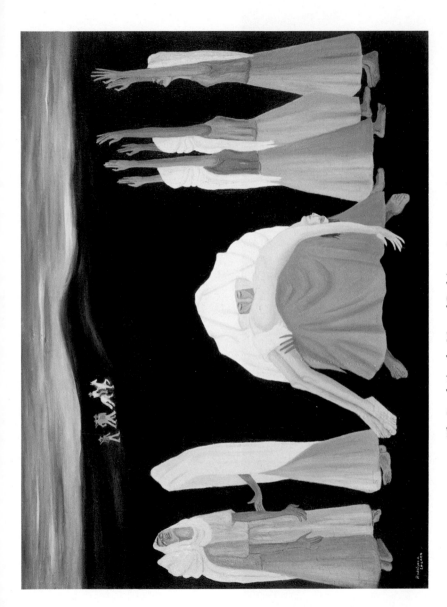

The Revolution, by Manuel Rodriguez Lozano, 1946,
depicting women mourning the victims of the Mexican Revolution. Oil on canvas.
The Granger Collection, New York

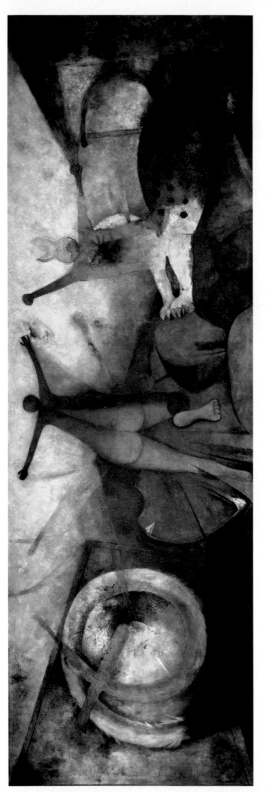

The Mexican and His World (*El Mexicano y su Mundo*), by Rufino Tamayo, 1967. Mural painting.
The Granger Collection, New York

Francisco "Pancho" Villa and Emiliano Zapata in the presidential palace, 1914.
Photograph by Agustin Victor Casasola

The execution of Padre Miguel Agustin Pro, 23 November 1927.
Left: Padre Pro at prayer; right: the moment of his execution.
ullstein bild / The Granger Collection, New York

Octavio Paz (1914-1998), in Frankfurt, Germany, in 1970.
ullstein bild / The Granger Collection, New York

that took Juana's life. Given the predictions of an impending "end-time," any sensitive person might have sought sanctuary in the quiet of a convent cell. As some of the early sonnets reveal, Juana was also keenly aware of the passing of time, including the loss of physical beauty. She was a devout nun, a genius, and a great poet; but she was also a vulnerable human being.

There are at least two legacies of Sor Juana that relate to the development of Mexican culture. There is, of course, the glory of her Spanish verse, her poetry and plays, commissioned by either the Church or the court. These works enhanced the spiritual profile of the saints, an important aspect of Mexican culture for generations to come. Further, her play *Lord of the Seeds* depicted the Conquest as, in part, a convergence of beliefs, suggesting that the indigenous religion was ultimately compatible with Catholicism.

The most lasting legacy, however, may be the least appreciated, and that is her contribution to a "theology of beauty." We will consider this in the next chapter.

There is also the legacy of Octavio Paz's passionate defense of Sor Juana as presented in his major work subtitled *The Traps of Faith*. While, as Catholics, we may lament the harshness of Paz's critique of the Church, we have nothing to fear from the truths he expresses.

Octavio Paz's study of Sor Juana was written over a long period of time, beginning with essays in the 1950s, and not completed until late in his life. It is highly speculative, and Paz admits that we can at best only catch a "glimpse" of the elusive Juana. He even remarks that "she was contradiction itself!" In some respects, perhaps the most significant, the book is ultimately more about Octavio Paz and his times than about the trials of Sor Juana.

Paz's effort to incorporate Sor Juana into his own intellectual and philosophical framework, and, in the end, even into a political context, results in both the weakness of the book and its value. While not convincing as a full account of Sor Juana or even of her significance, it is, on the other hand, a remarkable personal encounter between two great poets. Paz's "embrace" (his word) of Sor Juana does not "explain" her — an impossibility he himself admits, given the limited evidence — but does pose important questions about the relationship of art to faith, and belief to ambiguity. It is a rare and even touching meeting of two souls across a span of hundreds of years.

Paz states his central thesis about Sor Juana, her struggles, and the causes of her eventual silence in several places, both in *Traps of Faith* and in his introduction to Alan Trueblood's anthology of Sor Juana's writings. The source of the "persecution" of Sor Juana, Paz asserts, was her "love of letters," that is, her determination to be a free-thinking intellectual. The reason for her silence, or "being silenced," is because, as a woman, thinker, and poet, she challenged the rigid authoritarianism of the Church. Again, this conclusion is most significant in what it reveals about Paz's anxiety as to the precarious state of freedom of expression in modern times.

When this analysis of ideological despotism is applied to Sor Juana's circumstances, however, it is ultimately unconvincing. Paz makes, in this respect, an important admission. While he admires her poetry, Paz does not, he tells us, "take seriously" Sor Juana's theology, that is, her own personal efforts to articulate her religious beliefs — a curious stance, given who she was and tried to be. It reveals, I suggest, a blind spot exemplified by Paz's omission of St. Teresa's influence on Juana. As a poet, Paz understands and admires Sor Juana — indeed, his book is a kind of love letter over the centuries — but, as a critic, he analyzes her in terms of the ideological categories of his time. For instance, he compares Sor Juana's treatment with that of Soviet dissidents and, thus, searches out esoteric sources in her work that point to heretical tendencies; but there is no record of Sor Juana ever being charged with heresy.

As to the cause of her ultimate "silence," Paz indicts her confessor, the Jesuit Antonio Nunez de Miranda, and suggests that Nunez's personal ambitions played a role in his questionable spiritual guidance. Paz claimed that a letter of Sor Juana's discovered by a Mexican priest in the 1970s confirmed his suspicions of Nunez's complicity. But this "smoking gun" letter only reveals that Sor Juana dismissed Nunez as her confessor after he spoke of her "self-pride." This was at the height of her fame and court connections; and while the letter does reveal that there was a serious break between the two, it is not hard to see that there might have been two sides to the story.

What the letter further reveals is not only that Sor Juana defied this highly placed cleric, but that, in fact, her confessor had no real authority over her. Her position was secure enough to permit an extraordinary declaration of independence. Finally, what the documents, including this letter, do not explain is her silence. The premise of other scholars that Sor Juana relented to pressure because she was "worn down" seems the most speculative and in ways that, ironically, call into question Sor Juana's reputation as a strong and determined woman. There is no clear evidence that she was either "worn down" or intimidated.

When Paz wrote his final conclusion, the ideological blinders of the twentieth century were fraying, but still in place. Hitler and Stalin were dead, and Solzhenitsyn and other brave witnesses had exposed the cruelties and hypocrisies of communism, but the Soviet Union was still standing, however shakily. Paz, a veteran of the Spanish Civil War, had witnessed a century of fratricide rationalized by ideologically blinded intellectuals. His voice, in verse and prose, offered an eloquent appeal for liberty and civility. He was waging, in other words, a good and necessary fight. In Paz's eyes, Sor Juana was a seventeenth-century Anna Akhmatova, the great Russian poet reviled by the Soviets, and her story simply another chapter in the age-old "struggle between freedom and authority" and against what Paz decried as "ideological bureaucracy." Paz's true concern, his passion for freedom, was revealed in 1983 when in his last footnote he refers to his own times as having "known ideological persecutions on a scale greater than that suffered by Sor Juana." The evidence he sought in order to justify his portrayal of Sor Juana is insufficient, his conclusions perhaps even unfair, but his defense of liberty was both courageous and morally justified.

Paz the theorist and historian, however, is not always Paz the poet, and at times they are clearly in tension. He described Sor Juana as "a nun by vocation, but a poet by birth," so what is perhaps the most curious lapse in Paz's understanding of Sor Juana's choice of "silence" is his failure to mention the role of silence within poetry itself. This may seem a paradoxical phrasing, to speak of "words about silence," but Paz was never afraid of paradox.

It is understandable that the ultimate choice of silence would be clearly unacceptable, even offensive, to most modern writers. For some, the words on the page are the meaning and justification of life itself. To surrender even the attempt to "sign" could only be seen as a form of a willful self-destruction, or a capitulation to some oppressive outside force. But it is not only in the sublimities of mystical theology, but in the long tradition of poetry as well, that "silence speaks."

St. John of the Cross, whose poetry explores the obscure silence of the "dark night of the soul," was Sor Juana's closest predecessor in this apophatic poetic tradition. There is direct evidence of his influence as his works are seen among her books in the background of the Cabrera portrait. In describing the experience of God as "the Living Flame of Love," he wrote: "There is no way to catch in words the sublime things of God. . . . The appropriate language for the person receiving these favors is that they understand them, experience them within themselves, enjoy them, and then be silent."

The English poet George Herbert, who died in 1633, is another near contemporary. Unlike Sor Juana, he lived and died in obscurity; but, in many ways, he could be considered Juana's spiritual brother. He was a "devotional," that is, a religious poet who worked as a country parson, and the dates of the publication of his poetry, which brought him posthumous fame and honor, correspond to Sor Juana's most productive period. It is hardly likely that they ever knew of each other, but Herbert concluded his life and work in a spiritual state strikingly similar to that of Sor Juana. He wrote on his deathbed that his poetry reflected "the many spiritual conflicts that have passed between God and my Soul before I could subject mine to the will of Jesus my Master in whose service I have now found perfect freedom."

The verses of the nineteenth-century poet Gerard Manley Hopkins also capture Sor Juana's concerns. A Jesuit, Hopkins in his poem "Heaven-Haven" conveys the spiritual struggle of a nun "taking the veil" and describes her as seeking an inner peace "where no storm comes." In "The Habit of Perfection," Hopkins articulates a spiritual goal even more directly related to Sor Juana's: "Elected silence, sing to me, pipe me to pastures green, be the music that I care to hear!"

We could cite modern poets such as Rilke, Valery, or Eliot who speak of "words that reach into the silence, the stillness" and many others who recognize the limits of language and the significance of that frontier; but it is a poet closer to home who seemed most acutely aware of these boundaries, and, hence, the inevitable sign of silence. This poet was hardly blind to the relationship of poetry and belief. He thought that "by virtue of grace, humankind has an innate knowledge of divinity." He wrote further that even the comprehension of poetry is "a spiritual exercise." He recognized that silence could be a profound form of expression, and wrote that ". . . silence, after the Word, is based on a language — it is an encoded silence. The poem is the trajectory between these two silences — between the wish to speak and the silence that fuses the wishing and the speaking."

This great poet who offered us these insights was, of course, Octavio Paz.

A final speculation and some consolation.

What if, in seeking the asylum of her convent cell, Sor Juana was *not* playing it safe? She had never done so before. What if her "silence" was, for her and others, not a defeat but the culmination of her life and her work? Perhaps she had reached the path that led to silence as a form of surrender to God's love and the beatific vision that was the goal of every saint she had studied and venerated. One can reject this path and this goal — most people have — but it is a misinterpretation of her story, and even a disservice to Sor Juana herself, to negate what, in her own mind, would have been her greatest accomplishment.

We cannot know. We can only, with Paz and Tavard and countless others, speculate. Our consolation, however, is this: The depiction of Sor Juana as a victim of external forces or her own inner restraints may satisfy those prone to identify more with victims than saints; but we can be assured that our view of Sor Juana's life and work is much closer to her own.

We know from her own writing that Sor Juana's best-known poem, *Primero Sueno (First Dream),* was the only one of her many works that she composed for herself. "I have never written anything of my own free will," she noted, "but because of requests and commands from others; so I do not recall having written anything for myself except a little paper called *El sueno."* Even the title when published, *Primero Sueno,* has been variously interpreted. If, as Tavard speculates, a "second dream," a sequel, was to follow, it was never written or was lost. Another possible, even likely, interpretation of *"primero sueno"* in Spanish could be "first, I dream." As with so much of Sor Juana's life and work, we can again only speculate as to the ultimate meaning.

The poem is an extensive, highly ornate, and ambitious attempt to describe, first, the limits of the "soul's ascent," whether by intuition or discursive reasoning. The work reveals Sor Juana's vast knowledge of classical sources, and is thick, almost opaque, with images and symbols from mythology as well as esoteric and eclectic philosophy, much of which, however, would have been familiar to her readers. It also reflects her own misgivings and humility.

The ultimate ascent of the soul, past human wisdom, is to the contemplation of the divine, but, in *Primero Sueno,* consistent with her "theology of beauty," it is the human form that most reflects God's Glory.

From *Primero Sueno* (First Dream) as translated by Alan S. Trueblood:

> In short, I speak of man, the greatest wonder
> the human mind can ponder,
> complete compendium
> resembling angel, plant, and beast alike;
> whose haughty lowliness
> partook of every nature. Why?
>
> Perhaps that, being more fortunate
> than any, he might be lifted high
> by a grace of loving union.
> Oh, grace repeated often,
> yet never recognized sufficiently.
> Overlooked, so one might think,
> so unappreciated is it,
> so unacknowledged it remains.
>
> These then were the stages over which
> I sometimes wished to range; yet other times
> I changed my mind, considering it much too daring
> for one to try to take in everything.

"Beauty Ever Ancient, Ever New":
Sor Juana and the Theology of Beauty

Almost all visitors to Mexico admire the elegant designs, vivid colors, and the many artistic accomplishments one encounters at every turn; but to grasp the role of Beauty in Mexican Catholic culture, we must recognize that it is not merely a matter of aesthetic appreciation. If we take seriously, as we should, Sor Juana's theology, then we should explore, as she did, a deeply spiritual approach to all the forms of Beauty, including art, music, and poetry. It is appropriate in this context to capitalize Beauty because the underlying assumption of this approach is that Beauty is a face of God.

The word "Beauty" came into the Christian vocabulary from the Greek. It traditionally refers to a "harmony of proportions" derived from the classical view of the human body. Christians came to see something more, that is, a "proportion par excellence" that reflects our relationship with God. We are created, as human beings, "in relation to the whole," who is God. Beauty thus takes us beyond questions of art to a form of revelation.

Sor Juana's theology is not systematic in the manner of the great Scholastics, such as Aquinas. This is not a criticism. Beauty is an experience that lies beyond explanation or conceptual analysis. It cannot be limited by definition any more than our experiences of the divine in the sacraments or in nature.

Catholic theologians throughout the ages have developed a spiritual understanding of Beauty. St. Augustine's most quoted lines relate to his discovery of God in Beauty: *"Late have I loved you, O Beauty ever ancient, ever new, late have I loved you. You called, you shouted and you shattered my deafness."*

In modern times, theologians such as Karl Rahner, Bernard Lonergan, Josef Pieper, and, most particularly, Hans Urs von Balthasar have seen Beauty as fundamental to Christian doctrine. Similarly, John Paul II in his encyclical *Veritatis Splendor* described Beauty as inseparable from and, indeed, the "splendor" of Truth.

The philosophical roots of this Catholic tradition are found primarily in Plato and later Plotinus. Using Greek categories, Beauty was initially seen by the early theologians, Augustine in particular, as the "fourth Transcendental," that is, the fourth aspect of the absolute and awe-inspiring nature of God — the first three being God's Oneness, Goodness, and Truth. The Greek philosophers had originally viewed Beauty, that is, the experience of a profound harmony, as foundational to the other Transcendentals.

The medieval philosophers were more intrigued by the nature of Beauty than they were about the practice of art, which they respected as human labor. The breakup of the medieval order, as we have seen, had profound consequences for the heretofore-unified understanding of the world as God's creation. The attempts to create an organic synthesis of philosophy and theology by thinkers such as Albertus Magnus and Aquinas was challenged. Under these circumstances, when conceptual thought is conflicted and thus clouded, the redemptive role of Beauty becomes indispensable.

The Theology of Beauty is invariably related to forms of mysticism, in that the most profound Beauty is experienced as ineffable gift. Among the theologians who advanced this aspect of theology was St. Bonaventure, whose ideas about the nature of light are essentially mystical yet relate to nature and cosmology. Light as the source of energy creates matter and Bonaventure saw Light itself as beautiful and transcendental. Light comes from a simple, pure source that resists, by its very nature, fragmentation, distortion, and disharmony. This is the basis of an aesthetic that unites the body and spirit. We see this insight expressed in the Catholic creedal recognition of Christ as "Light from Light." Bonaventure's aesthetic theology related the mind and the senses to this illumination and thus validated art and images as "coming from above." This is Beauty as grace, but, again, not a concept so much as the description of an "enlightening" experience.

In the thirteenth century, as Umberto Eco comments, theology became increasingly concerned with "the things of this earth" and Christ became a paradigm of physical beauty. The early Renaissance artistic forms that were inspired by St. Francis and his followers, such as Dante and Giotto, in time became fused with a revival of Greco-Roman idealism that inspired, among others, Michelangelo. Art flourished, and artistic creations became virtually a "language of God's glory." The mystical theology that grounded this historical development was Sor Juana's inheritance. That she was not entirely original in this is no more of a criticism than the lack of systematic analysis. No one can be "original" about God or Beauty.

Sor Juana saw Beauty not only as a reflection of the Divine, the one God, but as an affirmation of the God-given nature of humanity. There was, for her, a kind of mirroring relationship in which the human perceives God in the glory of His creation while God sees Himself in the Beauty of human form. Her poetry primarily celebrates this human reflection of God's Beauty. That her poetry is rooted in her faith is self-evident. However, most of her praise of Beauty concerns the female form, including the female physical body. But her model isn't an aristocratic countess; it is the Virgin Mary — not the amiable maiden of popular art, but the exalted *Theotokos* of the Eastern Christian tradition, the graceful bearer of Christ.

What Sor Juana is seeking to reveal is the unity of the human and divine — a perennial theme in Hispanic theology. This is why her theological thought is so centered on the Incarnation and, finally, on the Immaculate Conception. Beauty as revealed in Christ is the theme of one of Sor Juana's major poetic works, *Divine Narcissus,* in which the mythic figure who gazes at his reflection in water symbolizes Christ's bodily manifestation in the world. The latter theological question, the Immaculate Conception, the Catholic dogma that Mary was born without sin, was a topic of serious debate at that time — in part, a Counter-Reformation response to the Protestant denigration of the role of Mary and the saints. It is beyond our purposes to examine these issues here but, again, just as with her Christology, Sor Juana is probing the relationship of the divine and human bodily form.

To fully appreciate the gift of Sor Juana's theology, we must first rid ourselves of some contemporary assumptions. Sor Juana is not a formalist or an aesthete devoted to abstract or minimalist forms. Art is meant to reveal God's magnitude, His *pleroma,* not His "leftovers." We must also recognize the inherent limits of any given culture to grasp this Beauty. Neither poetry nor prose is adequate. In fact, as Paz affirms, it is this encounter with the essentially inexpressible that creates poetry.

Finally, we must recognize the limits of our own time. Umberto Eco quotes E. R. Curius's astute observation that ". . . contemporary man places an exaggerated value on art because he has lost the feeling for intelligible beauty which the neo-Platonists and the Medievals possessed. . . . Here we are dealing with a type of beauty of which Aesthetics knows nothing."

Sor Juana's theology affirms that Beauty is revelatory, drawing us from the physical to the spiritual, and always revealing a higher, more mysterious harmony. This is an expression of the Mystery of the Incarnation. The incarnational aspect of Beauty can then lead us to the Resurrection, that is, to an intimation of a Beauty that is not subject to change. This Beauty has been described as a Mystery "imprinted on the heart's memory."

As we have seen, Sor Juana is a notable figure in a venerable Catholic tradition. The Beauty she expresses in her art and the Truth in her thoughts are one. They are based not simply on her own experiences, but on those of countless Christians before her. Our Christian experience of Beauty is, in the end, as mysterious and inspiring as our experience of God.

As we make our journey through Mexico, let us then be open to the uniqueness and ever-present forms of Beauty in art, nature, and people.

As St. Bonaventure taught, everything is united by Light which envelops everything. Light itself is beautiful.

And so are we.

To Stand Alone

Mexico's Nineteenth-Century Revolutions

The most grievous injustices in the New Spain of 1810 were not limited to economics. Social inequities abounded, and, importantly, spoke most directly to those capable of seizing power. The inherent antagonism was between the Creoles, sometimes calling themselves "Americans," and the Spanish-born Peninsulars, often called "Europeans."

Spain was foreign-dominated, that is, French-ruled, and, to make matters worse, insolvent. The Spanish government was continuously squeezing money out of New Spain by measures called "redemption" or *consolidacion*. These were, in effect, compulsory loans of funds intended to fund the "pious works" of the Church, that is, charities and hospitals. When the government was unable to pay interest on these "loans," the financial crisis worsened, and land and haciendas were then expropriated. With this, the owners, the *hacendados,* who were mostly provincial Creoles, turned against the regime in Spain.

Having attained considerable wealth, the Creoles resented their lack of status among the Peninsulars. A consciousness of a new and proud "Mexican" identity was growing. It is not accidental that the great symbol of this new national identity, the "dark virgin," Our Lady of Guadalupe, patron saint of the land since 1746, would become a battle flag.

The merchants of New Spain also had their eyes set on the cheaper goods available from England that the Spanish monopoly on trade denied them. But economic injustice was only one cause of the growing unrest. Events in Spain also inspired a desire for change in its colonies. King Carlos IV and his advisor Godoy had been overthrown in 1808, and their successor, Ferdinand VII, was imprisoned by Napoleon, who was hated by Spaniards as the great "atheist" and enemy of the faith.

When Napoleon was forced to retreat in Russia and Spain, the Creole revolutionaries realized that a restoration of a legitimate monarch in Spain would also restore royal authority in New Spain. They concluded that it was time to make their move and to declare independence. The instability of the Spanish Crown thus provided a pretense for the Mexican revolt of 1810. The motive of its initiators was, from the beginning, a separation from Spain. Ignacio Allende, the primary architect of the revolt, wrote to his ally Father Hidalgo that their ultimate intentions must be concealed, because the poor and the Indians were not interested in abstract notions like "liberty," but would fight in defense of the legitimate Spanish king. Local *juntas* or military groups were formed ostensibly for this purpose. The first battle for independence began in September 1810 in the small towns then called San Miguel el Grande and Dolores.

General Allende and Padre Hidalgo's uprising, however, led to their eventual capture and execution. In 1815, another revolutionary priest who took up the struggle, Jose Maria Morelos, was also defeated and executed. A period of fragile tranquility followed, but by 1820, the struggle had resumed under the leadership of Morelos's disciple, Vicente Guerrero, whose guerrilla army had holed up in the south. Other rebels, such as the Bravo brothers, who likewise had never surrendered to the central government, joined him. Significant events were also again taking place in Spain — the creation of a liberal constitution and the refusal of army elements to return to the colonies. In 1822, a subsequent Spanish government would reject the new constitution, but the independence movement would prove unstoppable. The anti-clericalism of Spanish liberals provoked a curious reaction among many high churchmen in Mexico. In the face of the loss of power in Spain, might not Mexico become the Church's best refuge? The Church leaders who had always looked to Spain for support were now moving toward a sympathetic view of independence.

Faith That Moves Mountains:
The Revolutionary Priests, Hidalgo and Morelos

In colonial New Spain, the seeds of revolution were found in the political alliances of the Creole landed elite in places such as Queretaro. This warfare against the Spanish empire, ruled by French royalty since 1700, led to several clashes, including violent attacks on the *penisulares,* as the Spanish-born were called. The leadership of the 1810 revolt was formed primarily by Creole military figures, such as Ignacio Allende, but the popular inspiration that gained the crucial support of the poor and indigenous came from a Catholic priest, Miguel Hidalgo. His famous *grito* or *"cry" (Viva Mexico!)* is still ritually offered by Mexican presidents on their independence day. The original *grito,* however, was *"Viva Mexico! Viva la Virgen de Guadalupe!"*

At this time, a significant division had appeared in the Church. The high churchmen were financially secure and comparatively compliant; however, the lower clergy, less educated, were often as impoverished as their rural parishioners. Others shared the interests of the small landowners, for example, the revolutionary priests Hidalgo and Morelos, both of whom had small holdings and raised cattle.

The leadership of the 1810 revolt came almost exclusively from a small social elite, the Creoles of the rich valley in the north known as the *bajio.* The cities of this area, Queretaro and Guanajuato, once the silver capital, and the town of San Miguel el Grande (now San Miguel de Allende) were relatively prosperous as the *bajio* was then the richest area in Mexico, with abundant crops of wheat and corn. The Indians were more assimilated into the Spanish culture than elsewhere, and there was a large population of *mestizos.* The ruling Creoles were considered "more Spanish than the Spanish," and yet it was here that the spark of a fiery rebellion was struck.

The leaders of the revolution, and ultimately its first martyrs — Allende, the Aldama brothers, and Abasolo — were all sons of Basque merchants. Typical of their class, they preferred military service over commerce and were officers in the local militia. These were, by and large, men of action rather than ideas; but the liberal ideals of liberty and tolerance, inspired by the French Revolution, were circulating in high circles in Queretaro and Guanajuato. Among the early supporters of independence were Miguel Dominguez, governor of Queretaro, and his wife, Dona Maria Josefa Ortiz, now celebrated as a revolutionary heroine. Historians of revolutionary change have noted that it is the frustrated ideals and ambitions of those of higher social rank rather than the truly oppressed poor that typically inspire a revolution.

The 1810 revolt, however, was led first symbolically and then militarily by a priest, Miguel Hidalgo y Costilla. Hidalgo's father had been a prosperous Creole hacienda manager who owned property and slaves. Miguel and a brother became priests while another became a lawyer. When a seminarian, Hidalgo had witnessed the expulsion of the Jesuits, including some beloved teachers, an event that undoubtedly created some bitterness toward the governing authorities. In 1790, he became rector of the seminary in Valladolid where he had been an outstanding student. However, he then apparently chose to serve as a priest in a poor rural area. In 1803, he moved to the small town of Dolores where he would later issue his historic cry for independence.

During his time at the seminary, two prominent bishops became his friends, Antonio de San Miguel and, most significantly, Manuel Abad y Queipo, a reformer with great sympathy for the poor. Ironically, it would be Bishop Abad y Queipo who would denounce the revolt, predicting that it would bring ruin to the country. He then excommunicated Hidalgo. Hidalgo's status in the Church was subsequently unclear. He had clearly been excommunicated, and there are dramatic tales of his being unable to offer absolution to dying soldiers. But Hidalgo was subsequently reinstated by other local Church officials, and then excommunicated yet once again. In any case, his critics never questioned the sincerity of his faith, only the prudence of his judgment.

These conflicts between ecclesial brothers reflected the deep divisions throughout the country. As with many of the revolutions to come, Mexico would be split into many pieces, the violence cutting across class and even family lines. One of Hidalgo's good friends had been the liberal governor of Guanajuato, Juan Antonio Riano, who opposed the revolt and who died during the famous battle of the fortified granary in Guanajuato. Hidalgo's and Allende's severed heads would be placed on the same granary's corner spikes following their executions.

The revolt initially had widespread support. Father Hidalgo had great credibility as a priest, and in an act of spiritual and historical significance, took the image of the Virgin of Guadalupe from the little church of Atotonilco and carried it as his banner. At first, it was the great houses and haciendas of the despised Peninsulars or "Europeans" that were looted, but the uprising quickly got out of hand. Crop failures in prior years had reduced an already impoverished lower class to near starvation. Now emboldened, they were eager for vengeance. The plundering soon became indiscriminate and extended to the property of Creoles as well and support for the revolution among this class began to fade. The opposing forces, some now led by Creoles as well as Peninsulars, were also better trained and equipped, and Hidalgo's ragtag army was eventually defeated. Hidalgo was captured and executed in 1811. The brief dream of independence seemed over, but it was to be quickly revived by yet another priest, Jose Maria Morelos.

Father Morelos, unlike Hidalgo, was from a poor family. His father had died in his youth and, after working at menial labor for many years, he became a priest at the then-late age of twenty-five. Hidalgo was one of his seminary teachers and, later, a friend. Morelos was serving in a poor parish in the south when he received the excommunication notice from Bishop Abad. He refused to circulate it until he met with Hidalgo, who convinced him of the righteousness of his cause. Morelos then joined the rebels, and his key role was to develop popular support for the revolution in the south. He was a better organizer than Hidalgo and subsequently proved to be a better general as well.

Following the defeat of Hidalgo and Allende, Morelos became the leader of the political and military course of the revolution. Again, his status as a priest gained the support of the poor especially. More than four hundred priests, mostly poor themselves, defied Church superiors to support Hidalgo and Morelos. Morelos's most valuable aide was also a priest, Father Mariano Matamoros, and the religious appeal of the revolt was evident when one of the rebel leaders, Manuel Fernandez, changed his name to "Guadalupe Vitoria."

In September 1813, while his forces were still in combat, Morelos assembled a congress to draft a constitution, which was completed the next year. It was both a republican and Catholic document, endorsing democracy, but establishing the Catholic Church as the sole religion. It also called for the return of the Jesuits. It is a matter of speculation as to the future direction this attempt at unification might have taken, but the constitution was never implemented. Nonetheless, it established the precedent of an egalitarian and representative government.

Despite his many remarkable victories in the field — he captured Oaxaca and the major port of Acapulco, though never Mexico City — Morelos was defeated by the royalist army and executed in 1815. He was reconciled with the Church at the end, and was seen praying before his execution.

History has been generous to Father Morelos, considered a man of great vision and unquestioned character. He is a Mexican icon, the famous Diego Rivera portrait of him depicting him with a sword in one hand, the constitution in the other. The city of Valladolid, site of the seminary, is now called Morelia, and the state is named Morelos in his honor.

Following the initial attempts to break free from the Spanish empire, New Spain became an aspiring empire itself, only now this was a Creole aspiration. This ambition was evident until the collapse of would-be imperial rulers, such as General Agustin de Iturbide, who declared himself an "emperor" in 1821. Iturbide achieved a nominal legal independence for Mexico in that year by peacefully overthrowing the Spanish viceroy, but his extravagant and oppressive "empire" lasted only two years. He was overthrown, in turn, by another general, Antonio Lopez de Santa Anna, who, though he proved to be equally ineffectual, would play a role in Mexican history for decades to come.

During this period following the failed revolution, an unfortunate, if not ominous, pattern had developed. Aspirants for power would proclaim an inspiring "plan" for the country — as did both Iturbide and Santa Anna — and then take power by force. The lasting consequence was to increasingly empower the army and its ambitious commanders.

The "Bad Neighbor Policy": Texas and the War with America

The so-called "Mexican-American War" of 1848, as we now look back on it, was a sad chapter in the history of both countries in that it left indelible scars and lasting resentments. It was, furthermore, probably avoidable, and, in fact, desired by few. The war was unpopular with Americans then, despite its incredible windfall in territory, and is still a discomforting chapter in our history.

A brief background:

As early as 1813, during the first revolution for Mexican independence, the province of Texas had declared its intention to be autonomous. In 1821, an American, Moses Austin, was then given the right to colonize in Texas by the Mexican government. By 1835, there were numerous settlers, including Mexicans, and such a growing self-sufficiency that, following some grievances, the Texans declared their independence. The military hero and would-be imperial ruler of Mexico, General Santa Anna, was recalled to suppress this rebellion. He lost the campaign at the legendary battle of the Alamo, and was himself taken prisoner by the Texans. A gallant and charming man, it is said that his demeanor saved him from execution. Texas, however, was lost and remained independent.

It was claimed that the government of President James Polk used the initial dispute over a stretch of land adjacent to the Rio Grande as a pretext for the war. Polk's Whig opponents in Congress, including Abraham Lincoln, fearful that this was a ploy by Southerners to extend slavery further west, strongly opposed the war. Some contemporary scholars who have examined the letters and diaries of Polk question this interpretation. It is their contention that Polk and his supporters had no real interest in a war with Mexico. They had ambitions, certainly, but these lay elsewhere.

The "manifest destiny" of America — a term coined at this time as a quasi-religious justification of the war — was seen primarily in terms of an expansion west to the Pacific. The port of San Francisco was the desired prize, not Texas or the desert wastelands of the Southwest. Whether this objective could have been obtained without war, we'll never know. In any case, both sides bluffed and miscalculated. Despite the defeat in Texas, the Mexican military command felt confident. The Mexican soldiers were expert horsemen with considerable experience in Indian wars, and this would be a war — the last of its kind — more of cavalry charges than heavy artillery attacks. The United States was larger and wealthier, but its army was not fully professional at that time, and many of the commanders were actually ambitious politicians. The advantage of industrial might in warfare would not become apparent until the American Civil War a generation later. Many of the celebrated generals of that later conflict — including Ulysses Grant and the Lee family — were comrades together in Mexico.

Mexico's miscalculation was based on the anticipation of a growing tension between the Americans and the English who were disputing possession of the Oregon territory. Some Mexican leaders, confident that the Americans couldn't fight two wars simultaneously, welcomed conflict rather than compromise. It was a serious mistake. In the end, there would be no war with England, and American military might, though at times stretched thin, prevailed in Mexico. Despite fierce resistance by the Mexicans, the Americans under General Winfield Scott ended the war with the capture of Mexico City.

Wars leave bitter memories, some carved in stone. There are prominent monuments in Mexico City to the military cadets *(los ninos heroes)* who committed suicide rather than surrender Chapultepec Castle, as well as to the *San Patricio* battalion. These were the numerous Irish Catholic soldiers who went over to the Mexican side and fought the Americans. Few of these impoverished and badly treated Irish immigrants were actually American citizens, but more than eighty were hung as deserters. A monument listing their names is in the *colonia* of San Angel. Their motives were probably mixed. Religious loyalty was undoubtedly important, but they were also promised land in return for their services. A devotion to St. Patrick, *San Patricio,* still has a special resonance in Mexico.

The loss of the war was catastrophic for Mexico, which lost a third of its territory, including Texas, California, Arizona, and New Mexico. The defeat was blamed on Santa Anna; but it engendered an anti-American legacy that exists to this day.

In some ways, General Santa Anna symbolizes this era in Mexico. The general was a quixotic figure, trying to preserve a passing way of life and the warrior code romanticized by Napoleon and imitated by so many other generals. In 1838, Santa Anna had served as military commander against the French, still ambitious imperialists, in the brief "Pastry War" — so-named because it was ostensibly caused by a financial dispute concerning a pastry chef. Santa Anna lost his leg in the battle, but emerged victorious and was once again a national hero. (He had the leg entombed in a monument in Mexico City.) Santa Anna regained power in the wake of his triumph and ruled the country until 1844. Perhaps more inefficient than despotic, he was then sent into "exile for life" in Cuba until recalled to fight the Americans. In 1853, Santa Anna became president for the fifth time. He attempted to establish a dictatorship, but his inept regime lasted only a few years. In 1855, Santa Anna was overthrown and sent into his final exile.

Following the American occupation, Mexico was close to financial collapse. The "War of the Castes," a violent Yucatan Mayan revolt, had broken out in 1847, and in central Mexico there was the beginning of agrarian revolt with violent attacks on haciendas. Once again under liberal rule, the government tried to recover financially by confiscating Church property, which was then auctioned to private bidders. However, as historian Jan Bazant notes: "Church funds could not save Mexico."

To the extent that conservative military leaders had re-established relations with the Church, both institutions had lost credibility following the military defeat of 1848. The Church had played no role in the war, but a new wave of nationalism emerged and the new men of a new class would now reign.

Liberal Ideals, Mexican Reality:
The Rise and Fall of Nineteenth-Century Liberalism

The heroic figures of Allende, Hidalgo, and Morelos are now honored in Mexico as are Washington and Jefferson in the United States; they initiated a revolution that eventually achieved Mexican independence. This, however, took many decades and, unfortunately, in Mexico's case, independence failed to bring democracy. By the mid-nineteenth century, despite its relative autonomy, Mexico's development was stagnant. The rule of would-be "Napoleons," such as Generals Iturbide and Santa Anna, was autocratic and inept, and the peace with the United States secured by the Treaty of Hidalgo of 1848, cost Mexico not only Texas and desert land, but the benefits of California's gold and shipping lanes.

In 1857, once again there was war. This time it was against the French and their imposed "Emperor," Maximilian, an Austrian nobleman. With the eventual expulsion of the French and Maximilian's execution, a lasting Mexican independence was finally secured. Benito Juarez, a Zapotec lawyer, became Mexico's constitutional president, presiding from 1867 to 1872. This began the era of liberal reforms.

For the most part, these reforms were aimed at the Church, which was considered by the reformers to have been an ally of the foreign *ancien regime.* This antagonism also reflected developments in Europe, such as the rise of secular nationalism led by a growing bourgeois class of urban industrialists. The Church, whose support was still strongest among the rural peasantry and traditional elites, was "dis-established" and most of its extensive property confiscated. Many of the remaining historic, monumental buildings in Mexico today are still recognizable as once having been seminaries, convents, and church-run hospitals.

A number of the liberals were antagonistic to religion itself, and their reforms were largely based on an ideology foreign to Mexican culture. We must try to understand, however, that many of these demands for change were justified by the circumstances. The Church was economically dependent upon an inherently unjust system. The bishops and canons received their often considerable income from tithes, and the religious orders from real estate. Even more damaging to the Church's reputation, the lower clergy depended upon a fee system, charging for marriages, baptisms, and funerals. For example, a marriage fee in a poor village might run from ten to seventeen pesos. A peon earned a peso a week and so a marriage could cost almost four months of earnings. Out of necessity, many chose not to marry and illegitimacy was common. In that the poor would have to borrow money for these fees, this system virtually enslaved the indebted peons. By paying off their existing loans, the owners, the *hacendados,* could in effect "buy and sell" peons. The injustice of this debt-service system was clear and inconsistent with Gospel teachings, and yet the Church had become dependent upon it.

In one notorious case, a village priest even refused to bury a dead child because the family could not afford the fee. This kind of abuse enraged liberal reformers such as the influential Melchior Ocampo, a wealthy *hacendado.* An anarchistic individualist, illegitimate by birth, Ocampo made the abolition of clerical fees his cause, if not obsession. His 1844 essay on the subject articulated the morality of the liberal campaign and made a significant additional point. The debt-service system was not just immoral but economically unproductive. This linkage between high ideals and economic development was central to liberal thought, and reveals the contradiction at its very heart.

Elected governor of Michoacan in 1846, Ocampo would become one of the most important liberal leaders in Mexico, serving as a cabinet minister in several future governments. Perhaps his most important contribution to the liberal cause, however, was the influence he exerted on a future leader. Sent into exile by General Santa Anna in 1853, Ocampo gathered other exiled liberals around him in New Orleans. Among them was the former governor of Oaxaca, a full-blooded Zapotec, the first Indian to rise to such prominence since the Conquest. His name was Benito Juarez and he was destined to transform Mexico.

Born in a remote village in Oaxaca in 1806, Juarez did not learn to speak and write Spanish until he was orphaned and migrated to the city. His struggle to acquire an education and his ultimate rise to power is legendary in Mexico, and his status is comparable to that of Abraham Lincoln in the United States. Juarez, like Lincoln, eventually became a lawyer. His hard work and pragmatic character then made him successful in politics and he became governor of his state in 1847. Exiled with other liberals during one of the not infrequent political seesaws, he met Ocampo in 1853. They became an effective team — the intellectually brilliant but personally erratic Ocampo was rendered more effective by the more moderate Juarez. Already a Mason, Juarez assimilated the then radically secular philosophy of Ocampo and put it into action.

Ocampo, Juarez, and other liberals, such as Guillermo Prieto and Miguel Lerdo de Tejada, both from urban, merchant backgrounds, joined the cabinet of President Juan Alvarez when the liberals returned to power in 1855. The temperamental Ocampo resigned after a few months, but Juarez remained and was increasingly recognized as the liberal leader.

The careers of Prieto and especially Lerdo are illustrative of that combination of liberal idealism and bourgeois ambition that characterized the age. Both were "pure" liberals and strongly anti-clerical. There is no reason to doubt their sincere commitment to individual liberty; yet their vision is inseparable from the middle-class ambition to acquire power and, most importantly, wealth and property. Lerdo became the Minister of Development, forming the early infrastructure of industrialism, such as the telegraph and the railroad. The liberals would finance much of this development through funds seized from the Church.

As we have noted, this was an historical development taking place throughout Europe, and, in some respects, coming late to the New World. The old aristocratic social order wasn't just dying; it was dead. A new class of financiers, property owners, and lawyers was now assuming control of all the Western societies. In many respects, the struggle in Mexico was between the Church, which had its base among the rural population and the poor, and this rising urban middle class. This conflict has been characterized by some historians as the "village priest versus the city lawyer." There was never any question as to who would win power.

Juarez, later to serve as Chief Justice of the Supreme Court before assuming the presidency, was the architect of legal reform, and most of it was aimed at the Church. The so-called *leyes Juarez* removed legal immunity from the clergy and to some extent from the military. These changes were so strongly resisted at the time that Alvarez was forced to resign and the more conservative General Ignacio Comonfort became president.

A Catholic revolt in Puebla was repressed and, subsequently, Church property in that state was virtually expropriated and the bishop expelled. Following this, despite Comonfort's futile attempt at compromise with the Holy See, a civil war broke out. This was the so-called "Three Years War" between the countryside conservatives and the urban-based liberals. The liberals ultimately won and returned to power in 1858. With the highly respected Juarez as president, the resistance of the Church, particularly the lower clergy and their poor constituents in the villages, was finally broken. The Reform Laws of 1859 confiscated all of the Church property and placed unprecedented legal restrictions on the Church — sanctions as severe as any of those imposed by Napoleon Bonaparte.

The confiscation of Church property was a turning point in Mexican history, not simply a divorce between government power and Christian faith, but a definitive step toward the creation of a bourgeois republic devoted to individual rights and property. Liberals set to work to foster democracy while simultaneously garnering the necessary human and technical resources for capitalist growth. This effort would quickly fail.

Benito Juarez had emerged as the unquestioned leader of the liberals after the assassination, death, and imprisonment of several other older party leaders. He understood the necessity for reconciliation, and through his patience, skill, and a reputation earned during years of sacrifice, he succeeded. He would ultimately rule as president for fifteen years. The first years, however, were perilous.

Mexico was debt-ridden and its European creditors formed an alliance bent on invasion and the restoration of stability. The English and Spanish governments, however, withdrew when it became clear that France's ruler, Napoleon III, had greater ambitions than mere financial restitution. This Napoleon, true to his inheritance, sought empire and domination. French troops landed in Vera Cruz in 1862 but were defeated by the Mexican army at the battle of Puebla on the fifth of May, *cinco de mayo*, celebrated as a national holiday ever since. The French army, nonetheless, brought in additional forces and a year later, in May 1863, Puebla fell. The French military commanders, Marshals Foray and Bazaine, seized control of the capital later that year and became, in effect, the rulers of Mexico.

Even this military loss did not deter the growing national pride of Mexicans. The desire for independence had become the core of a rising nationalism, as it had in most of Europe, and this was now identified with liberalism. The support of conservatives, royalists, and much of the Church for foreign intervention destroyed their credibility as an alternative to liberal power.

The French rule, ironically, proved to be a liberal one. In fact, one might argue that French policies, based on their revolution and Napoleon's dictates, were more liberal in many ways than those of Juarez and his colleagues. The French marshals appointed only like-minded liberals to governing positions, exiled the conservative leader General Miramon, and, consistent with Napoleonic anti-clericalism, no Church property or rights were restored. Even when the Austrian nobleman Maximilian was imported to be emperor of Mexico, the conservatives and Church were disappointed by his reformist views.

It was in the area of what we would now call human rights that the French went further than many Mexican liberals were prepared to follow. For instance, the oppressive "debt servitude," never abolished by the liberals, was ended by Maximilian's decree. The egalitarian French went still further. Appalled by the enormous gap between classes, new taxes were imposed on the rich, and efforts were made to restore some Indian communal lands. Modernization was extensive and some of it, the rapid development of the railroad, for example, was welcomed by everyone. Many liberals became supporters of the new regime, but their political base — the middle sector of the newly rich and property owners — were not pleased. Labor laws that abolished any peon's debt of more than ten pesos and even some child labor restrictions were seen as interference with property rights. The land was being broken up increasingly into individual parcels and banks and money-lending, much of it from foreigners, was financing the "new Mexico"; but this only created in property holders a new sense of entitlement. Many of the former Creole leaders were also dismissed by the French as superfluous, if not incompetent, and this too fueled the growing nationalism. All of these measures were eventually thwarted by the landholding interests. Such extensive land reform as proposed by the French — not the liberals — would have to wait for the next century.

Given the disappointment of the now-discredited conservatives and the resentment of many liberals, it is not surprising that when Napoleon withdrew his army in 1866, his short-lived Mexican empire quickly crumbled. Juarez and his allies had retreated north during the invasion, many ending up safely in the United States. There remains speculation still as to the role American government and business interests played in subsequent events; but it is clear that, following the American Civil War, financial support and even military supplies were provided for Juarez and the Republic.

The abandoned Emperor Maximilian, today viewed more as a pathetic, if not tragic figure than a despot, made his last stand against Juarez's forces at Queretero. He was defeated and taken prisoner, and, notwithstanding protests from European countries, was executed along with two of his military commanders in June 1866. Despite the international protests, the execution made its point. Mexico was now independent and would not tolerate foreign interventions.

By the summer of the following year, 1867, a rare degree of order had been achieved in Mexico. Juarez had again understood the task before him as that of pacification and reconciliation. Only about a hundred conservative supporters of the empire had been executed, a small number compared to previous periods of endless revenge and retaliation, and in 1870, a general amnesty was granted to the now politically defunct conservatives and other supporters of the empire. This was undoubtedly as prudent as it was benevolent, for, despite later political mythology, many Mexicans, including liberals, had supported Maximilian's futile effort to create an oxymoronic "liberal empire."

With the liberals returning to power, American interests once again became influential in Mexico. Similarly, though the restored liberal government broke diplomatic relations with both France and England, the London banks and the foreign railroad developers remained in place. Again, the liberal desire for democracy as well as capital development created social and political tensions.

In the presidential election of 1867, Juarez won nearly seventy percent of the vote, defeating, among others, the young war hero General Porfirio Diaz, the liberator of Puebla and Mexico City. Juarez's effectiveness, however, seemed to decline after the death of his wife. His primary advisor was now the French-educated doctor Gabino Barrera, who had embraced the philosophy of Positivism. This was a nineteenth-century belief that truth could only be determined by the techniques of science. This philosophy grew increasingly influential during the rest of the century in Mexico, but it remained an alien ideology for most Mexicans.

In 1871, seeking re-election, Juarez was challenged again by Porfirio Diaz, who charged that the president was creating a personal dictatorship. Juarez won only narrowly this time, with Diaz a close second. Diaz's warnings proved moot, for Juarez died of a heart attack the following year. Sebastian Lerdo, the Chief Justice of the Supreme Court, was the constitutional successor, but lacked Juarez's reputation and popular support. Lerdo's rabid anti-clericalism also ran counter to the more moderate Juarez's policies of accommodation. A bachelor, Lerdo had been dubbed "the curate" in recognition of his intellectual preeminence. But the term was telling. Many of the intellectual class were now aspiring to a kind of secular priesthood.

Meanwhile, the ambitious Porfirio Diaz had been waiting in the wings. Mexico's civilian rule after many years came to an end in 1876 when, in a military coup facing little opposition, General Porfirio Diaz seized power.

The liberal reform era was over, but the redistribution of wealth and property from one group or class to another would remain the implied promise of radical political movements and authoritarian regimes for the next hundred years. Promises, needless to say, do not produce development. Nineteenth-century lawyers in Mexico were neither economists nor industrialists, and the country they attempted to govern was still overwhelmingly rural and religiously conservative. The liberals had no choice but to ally themselves with the landowners, the latter tempted by the prospect of increasing their holdings at the expense of the Church and Indian communal lands. This "progressive" alliance of the urban educated elite and local landowners pitted against the "backward" Church, the indigenous, and the landless has been a pattern throughout Mexican history — as witnessed in Chiapas at the end of the twentieth century. "Progress" in this context requires careful definition.

In some respects, early Mexican revolutionary sentiments were as much reactions against political developments elsewhere as they were inspired by them. The Mexican revolt of 1810 may have been a protest against injustice; but New Spain remained a traditional and agrarian society, and it had no ideologue comparable to a Robespierre or Jefferson. In many ways, neither European nor American political ideals corresponded to the social reality in Mexico. The 1810 revolution also coincided with a widespread reaction against the extreme violence of the French Revolution. Similarly, in 1812, the now-independent Americans saw their attempt to incorporate parts of Canada frustrated. Americans view their 1812 war with England as simply a further step toward independence, but for Mexicans the conflict exposed American expansionist ambitions that could not have been reassuring.

In addition, Mexican rebels sought to proclaim a unique *Mexican* identity. Their radical vision was not that of the *sans culottes,* the destitute of the seething Paris streets, nor of the Yankee traders protesting unjust taxes on their prosperous trade. The revolutionary aspirations of colonial Mexico were closer to the Franciscan ideal — a desire to create a "new world" unspoiled by greed and privilege. Unlike the French or American upheavals, the Mexican revolution of 1810 marked the death of an old order but failed to create a new one. It would take decades to establish a lasting constitutional state, and the long reign of the dictator Porfirio Diaz would last until the beginning of the twentieth century. During this time, once again largely foreign ideas and values would be imposed on a society unprepared for the new capitalist order. Liberalism, whether American or British, could not take hold in Mexico because no real middle or entrepreneurial class had yet developed. The United States also possessed unique geographical and natural resources as well as a distinctive political history that made it a doubtful model even if Mexicans had desired to imitate it.

It should be noted that the prototypical "liberator-dictator," such as Mexican generals Iturbide or Santa Anna, and later Diaz, were found throughout Latin America during the century and beyond. As in France under Napoleon, equality and democracy were distant ideals having little to do with the reality of political life. At the end of the nineteenth century, politics, and not just in Mexico, would be characterized by a surfeit of ideologies — left, right, and pseudo-scientific — all of which in one way or another camouflaged the reality of ongoing violence and injustice.

The colonial period in Mexico that ended in violent revolution in many ways mirrored European events, including a prolonged war against the Church. During the French revolution of 1789, a wholesale attack was mounted on the Church, as well as the literal decapitation of the royal line. The actual revolutionary period — "the Terror" — was short-lived; it lasted less than a decade before it drowned in its own blood. Its aftermath, however, had a profound effect on the Church everywhere. Pope Pius VI had died what seemed an ignominious death in 1799 while an exile and prisoner in a French jail. Local priests, whether intimidated or disloyal, refused to attend to him and his death was officially recorded by the French as that of a "citizen" whose profession was "pope."

Napoleon, now a dictator, declared himself emperor and attempted to conquer the continent. During this time, Pius's successor, Pius VII, appeared utterly helpless in the face of Napoleon's now-absolute power. The pope was compelled to come to Paris in order to crown Napoleon "Holy Roman Emperor"; but, as Napoleon himself noted wryly, the pope "betrayed" him. The pontiff turned what was designed to be a humiliating recognition of dictatorial power into a triumphant march from Rome to

Paris, the pope greeted as he went by throngs of the surviving faithful. In Notre Dame Cathedral, Napoleon, however, had the last word when he took the crown from the pope's hands, and crowned himself.

By 1815, after years of papal exile, Pius VII, primarily through perseverance and personal example, managed to restore much of the prestige of the Church. However, for the rest of the nineteenth century, the Church would be not only profoundly anti-revolutionary, but anti-liberal as well. In 1823, Gregory XVI became pope and for more than a decade reestablished a rigid monarchial papacy. In reaction to the persecutions, Pope Gregory condemned all that was considered "modern" thought, including many of the concepts of liberty and equality. Gregory's reign anticipated one of the longest papacies in history, that of Pius IX. Greeted initially as a Church reformer who would be more tolerant of modern aspirations, the new pope would ultimately disappoint such hopes.

"Pio Nono," as he came to be called, was pope from 1846 until the end of the century. Not without reason, he came to consider himself "a prisoner in the Vatican" after the establishment of the anti-clerical Roman Republic in 1870, and his papacy remained largely defensive and resistant to outside influences.

In retrospect, the year 1870 marked a turning point in Church history. It was not only the end of papal temporal rule in Italy, but, arguably, the beginning of the end of the old order called Christendom — that is, the closing stages of the State-Church alliance, often uneasy, established by Emperor Constantine in the fourth century. In this respect, Pope Pius IX is an important transitional figure. Eventually, the Church, while struggling against forms of anti-religious modernism, would delineate and then affirm many of the liberal concepts of freedom and democracy. The struggle, however, lasted for more than a century.

The lasting heritage of the liberal period, in Mexico and elsewhere, was the recognition of the essential nature of liberty. During this era, Leo Tolstoy, the great Russian writer, wrote that the freedom of a nation begins with that of a single individual, clearly perceiving freedom as a spiritual condition. On the same page of his diary, Tolstoy noted, however, that only a truly religious person can see the ultimate purpose of this freedom.

What is perhaps most significant is that, in the end, the Church no longer possessed earthly power. For the first time in over a thousand years, the Church was protected only by the Holy Spirit and the support of its members. The popes were no longer "princes" comparable to secular rulers, but, like the Apostles, teachers who must persuade through words and example alone.

Gilded Glove, Iron Hand:
The Long Rule of Porfirio Diaz

It was actually after the period of mid-century liberal reforms that the "new Mexico" emerged, and this was under Porfirio Diaz. It is more than ironic that Diaz had warned of a potential dictatorship under Juarez, for that is exactly what he established himself, and with great success. The reign of Porfirio Diaz as virtual dictator of Mexico would last so long that it would be deemed an historical era: the *Porfiriato*. In many ways, it resembled the "gilded age" of late nineteenth-century America and the French *belle époque* of the 1890s. Increasingly, a society of small and medium-sized landowners, the *Porfiriato* was dominated by a business elite enjoying all the benefits of their new wealth and power.

Diaz's revolutionary and liberal credentials were as unimpeachable as his military heroism. He was born in the same state as Juarez, in Oaxaca City in 1830. His father was a muleteer turned innkeeper, and his godfather was a priest who later became a bishop. Following his mother's wishes, Diaz entered the seminary with the intention of becoming a priest, but, influenced by the liberal ideas of the time, rejected this path and studied law at an institute for science and arts where Benito Juarez was a teacher and mentor. Under his influence, Diaz joined the revolution as a guerrilla fighter, beginning a military career that would bring him fame and power. He fought in the civil war against the conservative forces, becoming a general at the age of thirty-one. His glory days came as the liberator of Puebla and Mexico City, and his political ambitions soon followed.

Diaz said that he favored democracy, but only when the nation was ready for it. Apparently, he decided that this was not going to be in his lifetime. This is not to say that Diaz's judgment was necessarily mistaken.

The poor continued to look to strong authority figures and those in the emerging middle class were looking out for themselves. Diaz, despite his pompous public image, was actually a skilled leader who picked capable men. He had learned much from Juarez and continued many liberal policies, as well as the division of communal land.

It is during the *Porfiriato* that the so-called *cientificos* became ideologically dominant. These were intellectuals who believed in what they considered to be "science" as the guiding principle of social development. As in Europe, the ideas of these social Darwinists also justified their oligarchy. One of their leaders, the mathematician Francisco Bulnes offered a "scientific" explanation of Mexican inequality, explaining that the people were naturally divided into "corn eaters" and the clearly superior "wheat eaters."

Though Diaz would himself attempt an alliance with upper-class conservatives, marrying into a distinguished Catholic family, the Church had remained the liberals' chief adversary. As early as the 1830s, however, some Mexican political leaders had moved to restore relations with Rome, although it was not until December 1836 that the Holy See even recognized the Mexican government. During that time, General Santa Anna had curbed liberalization and many in the liberal party, forced into exile, blamed the Church for their plight. The reform laws of the nineteenth-century liberal regimes not only banned female religious orders such as the Sisters of Mercy, but even forbade public religious processions. They had seized virtually all Church property but found themselves in a long dispute over how to dispose of it. There is no doubt that many liberals sincerely wanted to use this wealth to bring about genuine reform and relief for the landless; but, in general, the liberals, reflecting aggressive middle-class interests, moved too quickly. They had threatened not only the traditional rights of the Church, but also, to some extent, the position of the army, all the while failing to relieve the conditions of the poor. A backlash was inevitable. The *Porfiriato* reflected these unresolved social conflicts as it attempted to restore the privileges of class and rank while still fostering change.

What Mexico lost spiritually it attempted to replace with material development. The Diaz regime, in time, became aligned with, and dependent upon, foreign investors, especially the London banks, and American political and economic interests. In the last decades of the *Porfiriato,* the railroad lines were extended to Texas, and Mexico City was refashioned to resemble Paris. The *Paseo de la Reforma* was modeled after the *Champs Elysees* and, stretching from the central plaza, the *zocalo,* to Chapultepec, it remains one of the world's most remarkable boulevards.

Diaz shrewdly played American, French, and British interests against each other to his advantage; but, in the end, despite the nationalization of the railroads, foreign interests, particularly American, dominated Mexico. The overthrow of the Diaz regime in 1910 unleashed long-repressed desires for change, and the revolution that ensued became a virtual civil war, a bloody struggle that would last more than a decade. In the end, it cost more than a million lives; but this tragic struggle also created modern Mexico.

The long-term historical perspective, more than a hundred and fifty years later, is replete with ironies. In the struggle between "liberals" and "conservatives" — who "won"? Certainly not the countless dead the violent conflict left in its wake. During the revolutionary period of 1810 to 1823, it is estimated that the continuous warfare had cost Mexico more than ten percent of its total population. Following the massive expropriations, who "inherited the land"? Certainly not the poor or the indigenous. During the final years of the mid-century struggle, the liberal government and its conservative opponents both sold Church property to finance their efforts. The desperate liberals offered Church property to financial speculators for as little as a quarter of its value. The real victors were the financial speculators, an augury of the future.

The ironies abound. The liberal reforms, aimed not just at the clergy but ultimately at the Catholic faith itself, actually liberated the Church from its entanglement with the privileges and corruption of the social status quo. Further, the failure to create a modern state resulted in the continuation of the old autocratic order in a new guise, native oligarchies using "revolutionary" rhetoric but primarily eager to preserve their power and privileges. No one was more keenly aware of these anomalies than Mexicans themselves, the idealists and the impoverished, and by the end of the nineteenth century, revolution was again in the air.

There was another cultural anomaly in late nineteenth-century Mexico that has some resonance in our own times.

Many of Diaz's *cientifico* advisors believed that a modern education would be based on "science," that is, a positivist form of information. "Knowledge" meant accepting only truths based on observation and evidence. This supposition ignored the existence of any number of natural scientists who did not reject religious belief, a position based on distinctions between different types of knowledge.

The underlying assumption of the nineteenth-century materialists was a philosophical one. The world was initially seen as strictly determined by physical laws; however, by the middle of the twentieth century, this view had been largely replaced by the opposing concept of a physical world that is the manifestation of a primal chaos. The basis of both of these worldviews was presumably scientific observations that demonstrated either fixity or its opposite. There is, needless to say, an enormous gap between these contradictory assumptions and actual scientific work. The truth-claims of materialist philosophers such as Marx were not demonstrable by scientific observation or methodology. Their claim was a very old one and was Gnostic in character. It was the notion of an esoteric and exclusive knowledge based on the attainments of an elite. It was defended as "scientific," though it was not based on demonstrable facticity or scientific observation, but on an age-old desire for power.

Revolution, Repression, and Renewal

Twentieth-Century Mexican History

Twentieth-century Mexican history is not only complex and at times confusing, but also highly mythified. This blurring of hard facts by selective memory has been done by Mexicans themselves as well as other commentators. Foreigners tend to fall into two categories: romantics or cynics, and sometimes a peculiar blending of both. There are several excellent histories, cited in the bibliography, that strive for objectivity; but contemporary Mexican history presents a minefield of dubious ideological interpretations. Mexicans themselves are highly, even at times excessively, self-critical, though some tend to stress their uniqueness, as if detaching themselves from Spanish and American orbits could extricate them from the tangle of history.

Americans tend to use Mexico as a mirror of our own aspirations and concerns, including no small amounts of guilt and blame. Europeans, on the other hand, have been inclined to interpret modern history through the shattered lenses of political and historical theories, none of which turned out to have a predictive capacity. This conspicuous failure alone — for example, the inability to understand, much less predict, the fall of communism, or the weaknesses of global capitalism — should dispel the illusion that there is a "scientific" analysis available. Our effort, on the other hand, is simply to try to understand Mexican history as it sheds light on the journey of a Catholic people through the perils of late modernity.

Let's take a step back for an overview.

By 1910, the year that begins contemporary Mexican political history, foreign investment constituted two-thirds of the funding of the industrial base of the nation. Mexican interests were concentrated in land holdings and some degree of commerce. Further, since the early years of the century, there had been economic decline provoking social unrest. Strikes in 1906 and 1907 had increasingly turned violent, and anarcho-syndicalist ideas were spreading. The financial panic of 1907 then added to the political instability. The long-lived regime of Porfirio Diaz, for all its accomplishments, was clearly coming to an end, one way or the other. An idealistic liberal of the day proclaimed: "The successor to Porfirio Diaz should be the law." Unfortunately, this hope, too, would prove elusive.

It was an armed revolt in the north of the country that began a chain of events that led to Diaz's resignation and exile in France. The "Manifesto of San Luis Potosi," issued in October 1910, proclaimed the liberal and democratic ideals of the rebels and in June 1911 Francisco Madero, their leader, the son of rich landowners, triumphantly entered Mexico City to assume power.

Once again, the central issue was land reform. As it had been since its origins, Mexico was a country split by an immense gap, a chasm, between the owners and managers of the haciendas and ranchos, the *latifundia* system, and the impoverished lower classes of peons, laborers, tenants, and sharecroppers. It was an inherently unjust system enforced by law and more often by violence. The haciendas weren't farms as much as feudal domains often equipped with their own armed guards.

We should note, as we acknowledge this harsh reality, that Mexico was hardly alone in being an agricultural nation unable to solve the problem of a just use of land and labor. Much of the history of the twentieth century, even in the "advanced" countries, is a sad tale of the displacement of literally millions of people, either by law or force, from the land that had sustained them for generations.

The Mexican land disputes had resulted in endless litigation ever since independence. Justice was not, however, to be found in the courts, and the liberal program failed in its objective to create a class of independent farmers. The situation was even worse in the isolated areas of the country, such as the Yucatan where there was virtual slavery on the extensive sugar cane plantations, some worked by imported Yaqui Indians.

Such impoverishment and injustice without any seeming hope of redress constitutes, as always, a precondition for violent revolt. The revolutionary period of the early twentieth century was, indeed, to be marked by increasing violence and class hatred. This confirmed the predictions of earlier prophetic figures, such as Ortega y Gasset and, for that matter, Nietzsche, that the modern revolutions would be less about justice than about revenge.

The new liberal leader, Francisco Madero, attempted to take the reins of the brittle and discredited Diaz political machine. This would have been a futile effort, in any case; but a widespread agrarian revolt had already begun, and disorder was spreading beyond Madero's control. In the south, the "hot country" where Father Morelos had rallied his forces nearly a hundred years earlier, the revolt was led by the legendary Emiliano Zapata, a successful rancher with a strong sympathy for the indigenous tradition of resistance. His ideas of land reform were far more radical than those of the politicians in Mexico City. The present-day romanticizing of Zapata, however, obscures the complex internal conflicts. Some of the indigenous, for example, had indeed fought to retain their communal land; but there were ongoing fights among themselves, and between them and the cattle-owning *caciques,* the dominant community leaders.

By 1912, there were revolts throughout the country, and Madero, though widely respected for his integrity, floundered. A genuine liberal, he proclaimed: "Liberty can only flourish under the protection of the law." It was the noble sentiment of an idealist engulfed by lawlessness. In the north, the rebel leader who emerged as dominant was the equally legendary Francisco "Pancho" Villa. The stereotypical, even cartoonish, depiction of Villa (including portrayals in Hollywood movies) fails to capture his tenacity and military skill. Power now increasingly came from the barrel of a gun, and Villa proved to be the toughest among a growing number of competing gunmen.

The political situation deteriorated until it culminated in what are called the "ten tragic days" in February 1913. The details of the duplicity, treachery, and violence are too complex for this survey, but, once again, it was the military that intervened. Madero's supporter, General Victoriano Huerta, had effectively suppressed the major revolt in the north, but his loyalty to Madero and the law proved to be short-lived. The result was the murder of the legal president, Madero, and the seizure of power by Huerta and the army. The killing of Madero and his distinguished colleague Pino Suarez was justified by a phrase that would become a sardonic cliché in the years to come — "shot while trying to escape." No one, of course, believed this account, and a growing cynicism would keep pace with the violence.

One of the shadowy aspects of these "tragic days" is the degree to which influential American figures such as Ambassador Henry Lane Wilson and the financier J. P. Morgan were involved. Whether the Americans were sincerely trying to arrange a truce or compromise, or whether they were complicit in the ultimate outcome, is still debated. In any case, it is part of the mythology of the times that American interests were deeply involved in the power struggles in Mexico. Given the many events, including military interventions yet to come, there is much to support such suspicions.

Despite General Huerta's posturing as a land reformer, his unpopular regime was short-lived. A grim succession of violence and political murders now began. Armed revolts continued, especially in the north, possibly, if not probably with American aid, always accompanied by idealistic public manifestos. In time, another reformer, a former governor of Coahuila, Venustiano Carranza, would gain power. Clearly there were many political leaders, mostly middle-class intellectuals, earnestly attempting to create the conditions for liberty and democracy; but real power devolved to the men of arms, such as "Generals" Alfaro Obregon and his acolyte Plutarco Elias Calles, who had seized control in Sonora. A new generation of revolutionaries was emerging; but they were men of violence rather than ideals or ideas.

Obregon, Calles, Pancho Villa — these were the best known of the *caudillos,* the warlords with their own armies composed of "the hungry, the landless, and the vengeful" who would compete for power for the next twenty years, leaving countless dead and vast destruction in their wake.

By 1914, American intervention, whether justified or not, became overt as President Woodrow Wilson ordered a blockade of Vera Cruz to protect American interests. This created some odd bedfellows politically, as both General Huerta and the reformer Carranza denounced the American intrusion. Another brief and unusual alliance took place when Zapata and Villa, leading their own rebel troops, briefly took command of Mexico City. Unfortunately, this union led to no lasting peace or reform, only a memorable photo of the two famous revolutionaries in the presidential palace — a few seconds of elusive hope frozen in time. Later, fellow "revolutionaries" would assassinate both men.

A more ominous and lasting alliance took place between the ineffectual Carranza and the ambitious Obregon who, with his ally, Calles, was seeking the support of urban workers. We should recall that in 1912 anarcho-syndicalism was a highly influential ideology among revolutionaries around the world. Organizations in Mexico such as the *Casa del Obrero Mundial* (House of the Workers of the World) were capable of organizing mass demonstrations, especially in Mexico City, and thus a force to be courted by power-seekers.

In 1916, an assembly of more or less popularly elected leaders held in Queretaro attempted to forge compromises that could end the violence. These included new leaders such as Francisco Mujica of Michoacan who, in an augury of the future, rejected the old liberal *laissez-faire* policies in favor of a new nationalism that justified the expropriation of property. However, it was the army's candidate, Alfaro Obregon, who emerged as the unchallenged revolutionary leader. A self-styled "realist" who characterized political programs as "useless as rhymed prose," Obregon, as the literary reference suggests, was not an uneducated soldier. Many of the revolutionary "generals" were not career military officers but middle-class politicians and lawyers. These were the Mexican version of a "new class" emerging elsewhere in the world. Intellectuals obsessed with power, ruthless figures such as Lenin and Mussolini, were more representative of the age than the military dictators with their bemedalled uniforms. They would also turn out to be more lethal.

By 1920, with the murder of President Carranza, civilian rule again came to an end in Mexico, and Obregon became president and virtual dictator. He would rule for much of the next decade. That he did not become "president for life" was no fault of his own.

A shrewd politician, Obregon moved in several different directions at once. He secured labor support from labor leaders such as Luis Morones, a new force in Mexico with growing influence. Obregon also attempted to normalize relationships with business interests, and especially with the United States. A highly influential committee of bankers, including Thomas W. Lamont of the Morgan Bank, became his advisors. Nonetheless, due to its nationalist stance and land expropriations, the Mexican regime would not be officially recognized by the United States until 1923.

Obregon had many worries, and how he coped, or didn't, with Mexico's difficulties would establish a pattern for decades to come. He realized that the Americans, fearful of "bolshevism" following the 1917 Russian Revolution, could be blackmailed into economic compromises that were beneficial to Mexico — or, at least, to its ruling elite. By settling financial issues, the Americans, including the oil companies, could be held at bay.

New political realities had to be faced. The erosion of the power of the *hacendados* made Obregon depend upon a political base of workers and peasants. The elimination of the old regimes, traditional and liberal, had also left a power vacuum that had to be filled with a combination of populist politicians and army officers. This was an era of ambitious, even ruthless, "self-made men," and not just business tycoons.

The most important challenge for Obregon was undoubtedly the selection of his successor. As the constitution limited him to one presidential term, he was not the first or the last Mexican leader to view his successor primarily as an instrument for sustaining his personal power and influence. Not surprisingly, Obregon, with army approval, selected his old comrade from Sonora, Plutarco Calles.

Obregon and Calles both attempted major land distribution, and, to their credit, initiated a program of mass education, particularly in the rural areas. In 1910 there was a seventy percent illiteracy rate and more than one million indigenous Mexicans couldn't speak Spanish. One of Mexico's most illustrious cultural figures appeared during this era. Jose Vasconcelos, appointed Minister of Education by Obregon, became, in fact, the chief cultural architect of modern Mexico.

Formerly a journalist and Madero supporter, Vasconcelos was a highly idealistic but contradictory figure who promoted programs that were inspired, inspiring, and at times eccentric. He was anti-American and anti-Protestant, and saw Mexico as a nation defending its "idealism" against the forces of American materialism. He developed a theory about a "pure Ibero-American," that is, a new Hispanic race, which inspired his efforts to create a unique Mexican culture. Perhaps his most lasting accomplishment was his sponsorship of the notable Mexican muralists, the social realist painters who gave Mexico a "face," so to speak, now recognizable around the world. The three most celebrated of these painters were Diego Rivera, David Alfaro Siquieros, and Jose Clemente Orozco; however, there are many other distinguished artists whose work still decorates countless buildings and walls throughout Mexico.

Vasconcelos and his associates also led a revolution in education. The 1917 Constitution banned Church schools; the schoolteacher, thus, became a rival to the priest, a moral instructor and political indoctrinator as much as pedagogue. One of Diego Rivera's accomplishments was to promote a somewhat sentimentalized image of the self-sacrificing teacher serving the poor. Undoubtedly many such idealistic young people existed; for, through their efforts, one of the genuine accomplishments of the Mexican Revolution was a significant reduction in illiteracy.

Literacy, we are told, spurs a desire for liberty and equality; but, unfortunately, desire isn't realization. Mexico would not achieve a genuine competitive democracy for more than half a century.

The Twenties didn't exactly "roar" in Mexico, but by 1925, largely due to foreign capital investment, the economy had improved. There was an increase in oil production and silver mining, and ambitious highway and irrigation projects were initiated. American Ambassador Dwight Morrow, also affiliated with the Morgan financial interests, established the "Good Neighbor Policy" and stable relations with the United States helped to reduce Mexico's foreign debt.

What has been termed the *caudillo* or "warlord" tradition prevailed in politics as Generals Obregon and Calles consolidated their control. Obregon became president in 1920 followed by Calles, his puppet, in 1924. The congress then allowed General Obregon to run again as well as extending the presidential term to six years. It is widely believed that an agreement was struck behind the scenes between Obregon and his protégé, Calles, to "take turns" as president. The political stability, however, was superficial. There were abortive army revolts in 1927 and 1929, and though Obregon was re-elected in 1928, he was assassinated within the year. Calles would effectively rule Mexico for the next seven years.

Obregon was formally replaced by a transitional president, Portes Gil, who, facing widespread violence in the Catholic-dominated countryside, made efforts at a compromise with the Church. At the 1929 convention of the ruling party, however, Calles orchestrated the presidential nomination of his front man, Ortiz Rubio. In 1932 he would be replaced by Abelardo Rodriguez, another Calles figurehead. Real power was increasing in Calles's hands and this was opposed by only a few idealists such as Jose Vasconcelos.

It was during the years of first Obregon's and then Calles's rule that the most repressive measures were taken against Catholics which escalated the violence into a rebellion called the Cristeros War. More than ninety priests were murdered; many churches were closed, and several burned. After Obregon's death, Calles increased his already firm control of the army by disbanding the agrarian militias, allowing him to strike with little restraint at the Church.

The Cristeros War: "Viva Cristo Rey!"

War is always tragic, both in its loss of lives and in the seeds of hatred and revenge it plants. As Catholics, as Christ's peacemakers, we should never celebrate a war as a victory over others as much as we should recognize in it a moral defeat for all. Throughout history, however, Christians have recognized the sad necessity of "the just war," that is, a limited act of violence as the last recourse of self-defense. The so-called "Cristeros War" in Mexico in the 1920s is viewed by most observers as justified in this sense. After years of oppression, Mexican Catholics rose up to defend their way of life, which was being threatened by men who appeared to have little need to seek compromise. As with all wars, however just, the violence spiraled out of control and the Church itself took steps to end it.

Let us review the circumstances.

The Mexican Constitution of 1917 contained what was, in effect, a declaration of war on the Church. Provisions banned Catholic schools, outlawed the monastic orders, and forbade public religious processions.

Article 130 was directly aimed at the clergy, denying them the right to vote, to wear clerical garb, or, most pointedly, to criticize government officials. There have never been more oppressive measures taken against religion in any modern state outside of communist Russia and China.

The first anti-Church measures were undertaken during the reign of the ineffectual Venustiano Carranza. General Obregon, his military commander, having had Carranza assassinated, then took power. Known as *El Invicto,* "the undefeated," Obregon was ruthless but shrewd and applied the anti-Church restrictions selectively. His successor, Plutarco Elias Calles, no less brutal, was, however, even more fanatical in his hatred of Catholicism. Calles decreed that Catholic priests would be fined and imprisoned for five years for criticizing his government.

Predictably, with the survival of the Church at stake, Catholic resistance began to grow throughout this era. The National League for the Defense of Religious Liberty was formed in 1924 and in the following year, a Catholic political party, the Popular Union. The Mexican Association of Catholic Youth provided another source of strong resistance to government coercion. When the "Calles Law" was enacted in 1926, adding even more restrictions on the clergy, Catholic opposition to the government exploded. Catholic resistance became Catholic rebellion.

In July 1926, the Mexican bishops responded in strenuous but peaceful protest. They declared that all public worship would be suspended, and endorsed an economic boycott of government agencies, including transportation and schools. The central part of the country was particularly affected by these economic sanctions. Catholics throughout the country stopped riding the buses and streetcars, and Catholic teachers withdrew from public schools. These initial protests, striking at the politicians through the economy, were undercut, however, by the lack of support on the part of many wealthy Catholics more concerned about property than religious rights.

The extensive violence began in August when armed Catholics barricaded themselves, significantly, in the Sanctuary of Our Lady of Guadalupe in Guadalajara. The siege by federal troops left several dead and wounded. The sanctuary's defenders had run out of ammunition, but only in the form of bullets. The faith of their followers only grew more intense.

In the following days, government troops and agents went on the attack. A parish church in Michoacan was assaulted by soldiers, and among the dead were the parish priest and the vicar. In Zacatecas, government agents executed the priest and several Catholic activists. The response to these massacres was swift and forceful. A former army officer, Pedro Quintanar, led a group of ranchers in open rebellion and quickly controlled much of the State of Jalisco. By September, the uprising had grown to include elected officials, including the mayor of Penjamo in Guanajuato, who formed the first among many guerrilla bands in the mountains.

Further uprisings followed in Durango, Michoacan, Zacatecas, and Guanajuato, where the rebels were now led by a former general, Rodolfo Gallegos. Unable to match the federal forces in open country, the Catholic resistance took the form primarily of guerrilla warfare, and the Los Altos region of Guadalajara became the center of the insurgency.

The uprising took on an openly revolutionary character on January 1, 1927, when the Catholic youth movement selected as their leader a twenty-seven-year-old lawyer, Rene Capistran Garza. In the tradition of Mexican revolutionaries, Garza issued a manifesto announcing that "the hour of battle has sounded." Catholics throughout the country then joined the rebellion and the violence spread. Now conducting what was virtually a civil war, the resistance movement, *La Cristiada,* began to create an independent, separately governed area within central Mexico.

The prolonged war that followed, lasting until 1929, pitted the rebels against the federal troops, while various paramilitary groups emerged on both sides. As some Catholics, particularly in the middle class, collaborated with the government, the conflict began to divide towns and even families. The army, with vastly superior weaponry, was easily able to protect the larger cities. The government was, however, over-confident, one general predicting that the war will be "less a campaign than a hunt."

The over-confidence was understandable. The Cristeros — "soldiers of Christ" as they came to be called — were not, in fact, soldiers but a loosely organized force composed of rural Catholics led largely by religious idealists and spread out over vast regions without adequate communications. Garza resigned in frustration after a few months and then a more seasoned leader, Anacleto Gonzalez Flores, dubbed the "maestro" (teacher) by his young followers, was brutally tortured and executed by the army.

The nature of the rebellion was articulated by its victims. Gonzalez Flores not only forgave his executioners but said that he would act as their "intercessor before God." The most revered, and now canonized, martyr was Padre Pro — Miguel Agustin Pro, SJ — who, though clearly innocent of any crime, was executed in November 1927. A famous photo of the young priest, his arms held out in the form of a cross just seconds before his execution, is now iconic. Padre Pro was not, however, a Cristero soldier but a peace-loving priest. His brave shout before the firing squad was "Long live Christ the King!" But before that, he reportedly cried out: "With all my heart I forgive my enemies!" This, clearly, was not simply another political uprising.

The weakness of the Cristeros as a military force was predictable. Volunteers with a strong egalitarian bent, they were resistant to following orders, and a few resorted to banditry. Lacking leaders with military experience, the rebellion even at times turned to non-Catholic mercenaries, who, like many of their "revolutionary" predecessors, were more interested in power than religious ideals. Despite these inevitable weaknesses, the Cristeros' extraordinary bravery, based on their faith, prolonged the war for years. In a real sense, they were never defeated. The Cristeros succumbed, one might say, to politics, or even history, but not to force of arms.

While the Cristeros resistance had emerged primarily from the poor and powerless, a more singular and powerful voice had been raised in protest. In his encyclical of November 18, 1926, *Iniquis Afflictisque,* Pope Pius XI spoke to the world and the Mexican people about the "persecution of the Church in Mexico" in extraordinarily direct and adamant language. He described the leaders of the Mexican regime as a "small group of men" who had "no feelings of pity for their fellow citizens" and who had "done away with the liberties of the majority and in such a clever way that they [had] been able to clothe their lawless actions with the semblance of legality." The pope then carefully examined those measures in the 1917 Constitution aimed at the Church, including the denial of virtually all civil and political rights of priests. He itemized the further restrictions: "The vows of religious orders and religious congregations are outlawed in Mexico. Public divine worship is forbidden unless it takes place within the confines of a church and under the watchful eye of the Government. . . . All church buildings have been declared the property of the state (including) diocesan offices, seminaries, religious houses, hospitals and all charitable institutions. . . . It is not permitted to teach children their religion even in a private school."

After praising the clergy and the people for their bravery and steadfastness, and the bishops for their perhaps excessive forbearance, the pope called for prayers, particularly "to implore Our Lady of Guadalupe, Patroness of the Mexican people, to pardon all these injuries, especially those that have been committed against her, that she ask of God to return peace and concord to her people."

We might note that among his remarks was an indication of what would be the basis of the agreement that eventually ended the conflict three years later. "The bishops hoped that those in charge of the government, after the first burst of hatred, would have appreciated the damage and danger which would accrue to the vast majority of the people from the enforcement of those articles of the Constitution restrictive of the liberty of the Church and that, therefore, out of a desire to preserve peace they would not insist on enforcing these articles to the letter. . . ."

The Church hierarchy, never fully in support of the violence, began efforts to achieve at least a truce in the fighting. The Archbishop of Mexico, Pascual Diaz, was expelled from Mexico City following a rebel attack on a train that killed numerous people. Nonetheless, the archbishop and other prelates, following the mandate of their calling, continued to seek peace and reconciliation.

The Church was aided in this effort by the influential American Ambassador Dwight Morrow, the author of the "Good Neighbor Policy" between Mexico and the United States. Morrow arrived in October 1927 and is reputed to have played a key role in the behind-the-scenes negotiations. It is doubtful that Morrow, or anyone else, could have appealed to Calles on moral grounds; but there were undoubtedly good arguments to be made that the prolonged rebellion would hurt Mexico's economy.

The circumstances that led to an end of the Cristeros rebellion are too complex for anything but a brief summary. There were many players, so to speak. For example, the long-time liberal aspirant to the presidency Jose Vasconcelos mounted another political campaign, offering himself as a reconciler. There were also periodic outbreaks, some quite violent, among the military, and American oil interests, averse to disorder, probably played a role in the background. Former President Obregon, considered by many the architect of government policy even when out of office, engaged in several private negotiations with Church officials, who, in turn, went to Rome for consultations. By the end of 1927, however, there was still no sign of peace.

As they had clearly arranged, Calles was succeeded as president by Obregon in 1928. Whatever their plans, they were to be violently interrupted. One person convinced of Obregon's responsibility for the persecutions was a young school teacher named Jose de Leon Toral. Posing as a sketch artist, Toral managed to enter a post-election victory celebration and shot Obregon to death.

The assassin was described in the official press as a "Catholic militant" who held Obregon responsible for the often-brutal repression of the faithful. In retrospect, the documentary evidence suggests that this unstable young man was, indeed, the gunman, though, at the time, many Mexicans assumed that Calles, or perhaps the ambitious labor leader Morones, was the true "author" of the crime.

Following torture and a mockery of legal procedures, Toral was sentenced to death and an older woman called "Madre Conchita" was sentenced to twenty years' imprisonment for aiding and abetting him. The leader of an extreme Catholic group in which the unauthorized "nuns" were branded with crosses, Conchita, however sincere, was clearly as unstable as Toral and a compassionate priest urged that she be confined in a convent in Europe. Toral's trial was a travesty during which government officials shouted down defense witnesses, and the defense attorney, unable to be heard, had to be escorted from the courtroom for his safety. Toral later expressed regret for the killing. Following attempts on his life in prison, he was executed.

Calles, through a figurehead successor, Emilio Portes Gil, was now back in charge, and the Cristeros war would continue into 1929.

The Church once again took the initiative. An American Catholic priest, Father John Burke, was designated by the apostolic delegate, in effect, to represent the Vatican in the negotiations. An alliance was formed between the two Americans — Ambassador Morrow and Father Burke — and they took the opportunity presented by Portes Gil's "interim" presidency to again pursue a settlement.

Portes Gil made little more than verbal gestures toward reconciliation, still stressing the Church's need to "show respect for law and authority." The Mexican Church hierarchy, however, signaled their readiness to live with the legal restrictions as long as they were not vigorously enforced. A compromise was finally reached, which satisfied no one but brought the violence to an end.

The agreement of June 1929, known as the *arreglos* (arrangements), did little for the Church but end the most violent forms of repression. Restrictions on priests and religious practices remained; Church schools were still banned, as was direct political participation. The one-party, anti-religious dictatorship remained in place.

This settlement might seem a defeat — as it still does to some Catholics — but, in my judgment, this is shortsighted. The Church doesn't live by the time-frame of political tyrants or, for that matter, democrats. In 1929, though still under a repressive regime, Mexican Catholics returned to church, they and their priests now less molested than before. The sacrifice of Cristero lives, including saints and martyrs, had not only deflected the most violent attacks on the faithful, but — as could not have been seen at the time — they had redirected the course of Mexican political history. No other regime would again dare to mount such an aggressive attack on religion. In fact, within little more than a decade, a more serious compromise would be in effect, with a nominal Catholic becoming president. It would take another half century for Catholics and the Church to gain their full civil rights, and there remain deep prejudices still to be overcome within the Mexican political and cultural establishment; but the trajectory was changed in the bloody years of the Cristeros rebellion, and it was changed by the poor and the faithful. On May 25 of each year, Mexican Catholics honor the saints and martyrs of the Cristeros War. Most were Catholic priests who were executed for simply continuing their priestly duties despite the government prohibitions. Some were executed publicly as a warning to others, others were murdered in secret by government agents. They were canonized by Pope

John Paul II in May 2000. The Mexican political rulers during this era had made a serious mistake, one noted later by Russian observers. They had left the church bells in place. In Soviet Russia, bells had been removed and replaced, so to speak, by factory whistles, the new secular "call to worship" of industry and power. The Mexicans still heard the ringing of the bells, as they do to this day — signaling without words, another time, past and to come.

Garrido and the Red Shirts: Revolution and Fanaticism

Pope Pius XI, in his encyclical concerning the persecution of the Church in Mexico, described its instigators as "impelled by [a] fanatical hatred of religion" which spawned, in turn, an extraordinary cruelty. We hear so much about "religious fanaticism" in our times that it is salubrious to recognize the commonalities of this condition. The irrationality of those committed to what they consider a scientific approach to ameliorating the human condition is a curious hallmark of our times; but a chapter in the history of the Mexican twentieth-century revolution is illustrative of how not only brutality but irrationality can grow from an idealism unchecked by humility.

The rise and fall of Tomas Garrido Canabal, the dictator of the State of Tabasco, was a particularly violent chapter of the turbulent 1930s. Garrido's personal troops, formed in 1932, were called "Red Shirts" and their anthem was the communist *Internationale*. Garrido named his son Lenin and his daughter Liberty, which led to the quip that the only place liberty could be found in Tabasco was in her room.

Despite his rabidly left-wing rhetoric, Garrido's authoritarian policies were more akin to those of Hitler and Mussolini, as his uniformed goons regularly physically assaulted and intimated opponents.

Garrido had an extreme hatred of religion and of Catholicism in particular. The business card of one of his acolytes bore the legend "Enemy of God." Garrido's "atheism" was somewhat primitive, if not infantile, with pictures of Christ as a donkey used for target practice. The Red Shirts literally demolished most of the churches in the state, desecrating whatever they could seize, and, like the Nazi youth, burning books and relics in public bonfires. The destruction of churches was so extensive that Graham Greene commented: "Garrido did his job well; he knew the stones cry, and he didn't leave any stones."

What lent a particularly bizarre aspect to Garrido's regime were his attempts at an extreme regimentation of his subjects, a policy not easily compatible with the Mexican temperament. Women, for example, were forbidden to wear makeup or short hair. In time, his extremism led not only to great viciousness but to ridiculous edicts. Christmas and the display of crosses were banned, and, still more absurdly, the most common of Mexican expressions, *Adios* ("to-God"), was suppressed. The wackiest of Garrido's regulations was that all children had to be in bed before eight or their parents would be fined. In that the police could keep half the fine, this led to policemen peering into windows at night, looking for miscreant children out of bed!

Membership in the Red Shirts became obligatory for all males in Tabasco between the ages of fifteen and thirty, and the ambitious Garrido, who had risen to be a minister in the Calles cabinet, attempted to employ them as storm troopers to increase his prestige and power in Mexico City. This led to violent clashes with Catholics in the capital, including the slaying of worshippers outside a church in Coyoacan.

General Cardenas, later to moderate his own policies and restrain the extremists in his government, initially supported Garrido's violent campaign, praising it in 1934 as a "laboratory of the Revolution." The violent clashes, however, grew in intensity and frequency, and this, along with his tactical error of supporting Calles against his successor Cardenas, led to Garrido's eventual downfall and exile.

A generation or more of Catholics paid heavily for Garrido's extremism; yet, in time, even deep wounds heal. I spoke to a Mexican missionary priest who has worked in Tabasco in recent years, and it was his opinion that the tyranny and destruction had been in a mysterious way a blessing, in that it ultimately strengthened the faith of the laity who for years had only fugitive priests to serve them. Such deprivation isn't always destructive, he said, as long as it leads to stronger personal relationships within the family and the Church.

Garrido, an embarrassment to true revolutionaries, is now largely forgotten; yet he has a lasting memorial, though one he wouldn't appreciate. His fierce persecution of the Church provided the background for Graham Greene's classic novel *The Power and the Glory*.

Following the conclusion of the Cristeros war, Plutarco Calles managed to hold on to power for a few more years. Proclaimed *jefe* and "chief of the nation," he had shaped a single party system, which then promoted him to "Supreme Leader of the Revolution." A man who had once been an obscure, sickly school teacher emerged as a virtual dictator. Fortunately for Mexico, this wouldn't last. By 1930, the "Supreme Leader" was declaring that the chief goal of the Revolution, land reform, was "a failure" and he began to cut back land distribution. The world Depression of the 1930s then hit Mexican export crops such as cotton, cutting them by half. In 1933, the Party adopted a "Six Year Plan," a socialist approach to agrarian reform that, in effect, ended the hacienda system, but not the poverty and misery of the land workers and landless.

This failure to solve the problems in the countryside, social and economic, was the primary reason for Calles's ultimate downfall. Groups of discontented farmers, the so-called "Agrarian Leagues," played a key role in bringing another general, Lazaro Cardenas, to power in 1935. The Mexican revolutionaries, unlike their European counterparts in Russia or Spain, were finally able to transfer power without endless bloodbaths.

Initially, Cardenas's ascendancy seemed to signal a continuation of Calles's radicalism. Cardenas spoke openly in Marxist terms about "class struggle" and the need to organize "proletarian workers," and his long-time mentor, Mujica, was a self-proclaimed socialist. With increasing unrest — twelve hundred strikes in 1935 alone — new and powerful labor leaders such as Lombardo Toledano were emerging. Many were clearly communist ideologues, though not necessarily pro-Soviet. Ideological labels are, in fact, misleading during this period, as the often-bloody conflicts were more about power than ideas. Following an attempt on President Ortiz Rubio's life in 1930, for example, more than sixty liberal supporters of Vasconcelos were tortured and killed, condemned as "reactionaries" betraying "the revolutionary family." Vasconcelos himself counted on a violent revolt within the military to bring him to power. To further muddy the ideological waters, the Soviets under their paranoid leader, Stalin, considered the freewheeling Mexican revolutionaries to be "agents of American imperialism"!

Cardenas, once in power, moderated government policies. He sent Calles into exile in 1936, and formed an alliance with President Roosevelt, who, facing imminent war, became, if not a partner, at least a friend. It was during this time of a forced economic and political truce, so to speak, that Cardenas became a Mexican national hero by nationalizing the country's oil. The companies cried foul, but Roosevelt made no serious protest. The war soon came, and while the oil was now wholly "Mexican," the refineries remained largely in American hands.

Lazaro Cardenas: The President Who Learned to Listen

It is risky to interpret the historical figures of another nation, and downright dangerous if some demythifying is involved. It is also presumptuous for an outsider to gauge the full significance and symbolism of some figures. Americans would be uneasy, if not resentful, to hear Lincoln, Roosevelt, or even John F. Kennedy "de-constructed" by foreigners.

Our purpose in viewing the contradictory aspects of Mexico's most beloved president, Lazaro Cardenas, is not, however, to diminish his reputation or discount his accomplishments, but to seek a better understanding of the internal conflicts within Mexican historical development.

Official Mexican history, the school-book version, presents Cardenas as an almost messianic benefactor of the poor and indigenous. His few critics, however, saw him as a "failed messiah" who was ultimately rescued by foreign support, particularly that of the Roosevelt administration. What seems indisputable is that the Cardenas "revolution" was highly pragmatic; that it prolonged a one-party state; and that, despite its expropriations, allowed considerable foreign investment.

Mexican political mythology, similar in this respect to the American, is that Cardenas, like Franklin Roosevelt, "saved us from communism." Whether this is an accurate assessment is too speculative for our present concerns. What is clear is that Cardenas, a judicious man who, as governor of the agrarian state of Michoacan, had learned through trial and error how *not* to govern, and particularly how not to govern peasants.

By the time Lazaro Cardenas came to power, a socialist program for Mexico was well under way. In 1931, a government educational system, designed by a Marxist, Narciso Passolo, was in place, and throughout Mexico, nominally socialist, or at least populist, politicians and parties were dominant, many closely aligned with radical labor leaders and agrarian leagues.

Despite the existence of a feminist movement as early as the 1920s, women's rights were "delayed" in Mexico. Only four states supported Cardenas's initial proposal to grant women the vote, and one, Yucatan, later annulled it. This was primarily due to the fear of the revolutionaries that Mexican women were inherently religious and thus conservative. Once the vote was granted, their fears would prove to be amply justified.

The campaign against the Church had intensified during the Thirties and included a national radio program on Sunday designed to replace religion with "culture." Perhaps the most naked, though clearly futile, attempt to dislodge the Church was the creation of a rival institution, the absurdly named "National Orthodox Apostolic Catholic Church." Its obvious political purpose was made evident in that its leader was a Mason.

On a more ominous note, there were signs of another possible armed revolt. Many churches had been destroyed and the papal envoy and more than two hundred priests had been expelled. The Cristeros uprising in the 1920s had cost seventy thousand lives and the expenditure of more than half the national budget. Another such outbreak of violent protest was seen as catastrophic, and yet seemed possible.

Meanwhile, President Cardenas was "listening," and carefully to the common people. Cardenas was a deeply moral man, in fact, a strict moralist who seriously proposed the prohibition of alcohol and gambling, and tried to close the houses of prostitution in Mexico City. A massive procession in the capital in 1938 honoring the Virgin of Guadalupe undoubtedly also had an effect on any politician sensitive to public opinion. There is evidence, though, that Cardenas had already learned some valuable lessons.

In her study, *Setting the Virgin on Fire,* historian Marjorie Becker takes a close look at Cardenas's reign as governor of Michoacan prior to his presidency, when the campaign against the Church and religion was at its height, and when the rural poor began to resist these policies. Becker's analysis tends to dispel the "progressive" mythology and yet is sympathetic to Cardenas's efforts to improve social conditions. It is his failed efforts to transform the culture, however, that expose the most significant contradictions in Mexican politics and history.

The revolutionary movement in Michoacan, under Cardenas, had attempted to gradually transform Catholic beliefs into a kind of moralistic secularism. Over several years, efforts were made by government educators, for example, to separate Indian art and dance from their traditional rituals. This led to a largely artificial folklore that might appeal to tourists but couldn't possibly replace religion. Such efforts would fail in large part because the most ardent *Cardenistas* were middle-class intellectuals and school teachers who disdained what Marx had called the "dark and monotonous" countryside. "Progress" for them meant, in effect, rescuing the peasants from their own way of life, and this, of course, meant a rejection of their most fundamental beliefs. The radicals who opposed religion in all its forms were, however, a minority who often disagreed among themselves when it came to tactics. The more moderate tried to distinguish between an "acceptable" Catholic faith and "fanaticism," which, unfortunately, meant, to them, the actual practice of the religion. In the long run, not only would these attempts to eradicate religious belief fail; they would provoke a strong and at times violent backlash.

Becker concludes that Cardenas's choice of Avila Camacho over the radical Mujica as his presidential successor was less a concession to his conservative opponents than to the demands of the rural poor and indigenous for a restoration of their Catholic traditions. The attempts to "revolutionize" the poor from on high, including the efforts to promote indigenous culture as a counter to their Catholic faith, had largely failed in Michoacan. By 1939, after years of persecution and marginalization, what Becker calls "Catholic fervor" was more evident than ever.

As president, Cardenas created a cult of personality, which while leaving an historical legacy wasn't sufficient to govern the country or to develop its economy. Cardenas, however, "knew how to listen" and, though personally opposed to all forms of religion, allowed a restoration of church services. Cardenas himself refused to be married in a church; but he realized that it would be wise to allow others to do so.

The irony is that while seeming to retreat from revolutionary principles — anti-religious and collectivist — Cardenas actually redeemed the

Mexican revolution by making it acceptable in the eyes of the poor, whom it was originally meant to serve. The leaders that would follow were "revolutionary" only in rhetorical terms; but they were able to retain power and even, to a great extent, to stabilize the country.

Following the ideological *zeitgeist* of his era, Cardenas believed in a kind of secular mysticism based on nineteenth-century notions of historical laws. The poor and indigenous believed, as they always have, in "invisible realities" — a God who creates a mysterious cosmos and loves His creatures. There is no way to reconcile these radically different perceptions of human life. Cardenas, to his credit and to the lasting benefit of his nation, called off the fight. Mexico would have no official ideology, only slogans. While Cardenas was their able instrument, it was the poor and the indigenous who redeemed the Mexican revolution, and they did so through their Catholic faith.

The adulation of Lazaro Cardenas remains a political staple in Mexico as he is understandably considered a national hero for his nationalization of oil and efforts at land reform. What he was unable to do, however, was to establish genuine democratic procedures, if, indeed, that was even his aim. His choice of the moderate Avila Camacho was sensible and had a stabilizing effect, but the Camacho election was clearly as rigged as those that would follow. When the celebrated Mexican comic Cantinflas announced jokingly that he himself was going to run for president, a friend protested: "Who would vote for you?" Cantinflas shrugged: "Who voted for Avila Camacho?"

The Conditions of Existence:
A Footnote on Land Reform

The central question of justice and equality throughout modern Mexican history has concerned the issue of land reform. The indigenous lands, originally held communally, were first divided among the Spanish conquerors and the Church; a harsh and essentially feudal system prevailed into the colonial period. The haciendas, often huge parcels of land, depended upon the labor of the peasants, indigenous and *mestizo*. After the nineteenth-century revolution that created an independent Mexico, the Spanish were expelled and the vast Church land holdings were seized. The first attempts at land reform were initiated; but, by and large, the land now became the private property of the upper classes.

By the 1930s several attempts at land reform, the *ejido* system, theoretically a kind of collective farm, had been attempted but, despite the distribution of large amounts of acreage, had largely failed. One might note that this failure was hardly unique to Mexico. Attempts to create collective farming were failing around the world, and in places such as Russia and China accompanied by horrific losses of life and liberty.

In many ways, though now largely privatized, land remains an issue in Mexico. The North American Free Trade Agreement (NAFTA), whatever else it might have accomplished, is viewed by many rural Mexicans as a threat to their way of life. It was on the day of the signing of that agreement that the abortive uprising among the land workers in Chiapas began. This was not a coincidence.

Those of us Americans, now an overwhelming majority, who have been raised in urban centers may have trouble understanding the attitude of previous generations, even in our own country, about the significance of land possession. Urbanites may recognize the access to land as a matter of economic and political justice; but people raised on land they have worked for generations possess a much deeper perception of its value. For them, it is fundamentally a spiritual question.

Two of the sages of the latter part of the nineteenth century, Leo Tolstoy and John Ruskin, addressed this question perceptively. Tolstoy observed: "The land, like our character, cannot be the object of buying and selling. Behind the buying and selling of earth is the hidden process of buying and selling a personality." John Ruskin had a similar perspective: "The bodies of men and women, and, even more important, their children, should not be bought or sold. So, too, the water, the land and air, because these things are necessary conditions of this existence."

It is easy to see that this viewpoint, shared however inarticulately by vast numbers of peasants and even some wealthy landowners, was incompatible with the new age of industrial development. "Land reform," however well intentioned, did not and could not address this fundamental loss of meaning and identity.

The Twenty-first Century: Past as Prologue?

The Second World War transformed Mexico as it did America and the rest of the world. In 1940 President Cardenas prudently chose a political moderate and nominal Catholic, Avila Camacho, as his successor, and with Mexico's support of the American war effort, politically and economically, an era came to an end.

The aftermath, from the 1950s on, is considered to be Mexico's "post-revolutionary" period; but, in some ways, this is misleading. The revolutionary rhetoric remained, as well as the one-party state, for decades; but the changes in Mexico in the second half of the century were as far-reaching — though fortunately less violent — than those of the early years.

It isn't the purpose or prerogative of this book to evaluate Mexican politics, past or present. Our interest has been in how the Catholic faith of Mexicans has shaped its culture and social development, or, at times, resisted it. What we can observe in the political arena is that Mexican Catholics — on both the "left" and "right" of the spectrum — have attempted to integrate their faith and Church teaching into public policy.

In the 1970s a movement primarily among Latin American theologians referred to as "Liberation Theology" became influential in Mexico. It led, however, to many conflicts within the Church, and its influence has gradually diminished. What proved to be the most controversial aspect of this theology wasn't the admirable commitment to the poor, or innovative proposals for community organizing (the "base communities"), but the use of a Marxist ideological framework to interpret history. The concept of class struggle derived from Marx relativized Christianity and its message into a limited stage of historical development. Much of Liberation Theology had stressed the need to sustain a Hispanic identity forged in opposition to Eurocentric theology. Yet much of the theory was grounded in the most thoroughly European ideology in history: the materialist interpretation of culture by Marx and Engels. As the political rhetoric became more revolutionary, the "poor" of the Bible increasingly came to resemble the exploited "proletariat" of communist doctrine. The plight of the poor and the struggle for justice, central to the Gospels, was transformed ideologically into modern class warfare.

Class warfare was clearly not the intent of the Liberation movement or its major theologians; but some priests, particularly in Central America, interpreted these "radically new" ideas as a sanction for violence and guerrilla warfare. By 1979, the bishops of Latin America, meeting in Mexico, were obliged to address those ideological elements that were clearly inconsistent with Catholic teachings; but they did so while reaffirming the Church's "preferential option for the poor." The danger wasn't that some aspects of Liberation Theology were "radically new," but that they were "radically old" in rationalizing political violence and hatred.

The best thing that happened to the Liberation theorists was the fall of the Soviet Union, and not just the failure of Marxism but of all the utopian variants enamored of power. Liberation Theology, divested of Marxism, might yet provide alternatives to both capitalist globalism and State authoritarianism.

At the beginning of the twenty-first century, Mexico faces serious social and economic problems, especially the prolonged and violent drug wars. Yet it should be recognized that considerable progress toward a genuine democracy has been made in the last decades.

In the year 2000, the first candidate from an opposition party to win the presidency, Vicente Fox, generously acknowledged the role of his predecessor, Ernesto Zedillo, in allowing a free election to take place. Fox served the single term allowed by Mexico's constitution, and his successor in 2006 was Felipe Calderon, also from the *Partido Accion Nacional* (PAN), originally founded by Catholic activists. Fox, a devout Catholic, openly defied the previous prohibitions of religious expression by political leaders. In his memoir *Revolution of Hope,* Fox revealed his deep reverence for Pope John Paul II, and the spiritual influences of Gandhi and Martin Luther King on his life and work. He expressed sentiments common to many Mexican leaders when he declared that while Mexico sought material progress, "our soul was not for sale."

Fox described the "best values of Mexico" as "family, church, work, compassion," then adding, somewhat whimsically, " — and *huevos rancheros.*" He also candidly admitted Mexico's "worst traits," including corruption, inefficiency, and authoritarianism, though he was confident that "these are fast fading into memory."

"In Mexico," he concluded, "journalists will criticize me for saying this, for airing our own dirty laundry. But the fact that they are free to do so is proof positive of how far we have come."

We can only admire the courage and tenacity of those Catholics, whatever their political orientation, who are willing to grapple with the inherently messy and even corrupting realities of political life. The danger inherent in political commitment, however, is not merely corruption. To live as a Christian is to refuse to demonize other people into "enemies." This temptation will always confront us whatever our historical circumstances. It is the mysterious nature of forgiveness even more than that of securing justice that reveals a source of life beyond our own powers.

Progress and Peril

Mexico and the Crisis of Modernity

While the paradigm shift provided by Mexican history helps us to better understand our own past, Mexico's encounter with modernity is perhaps of even greater value. Mexico is, again, unique. It has been virtually engulfed by America's celebrated individualism and, at times, enticed by Europe's ideological alternatives, yet has somehow remained apart from both.

At the end of the twentieth century, Mexico, as it typically does, offered a spectacle of striking contrasts. The "drug wars," the violent conflicts between large gangs of *narco-traficantes,* major drug dealers, were intensifying, and the image of Mexico as lawless and dangerous was seriously harming tourism. These conflicts were exaggerated by the American media; yet, whatever the scope, this civil disorder was a troubling symptom of an inadequate system of law and justice. On the other hand, Mexico now has a democratic multi-party system in place, and, in turn, greater civil and press freedoms.

There is a connection worth noting between the growth of democracy and the outbreaks of violent lawlessness. Despite significant differences, this development is similar to that in Russia following the demise of the Soviet system. In both countries, a one-party rule, often by local bosses, was despotic and corrupt, but relatively effective in limiting lawlessness. Deals could be made without the restraints of law or justice. Similarly, the loss of a moral foundation among the political elite due to a long and relentless secularizing process resulted, inevitably, in the dividends of widespread corruption and cynicism.

We are, however, seeking a broader perspective than political developments can provide.

Modernity, in the limited sense that we will employ, refers to that historical period in which the central organizing idea, and the principle by which cultural life could be assessed, became the creation of the autonomous Self. This autonomy, affirmed in terms of freedom and power, was to be achieved through reason and science, undergirded by the concepts of evolutionary biology and the attainment of a "higher" consciousness. Clearly, these premises would suggest, if not mandate, a break with the past, and an anticipated "progress" toward, if not a "new" human being, at least a more fully developed one.

Modernity — the modern world — came to mean something different to each of the groups shaped by it. For nineteenth-century entrepreneurs and intellectuals, it meant greater liberty; for the middle class, it signified material advancement. For the rural poor, however, modernity meant a loss of place, land, and village, and an impoverished life in urban slums. For traditionalists, it meant a loss of cherished values; for the *avant-garde,* unknown territory. As it came to an end, modernity meant whatever we imagined it to mean.

As an historical period, we will locate the origin of "modernity" in the French Revolution of 1789, and its terminus in the collapse of the Soviet empire in 1989. For all its inadequacies, this framework provides at least a tidy time-period of two hundred years. Of course, the origins of the "modern," intellectually and spiritually, lay much further back, and we are still attitudinally "moderns" in many respects, even if, at times, we might feel distinctly "post."

It is our assumption that while many of modernity's associated hopes and attitudes have been retained, especially in popular American culture, this historical period is now over. Aspirations to create a "new human" or an "advanced society" through technology might still linger, but there is no longer a consistent set of ideas or principles to make this project coherent.

We are reaching a point, I suggest, that we can now look back and ask: What did this "age of modernity" mean to Americans and to Mexicans?

The sociologist Gunnar Myrdal described mid-century America as a "nation of Hindus governed by Swedes." His insight was that while the cultural elite was increasingly secularized, the vast majority of Americans remained traditionally religious. This gap has been even more pronounced in Mexico. Such an enormous gulf, economic and social, between the educated upper classes and an overwhelmingly poor majority hasn't been part of American life for more than a hundred years — that is, not since the waves of poor immigrants in the nineteenth century began their socially upward climb.

Mexicans and Americans experienced this two-hundred-year modern era in quite different ways, particularly in the enjoyment of its material benefits, but also in terms of personal liberty and opportunity. What was most "modern" in Mexico was often the radical secularism of a small cultural elite and the expansive lifestyle of an even smaller group of the newly rich. The best aspect of modernity for most Americans, on the other hand, was the growth of a large middle class and their eventual creation of a suburban subculture.

Not surprisingly, many thoughtful Mexicans looked for alternatives to what seemed an unsuitable American model for their future. Many intellectuals turned to the even-more insubstantial utopian ideologies of the past. A few Catholics looked to their own forms of radical alternative, such as Liberation Theology; but others simply locked the door and waited for the storm to pass. In some respects, we're still waiting.

However, to appreciate the Mexican experience, we need to look beyond the meaning of modernity in sociological or political terms.

Though the reign of absolute Reason has eventually waned in Western thought, the autonomous Self remains the goal of modern society. Traditional concepts of duty, virtue, indeed, of tradition itself, are no longer normative. By the end of the nineteenth century, the human will, especially the "will to power," had replaced reason as the key to a self-defining and, hence, "free" lifestyle. In time, modernists, that is, those thinkers who saw enlightenment primarily in terms of future development, tended to fall into two categories: determinists and absurdists. Determinists presumed to use scientific methodologies as means of liberation and sought to find "laws" of development. Absurdists, on the other hand, seemed, in some eyes, even more "modern" (or even "post"), but were actually returning to an earlier, ancient mindset. They saw creation as arising from primal chaos, without inherent meaning. This perception usually encouraged an antinomian view of behavior, though not necessarily bad manners. In many ways, these attitudes remain at the core of the modern legacy.

The lasting meaning of modernity, however, has emerged in the writings of its critics. This was anticipated by prophetic figures in the latter part of the nineteenth century, such as Ruskin, Tolstoy, Kierkegaard, and Dostoyevsky. The French philosopher Maurice Blondel risked Church censure at that time by pointing out that the freedom demanded by modern thought was essential if the limits of human knowledge were to be understood. For the next hundred years, the critics of modernity were able to reconstitute a continuity between the present age and the past. This was a valiant effort of inestimable importance, as it revealed the true value of modernity.

The early conservative critics tended to see modernity as a somewhat predictable stage of history, but not a progressive one in a positive sense. There were numerous distinguished historians, such as Toynbee and Dawson, who perceived the West, and Europe in particular, as having been in a stage of decline as early as the end of the nineteenth century. A loss of confidence in the society's values among its own elite was usually cited as the telling characteristic of a declining civilization. Matthew Arnold's poem "Dover Beach," with its lines about ominous "clashes by night" captures the dark mood that appeared a generation before the Great War. Other symptoms often alluded to include a loss of inherent meaning in work, and pansexuality.

What we most commend in the critics of modernity — prophets and direct witnesses — isn't just their acumen, but their courage. It was their willingness to confront and assess the meaning of the devastation of the two world wars, the rise of totalitarianism, and the horrors of fratricide and genocide that provided the essential context for an ultimate critique of modernity. We can celebrate advances in medicine, communications, and environmental awareness; but to ignore the pivotal violent events in modern "progressive" history, from the French

Revolution and its "reign of terror" to the Gulag, is to ignore the image in our collective mirror.

The conclusion of these many observers most pertinent to our interests was that modernity had produced an increasingly anxious and alienated state of mind due to the loss of community, tradition, family ties, and a concept of meaningful work. There has also been an accompanying loss of the "rites of passage" into adulthood and corresponding sexual preoccupations characteristic of arrested adolescence. The spiritual crisis of modernity has produced a range of reactions as well. One of the later manifestations has been a "thwarted mysticism," that is, a sincere, but ineffectual attempt to invent an individual "spirituality" without ties to either community or tradition.

Americans have responded to the loss of modernist certainties in reason and power in two fundamental but contradictory ways. We deplore the loss while simultaneously denying it. As the external threats of totalitarianism, left and right, diminished, uneasiness about the goals of unlimited wealth and the status it provided seemed to increase. Curiously, by the end of the twentieth century, Americans, though with unprecedented national wealth, seemed to become more "religious" rather than less as in Europe. Yet the materialist goals and mass consumerism, if anything, grew more dominant, and relativized moral standards provoked even more confusion and discord. The chief characteristic of American moral discourse, as philosopher Alasdair MacIntyre observed, became "interminability" because the underlying contradictions were not addressed. This unresolved inner conflict — between at least nominal Christian values and a clearly contradictory way of life — produced, not surprisingly, an atmosphere of guilt and accusation. Political rhetoric, evasive of the underlying moral questions, became inflamed, and talk-radio rants became the norm. American partisan politics is now the arena by which we distract ourselves from our real problems.

American leaders — political and cultural — have responded to the loss of a unifying moral covenant by largely denying the problem. They have maintained a central American myth: the illusion of American "exceptionalism." Rooted in nineteenth-century idealism, this is a vision of an America that is somehow exempt from history. Any suggestion that we are susceptible to decline, much less fall, produces predictably harsh denunciations of an unwarranted pessimism, if not outright disloyalty. F. Scott Fitzgerald reflected on this refusal to confront the reality of natural limits as a national characteristic. "Americans," he observed, "believe in only the green light." A collision in the intersection of history was inevitable.

We American Christians seem as prone to this state of denial as our secular compatriots, and are often as intent to succeed as any other market-driven competitor. We are particularly in peril, however, when our vaunted individualism leads us to want to distinguish ourselves from others in this way. This desire for worldly success and recognition is especially self-deluding when it is, however unconsciously, disguised as altruism. Such "success" contradicts the Christian spirit of selfless disinterestedness.

We mustn't confuse this recognition of the historical reality of rising and diminishing power with a political posture. The expansion or contraction of American power will have serious effects, which must be addressed, but it will not change the meaning of our lives as Christians, nor our moral obligations.

Mexicans, while increasingly absorbed into the American cultural market as well as the economy, retain a distinct difference in their response to modernity, as we shall see in examining the insights of Octavio Paz. The modern crisis has only deepened the contradictions within Mexican society, and many have responded by retaining the comforting status of victimhood. This posture has engendered a curious symbiosis in that "victimhood" is increasingly a prerequisite status for sympathetic attention in the United States. As Renc Girard has warned, we are in danger of replacing the liberal notion of justice with a "cult of misfortune" that sees, if not glorifies, everyone as a "victim." We are at even greater risk when this takes the form of a Christian romanticism that misconceives our mission as the removal of the Cross from the world and history.

Where are we now?

"Postmodern" is the preferred academic category for "where we are now." While this term may be useful in defining the diminishing or lost characteristics of modernity, in the end, it offers only a blank page, or, worse, a scrawl of defiant despair.

A Catholic perspective on the crisis of modernity might begin with the recognition that the first half of the twentieth century was the most oppressive and dangerous period for Christians and Christianity since the persecutions of the Roman emperors. Countless Christians died for their faith in Russia, China, Germany, the Middle East and, one must add, Mexico. Many churches, including some of the most sacred sites, were destroyed or deliberately desecrated. There was widespread apostasy, particularly in Western Europe, and, perhaps most troubling, deep divisions among Christians. This is the background for the crisis of belief — not just doubts about religious dogma, but, ultimately, disillusionment about belief itself.

Louis Dupre, an astute observer of modernity, has recognized that our understanding of the past — or present — depends more on "epiphany" than discourse. We have a "lust for consensus," but what we need first is gratitude for "the Glory of Being in itself." The nihilism of our age is less a philosophy than it is a form of memory loss. We are "forgetful of Being." When we seek the truth about history or suffering — synonymous to some — we must see the truth as coming more from participation and disclosure than analysis. This insight was at the heart of Focolare founder Chiara Lubich's appeal to us to share in the "Cry" from the Cross, which unites us with humanity and enables us to more clearly see the story we share, and without despair.

George Steiner referred to the end of the twentieth century as constituting an "after-Word" to a departed culture; but the novelist Walker Percy was even pithier. We have entered, he suggested, "the no-name new age." Percy, a Catholic, undoubtedly meant to suggest that the lack of a "name" pointed to a loss of a transcendent meaning or goal. As Graham Greene, another Catholic novelist, described it much earlier, our condition is now one of "little hope, and no forgiveness."

Yet this condition, shorn of false hope and certainties, could be a prelude to something new and authentic as much as recognition of what is past. We may now be able to better discern the real gifts of modernity. While they may not be permanent, or even long-lasting, the "fruits of modernity," to use Jacques Maritain's phrase, are the affirmation of an essential freedom of conscience and the recognition of the universality of the human condition. These are the gifts for which we should be most grateful. Where are we? By returning to our timeless sources, perhaps we are finally achieving the "progress" we sought all along. For the ancients, humility and gratitude were the most reliable signs of wisdom. If

Romano Guardini and other earlier observers were correct in anticipating a spiritual response to the modern crisis, then we might anticipate a serious search for the roots of the sacred in all traditions. In Mexico, we will have to dig less deeply than elsewhere to find those roots.

A loss of the sense of the tragic constitutes one of the most serious losses in contemporary consciousness. The tragic is not merely a deeper degree of sadness or pain, but contains a great potential for revelation. This is another way of saying that we've lost our ability to respond to the fullness of life that includes the redemptive nature of suffering. In current times, no Christian concept has been more rigidly resisted or resented than this. Yet there remains in Mexican culture a residual Catholic attitude toward suffering. It stems, of course, from the perception of the suffering of Christ as the prelude to new life.

As our observations about Sor Juana and the Theology of Beauty suggest, we might also find in Mexico a path of redemption in Beauty. This would include art, myth, and poetry, and Mexico is rich with these treasures.

While Mexico is best known for its pictorial and plastic arts, we can also see that a poetic response to the crisis of our times may be at least as valuable, if not more so, than analysis. Poets and saints both wander the desert wastes until they are purified and are then able to return to others. Many of us are wandering in a wilderness disguised by its urban metal, plastic, and electronic veneer. Poetry, as with art, can be a path by which we return to our origins, and recover our lost languages and symbols. Our journey into Mexico continues on this path.

The Solitary Mexican: God, Mexico, and Octavio Paz

In assessing the causes and effects of our modern condition, most of the critics we have drawn upon were Europeans who had directly witnessed war and oppression. Others, such as Christopher Lasch and Philip Rieff, were Americans who were able to look beyond affluence and dominance to describe our spiritual disorders. In different and yet remarkably similar terms, all of these observers have provided a not-always-welcome but truthful picture of our times. No one, however, was more insightful and courageous in describing his own culture and people than the celebrated Mexican poet Octavio Paz, whose mid-century book *The Labyrinth of Solitude* is truly a classic in that it is a timeless, perennially relevant work.

Paz's remarkable accomplishment was to see himself and his culture with such clarity that, drawing from Mexican particularities, he was able to depict the universal condition. It is through his eyes — the sensibility of a poet more than a philosopher — that we can best see what Mexico might offer us as a response to our shared modern condition.

Octavio Paz died in 1998 at the age of eighty-four after a full and remarkable life. He resided for some time in France and India, fought for the Loyalists in the Spanish Civil War, founded a major journal, wrote highly influential works on art and culture, and was given the Nobel Prize for literature in 1990. He was one of the twentieth century's most illustrious poets, arguably the greatest in the Spanish language.

With all of his accomplishments, he was, above all, a poet, and, as such, he lived in, with, and among paradoxes. He was, in many respects, a very modern man, but with a traditionalist sensibility. Such profound contradictions undoubtedly made him a great poet, for poetry, like religious faith, comes alive somewhere beyond the range of conceptual analysis.

It is not because Paz was Mexican and Catholic, but because he was Mexican and was *not* Catholic that he serves as a guide to Mexico's confrontation with modernity. In this way, he embodies the confrontation. Even though at times a harsh critic of the Church, Paz is unique among the intellectuals of his generation in avoiding what the historian Samuel Huntington described as the most serious analytical error of the century. Paz took religion seriously, understanding that a shared spiritual belief was an essential characteristic of the human species. This awareness, in great part, was due to his sensitivity to his — and Mexico's — indigenous heritage.

Much of twentieth-century poetry concerns time and death. In fact, an anthology of early modern poetry following the great wars could easily be catalogued under necrology. Paz's awareness, however, had much different roots than the despair induced by war so common to the British and Europeans of his generation. In his own way, Paz, through his poetry, sanctifies time. He absorbed an indigenous perception of time — and therefore death — which was cyclical and not what Paz dismissed as modernity's "empty abstract measurement."

"Time and eternity," he advised, "are not opposites." Time, for the indigenous, Paz noted, was a concrete force, a substance that is perpetually being "used up." The central question for the Aztecs was, then, not how to hoard time or escape death, but how to "reinvigorate" them. This concept of death — almost incomprehensible to us moderns — brings us to the heart of the matter and to the tension between American and Mexican cultures: A profound difference in the perception of death inevitably results in an equally contrasting view of life.

We need not follow Paz in his full embrace of the indigenous past, for, as Catholics, we follow a different path. We must recognize, however, that for many contemporary Americans and Europeans, life terminates, as Paz puts it, in a "useless death without end." He concludes that a "truly modern consciousness" is one which eventually "turns upon itself." Human knowledge, taken to its limits, can only result in futility and despair.

Paz recognized the force of this modern despair, and his work at times reflects it; but he also saw other possibilities, and looked to his culture's past for hope and inspiration. Aztec society viewed voluntary self-sacrifice as the highest expression of its doctrine of life and this reflected an acceptance of human limitations. The ancient concept of the "eternal return," a form of rebirth, is thematic as well in Paz's eloquent poetry.

In contrasting the Mexican and American cultural attitudes of his day, Paz was not sparing of either. He saw modern Mexicans as increasingly "hiding from life" as well as death behind the alternating "frenzy and passivity" of their *fiestas* and wakes. He described this as a cycle of "intimacy and withdrawal" — a burst of fireworks followed by silence. This insight seems close to that of anthropologists who note the frenzied extremes that characterize a ritual when it loses its spiritual core. To the extent that the Mexican *fiesta* has become mere custom, or, worse, a tourist attraction, it loses its ability to transcend itself, and fails to purge the participants of their fears and anxieties.

An obsession with death, though repressed and thus made more obsessive, was, for Paz, a chief characteristic of modernity. He therefore viewed the Mexican, in this respect, as an even more "modern" person than the American because of the more direct awareness of death in ordinary life. He observed that Americans were attempting to cope with death by filtering it through crime fiction and gangster movies. This observation was made at mid-century, around 1950, before the media avalanche of theatrical mayhem and horrors — and there is no evidence to suggest that this trend is diminishing.

Paz's insights provide a bridge between American and Mexican spiritual conditions. This becomes apparent when his analysis is compared with that of Christopher Lasch less than a generation later. There is a clear link between Paz's "solitude" and Lasch's use of "narcissism" as metaphors for the toxic element in an American culture increasingly fixated on youth. One of the distinctive characteristics of adolescence is a painful sense of solitude and extreme self-consciousness. This is part of normal development, a stage moving toward maturation. If this process is thwarted, however, death is, then, anticipated as the final and absolute isolation. This arrested narcissistic stage provokes only a "monologue," an endless echoing of our isolated thoughts and words.

Paz's concept of "solitude" seems comparable to Lasch's "cultural narcissism" when it is seen as the "mask" that conceals the Mexican soul. Paz believed that this self-concealment reflected an essential dualism in Mexican society. It is the result of the outer ritual deprived of the inner faith — a modern condition, but one that is as old as the human race.

However, more importantly, Paz saw that solitude could be redemptive as well as self-destructive. Here his affinity to Miguel de Unamuno, the Spanish philosopher to whom we referred earlier, becomes clear. Unamuno had affirmed that solitude, as it relates to an admission of human limitations, can bond and unite us. Unamuno wrote that "only in solitude do we find ourselves, and when we find ourselves, we find our brothers in solitude."

As a poet, Paz knew that poetry nourishes and sustains a common language. Language, he insisted, retains a "magic power," that is, a spiritual dimension that suggests a life beyond our own. This is the aspect of religion that the pioneer psychologist Carl Jung saw as inherently healing. Paz compared "verbal representation" to the creativity of biological reproduction. The loss of a common vocabulary — poetic or religious — isn't simply then a cultural loss or a moral problem, but a sign of decadence and dissipation.

Solitude as a form of redemption is, I suggest, an interpretive key to Paz's thought and poetry. By "solitude," Paz means specifically "the feeling and knowledge that one is alone." He sees communion and solitude, however, as complementary opposites. The mysterious and redemptive power of solitude is that it strips us of our last illusions; and, alone in this respect, we are drawn toward an ultimate, equally mysterious union.

Paz resisted any specific religious heritage; but some of his conclusions can be read as a kind of exegesis of his own spirituality: "To live is to be separated from who we were in order to approach what we are going to be in a mysterious future." His dialectics also point to a metaphysical end. He wrote that the "most profound experience life can offer us [is] that of rediscovering reality as a oneness in which opposites agree."

Paz conceived of society as an organic unity in which the individual is literally part of a body. Therefore, he wrote: "No one is either saved or damned on his own account." It is hard to miss the Christian overtones, with the Body of Christ as the ultimate organic unity. However, Paz offers an anthropological or even mythical viewpoint rather than a religious one. He believed that primitive religion emerged as a means of avoiding social dissolution, an insight that resonates with that of Rene Girard. Paz's solitary "exile," in this context, seems close to Girard's description of the function of the sacrificial victim. When societies collapse, Paz noted, there is "a sense of guilt, or solitude, and expiation plays the same role as it does in the life of an individual." In this respect, Jesus of Nazareth seems the most pivotal "solitary" or "exile." I strongly suspect that Paz would agree.

Despite all the similarities of his conclusions, Paz was far from being a Catholic or formally religious. There is a distinctly modern side to much of his thought that is expressed in existential and even psychoanalytical language. He saw solitude also in Freudian terms, as a self-awareness that was in tension with a universal longing to return to the safety of the womb. The existentialist overtones are similar to those of Albert Camus when Paz declared that a man "invents himself" by "saying no," as a declaration of existential freedom. "Self-invention" here can seem primarily negation and "longing" can suggest merely a need for escape.

It is not surprising that we should find some aspects of Paz's thoughts incompatible with our own beliefs and Christian faith. It is the differences, however, that provide the bridge that we desire. It is the unity of opposites that we must seek and accept. St. Teresa, in her direct and illuminating way, went to the heart of contradiction when she asked: "Is birth death and is death birth? We do not know." This is the Mystery of the Cross, and we must not run from it.

Paz himself was a modern Mexican lost in his own "labyrinth of solitude." He used words as a poet, not a theorist, and allowed his genius to guide him through the labyrinth of ambiguity and doubt without expecting to find an exit. He acted out what he believed: that it is the solitary, whether saint or poet, who, purified by exile, must return to the world to preserve the unity of his people. Following the collapse of religion and utopian politics, Paz hoped that there would be the revelation of a universal human condition. It is on the basis of a shared existential condition, the acceptance of an unwelcomed freedom, that Paz proposed to build the future. We might share the hope of a greater acceptance of a universal condition; but what Paz's honest appraisal confirms for us, as Catholics, is that we have reached the end of the modern illusion of human autonomy.

Almost all of Paz's contradictions are ones he exposed himself. Paradox is his theme, as he endlessly observes how opposites unite. Life and death are one and time is not fixed, but "living." The *fiesta* and funeral renew us and make us contemporaries to all who have lived. Our life matures, Paz asserts, when "time takes on meaning and purpose." Paz refers to "our fear of being" and seeks a "nakedness" that binds us. In this sense, he is part of the ancient biblical covenant that binds us to simply "love one another."

Paz saw that the Mexican search for unity had become a search for the lost mythic unity of the ancient past, or, conversely, a unity based on the modern project of self-invention. It is while bravely confronting the failure of these efforts that Paz's own human limitations become apparent. His talent and integrity were exceptional; but few of us transcend our own time, and none of us can do so through our own efforts. We are all, like Paz, "time bound" without the grace of the epiphany we call Revelation.

Paz, I believe, discovered a revelatory light only in his poetry. It is this magnificent poetry that passionately fuses the spiritual legacies of Mexico. This is most evident in the concluding stanzas of Paz's most celebrated poem, inspired by the ancient Aztec solar calendar, *Piedra del Sol* ("Sunstone") as translated by Eliot Weinberger.

door of being: open your being,
and wake, learn to be, form
your face, develop your features, have
a face that I can see, bread, rocks, and a fountain,
source where all our faces dissolve
in the nameless face, the faceless being,
an unspeakable presence of presences.

I want to go on, to go further, and cannot:
as each moment was dropping into another
I dreamt the dreams of dreamless stones,
I heard my blood singing in its prison,
and the sea sang with a murmur of light,
one by one the walls gave way,
all of the doors were broken down,
and the sun came bursting through my forehead,
it tore apart my closed lids,
cut loose my being from its wrappers,
and pulled me out of myself to wake me
from this animal sleep and its centuries of stone
and the sun's magic of mirrors revived
a crystal willow, a poplar of water,
a tall fountain the wind arches over,
a tree deep-rooted yet dancing still,
a course of a river that turns, moves on,
doubles back, and comes full circle,
forever arriving:

The noted Mexican-American author Richard Rodriguez, who called Paz the "voice and soul of Mexico," remembered that the great poet always concluded his readings with lines from his poem "Brotherhood":

I am a man. Little do I last. And the night is tremendous.
But I look up. The star is right.
Unknowing, I understand, I too am written,
And at this very moment, someone spells me out.

"Who Do You Say I Am?": Modernity and Identity

The critical examination of the crisis of modernity — with all its possible causes and ramifications — might seem a lofty intellectual enterprise far from our daily concerns. Yet, whatever the terms of analysis, the crisis signals a loss of belief that strikes at our very identity and closest relationships.

A form of *crisis* — a word implying the necessity of life-changing choices — is now recognized as the common predicament of humanity at the beginning of the twenty-first century. It implies the possibility of irretrievable loss; but the risks go beyond institutional failures, or the collapse of ideologies and empires. These losses confront us in various ways, but the most perilous loss is that of identity. Traveling or living in another country can make us more keenly aware of the strength or fragility of the components of our identity.

But what do we mean by "identity"?

Let me first suggest what identity is not. Perhaps the most common characteristic associated with identity is, unfortunately, the attitude that excludes or even negates others who are different. This tells us simply, "I am not like those others." This is the key element, for example, that forms street or prison gangs composed of young men who have only the bonds of a highly accidental geographical boundary — a neighborhood in which they live quite by chance, yet defend as if a homeland. They make deadly enemies of others who live on the other side of the street, despite the fact that they are of the same race or ethnicity. This tendency to unite through conflict and exclusion may seem irrational; yet a territorial sense of identity probably goes back to our most primitive origins and instincts. Needless to say, this "negative" form of identity clearly contradicts the Christian principle of "love your neighbor," let alone the command to "love your enemy."

A more modern version of identity is based on abstract beliefs and loyalty to a system of ideas around which identities are assembled. These concepts are used, again, to bond people and, at times, do provide significant distinctions. These "value systems" might be consistent with the Gospel; but to the extent that they remain abstract, they are arbitrary. This is especially true if the essential commitment is political. Loyalties shift and people migrate. One can go from "right" to "left" almost instantaneously and then back again, or "lose a faith" and then regain it. Under these circumstances, if by "changing your mind," you can, presumably, change your identity as well, then, clearly, this concept is unstable and deficient.

One can seemingly solve the identity problem by defining it narrowly, as simply biological or historical. "I am who I am" by virtue of birth, parentage, and location. This may or may not create lasting obligations, but it does give some weight to kinship and collective memory. The breakup of families and mass migratory patterns in modern times, however, has made this form of identity increasingly less certain or lasting.

If identity, whether defined by biology, race or ethnicity, moral or political commitment, is experienced as arbitrary and transitory, then one might conclude that identity is simply accidental, and thus meaningless. The temptation, then, is to say, "I am whoever or whatever I decide to be." This renders identity utterly arbitrary and transitory — but now we have a serious problem. It is precisely because this form of accidental identity cannot provide the sense of "being and belonging" that gives life purpose and meaning that we experience this loss as a crisis.

Increasingly, this crisis has grown acute and has produced a dangerous form of false identity, which disguises its falsity by creating myths and bigotry, and, ultimately, produces violence. Nationalism, racism, "ethnic cleansing," "holy wars," political extremism, and religious fanaticism are all related to a loss of genuine identity. They stem from a desperate attempt to invent and affirm one's self through the negation of the "others" unlike ourselves. This desperation creates a far more dangerous situation than one viewed primarily as a psychological condition, however painful. Contemporary observers, such as historian Niall Ferguson, author Gabriel Meyer, and the Sudanese scholar Francis Deng, suggest that this identity crisis is a primary cause of the "genocidal impulse" so evident in the last decades.

Their analysis relates in ways to the traditional religious concept of the "demonic." Theologians such as Paul Tillich have recognized that a "demonic force" — an overwhelming impulse toward evil and destruction — arises from the futile attempt to endow the transitory with a transcendent permanence. It is, in other words, a form of idolatry. One can be a patriot and defend your fellow citizens, even with your life. But when this otherwise commendable commitment is attached to a political entity, nation, party, or movement that has no fundamental relationship to God, this is idolatry. Nationalism or ethnocentrism based merely on human desires will inevitably degenerate into tribalism.

The Christian path has always required a painful break with one's tribe. Jesus makes this clear when he tells his new followers that they must forsake family, mother and father, everything and everyone, for his sake. Permission even to bury the dead is not granted if it interferes with overriding divine imperatives. In many respects, this renders Christians "homeless." We come to see that to be fully human is to be a displaced person, a pilgrim in a strange land. In this life, we are all immigrants and are meant to be.

In this light, what does it mean to be "Mexican"? What does it mean to be "American"? To probe the nature of another's identity is, inescapably, to further question our own.

The contemporary American attempt to shore up an uncertain identity through the acquisition of wealth and power, or worse, through identification with the "celebrity culture," is failing. It is as artificial as the Mexican pretense that they are reconstituted Aztecs. What we have increasingly in common is a sense of a lost or diminishing identity, sometimes put further at risk by assimilation. The retired American "ex-pats" in Mexico are as exiled as the Mexican migrant workers in Texas and Arizona. We have far more in common in this search than we may wish to admit. The particulars of Mexican identity, the markers that set Mexicans apart, are undoubtedly unique from several perspectives, historically, culturally, even racially. Millions of Mexicans now live in the United States. Many become citizens and their children sometimes speak little Spanish and prefer Big Macs to tacos. If we lose or disregard the particulars that provide "negative" bonding and those which are clearly fragile and transitory, what's left? Angry confusion, or an open door?

One of the prominent theologians at the Second Vatican Council, Father Henri de Lubac, addressed the central question of identity by noting what he called the "loss of ontological density." As the formidable phrase suggests, this is a subtle philosophical concept; but, rendered into simple terms, it means that we moderns no longer have any real confidence in the importance or significance of our own existence. This insight recognizes the gradual loss of a sense of being itself — that is, a fundamental identity that comes from being an integral part of God, nature, and society — and in that order.

The crisis of identity is, then, not simply a loss of the particular ties to family and place, as important as they are, but a more fundamental loss of connection to God's creation and the larger world around us. The Church has recognized and addressed this anxiety in contemporary terms. The concept of Catholic "personalism" — developed by esteemed figures such as Jacques Maritain and Emmanuel Mounier — has been a direct response to the conditions created by a depersonalized mass society. So have been the growing lay movements, such as Focolare and Communion and Liberation. The crisis of identity and belief was addressed directly by Pope John Paul II, whose writings provide a fuller understanding of the dual crisis, and how closely they are related.

What we have in common is a contradictory human nature. Conflict, rivalry, and violence are part of that nature; yet there is also longing for union and an impulse for self-donation. But if the impulse to love and even to give one's life for others is arrested at some lower level by fear and self-interest, the result will be either an isolated and anxious self, or some form of tribalism. For all of our analysis of the "modern condition," there's nothing new in this. We must be aware of our own tribalism. The answer is not to just become more "Catholic," but to become more human. It should ideally mean the same thing.

To the question, "Who do you say that I am?" posed by Jesus to his disciples, Peter replied, "You are the Son of the living God." Jesus knew that Peter didn't grasp this truth through human means but through God's own revelation. Modern men and women are equally unable to answer, "Who am I?" without the guidance of God's grace. While it is through the grace of God that we come to know our real selves as children of God, on our part, we must confront the obstacles — the sources of fear and confusion — that blind us to our true being.

Strong Faith, Deep Roots

The Faith and Beliefs of Catholic Mexico

The historic encounter that is now taking place between the two cultures, American and Mexican, has many dimensions and has provoked, at times, fear and controversy. But what is its larger meaning for us as Catholics? There is a "mystery of vocation" that confronts a people as well as individuals. An understanding of that vocation requires spiritual discernment.

The Catholic faith and beliefs of Mexicans is that of the universal Church; but what are the distinct cultural expressions of that faith which Mexicans offer? I would suggest that the most valuable are those which do not separate Mexicans from others, but which reconnect us all to those aspects of Catholic tradition that are sometimes neglected or forgotten. When our distinctions lead us to a greater understanding of the nature of that which unifies us, then we are truly "Catholic."

Let us first recognize what we share, not just in the realm of ideas, but in terms of vital personal relationship.

The Mother of Us All: Our Lady of Guadalupe

The Virgin Mary has appeared to different people in various places and circumstances. Some of these appearances are accepted by the Church as authentic and inspire reverence; others are not. The one we shall consider now is an important, indeed, central, part of our spiritual journey into Mexico. No more profound devotion exists within Catholicism, or one with such extensive consequences for a people, as that of Our Lady of Guadalupe. Yet, in some respects, there are still many unanswered, perhaps unanswerable, questions connected with this extraordinary event that still provoke disputes. Nothing is served by avoiding the difficult questions or the controversies; but we must engage them in ways that deepen and enhance our faith.

The story of the appearance of the Virgin Mary as Our Lady of Guadalupe to the Indian convert Juan Diego on a small hill near Mexico City in the sixteenth century is among the most fascinating, enigmatic, and inspiring stories in Church history. The papacy of John Paul II, given his personal devotion to the Virgin, made Our Lady of Guadalupe an even more universal figure. Between 1979 and 2002, John Paul II made five trips to Mexico, where he was greeted by crowds literally in the millions. His last visit to the Shrine of the Virgin in August 2002 is fully and sensitively described by Paul Badde in his book *Maria of Guadalupe.*

The story of the Virgin of Guadalupe is the essential chapter in the history of the Mexican people, in that her image created and unified them, and later served as the banner of their struggle for independence. The Virgin of Guadalupe provides, as Octavio Paz concluded, the Mexicans' only true symbol, and, as the poet observed, such symbols relate to that form of myth which is revelatory. Beyond that, given the amazing imagery, this story could well be called a "cosmic drama."

The year, acknowledged by most chroniclers, was 1531, and the setting was a small hill called Tepeyac overlooking the large lake Texcoco upon which Mexico City had been built. While not certain, it is presumed by most scholars that the hill had once been the site of a temple dedicated to an Aztec goddess called Tonantzin, among other names. She was, it is believed, the goddess of birth, health, and renewal.

The basic outlines of the story, the historicity of which is still disputed by some, are relatively simple to relate.

The Indian Juan Diego hears beautiful birds singing at the top of the hill, so melodious that he wonders if he has not entered heaven. He then encounters a beautiful woman dressed in a traditional native mantle and bathed in sunlight, who identifies herself, in the elaborate and poetic Nahua language, as the Virgin Mary. She tells Juan Diego that she is the mother of the one true God, but also his mother and the mother of his people. She then asks Juan Diego to go to the bishop of Mexico and tell him of her request that a temple be dedicated to her on this hill. The story has some twists and turns as the bishop and particularly his servants are naturally dubious of Juan Diego and his request, and then the illness of Juan Diego's uncle intervenes. The Virgin appears four times to Juan Diego ("the four apparitions") and, finally, gives him some wondrous roses as the proof of her presence that the bishop had requested.

When Juan Diego presents the roses to the bishop, a miraculous image of the Virgin appears on the Indian's rough garment (the *tilma*), and the bishop and all present kneel in tearful prayer. A chapel dedicated to the Virgin, Our Lady of Guadalupe, is then erected and becomes a center of a major devotion.

As to the story's location, originally referred to as the sanctuary or the *ermita* (hermitage), a larger church was constructed on the hill in the seventeenth century, and by the 1790s, Tepeyac included a basilica with a large dome and towers, the 1749 Collegiate Church and the Chapels of *Cerrito* (little hill), *Indios,* and *El Pocito* (little well or the miraculous spring). A convent of the Capuchin order was established to provide assistance to the increasing number of pilgrims. The village was designated a *villa* (town) in 1751 and in 1822 made a city — Guadalupe Hidalgo — before being reduced to a suburban precinct in 1931. During this period of religious repression, a bomb exploded near the basilica's altar but, again miraculously, the *tilma* was undamaged. The new basilica, erected in 1976, is one of the world's great centers of religious pilgrimage.

The *dramatis personae* of this story are among the most remarkable figures in Mexican history. However, we might want to begin with the central figure — Mary, the Virgin Mother of Our Lord Jesus Christ.

While the role of Mary in salvific history has, if anything, increased during the last century, we might remember that the figure of the Virgin Mary was a source of controversy in the early Church. In A.D. 430, a priest who was a follower of the Church Father Cyril of Alexandria gave a Christmas sermon praising the Virgin as "the mother of God." This is now a common and accepted title; but, at that time, it was an honorific associated with Isis and Diana and other female pagan deities, who were likewise called "bearers of gods." The use of this term — in Greek, *theotokos* — was therefore denounced by another Church patriarch, Nestorius, as indicative of paganism. Nestorius argued that Mary is the "bearer of Christ" in his human nature, but not as "theos" or God. Nestorius himself was not unreasonable in his arguments, but his followers often were, and this "Nestorian" view was rejected in 432 at the Council of Ephesus, and then again in 451 at Chalcedon, where Mary was declared to be the *Theotokos,* the "Bearer of God," the term still most commonly used in the Eastern Church.

This was the declaration of an important truth that went beyond the intricacies of what, at times, seems the convoluted language of the early Christological debates. The question "Who is Mary?" addresses the even more crucial question of "Who is Jesus?" By defining Mary's significance, the Church, at the Councils of Ephesus and Chalcedon, clarified and affirmed both the divinity and humanity of Jesus Christ, and the Trinitarian nature of God. The Mother of God is never a bystander.

One of the first accounts of an appearance of the Virgin Mary situates the event on a hill in Rome during the fourth century. A pattern is clearly established in this story, considered legendary in that it is not based on official Church records or other testimony. The pope is looking for the proper site for a church when the Virgin appears to him, and snow miraculously begins to fall in August, on the top of the hill, now the location of the magnificent Church of Santa Maria Maggiore. This first image of the Virgin was reportedly that of an empress.

Her central importance in Church history was reaffirmed by the proclamation of the dogma of the Immaculate Conception (Mary conceived without sin) in 1854. Another pattern of Marian appearances began following this declaration, which has created major centers of devotion, such as Lourdes in France, Fatima in Portugal, and Knock in Ireland.

Many of the devotions to the Virgin are based on appearances and miracles, some of which relate to legends and even to the discovery of icons and statues in the ruins of Byzantine churches. These icons or holy images, beyond their beauty, invariably attest to the Incarnation of Christ. Wherever Mary appears, she affirms the faith and Church teachings by rendering them into very human actions and, most importantly, images.

Indeed, the "story" of Mary herself has often been told far more eloquently through images than through narratives. We might recall Velasquez's magnificent rendering of Mary as *Queen of Heaven*, Caravaggio's *Ave Maria, The Virgin of the Rocks* of Leonardo da Vinci, Rembrandt's 1500 painting of the *Pieta,* Titian's *Assumption,* and the many different images of the Virgin as mother, bride, queen, and protectress.

The appearance of the Virgin Mary as Our Lady of Guadalupe in sixteenth-century Mexico has some unique and fascinating characteristics, and while they remain within the pattern of her many manifestations, there is an unprecedented and extraordinary nature to the event. She is young, pregnant, and the content of her message is not a warning or admonition, but purely one of loving reassurance.

When the Virgin appears to Juan Diego on the hill of Tepeyac, she is not described as merely a "beautiful woman," but as "noble and virtuous." She is clothed in blue and pink, and wears a jade ring, mixing Christian and Aztec symbolism. The decorated garments are merely a few of a galaxy of symbols, including the colors themselves. Colors were considered sacred by the ancient indigenous cultures in that they represented stages and levels of creation. We must remember that the indigenous mode of communication was traditionally visual. Hieroglyphic paintings were even used, according to the historian Prescott, for legal documents and court records. Numerous scholars have demonstrated that the image of the Virgin of Guadalupe is, indeed, an ideograph — an image filled with numerous, interrelated symbols and signs. This rich symbolic language also expresses the message she brought to the New World.

The other major character in this remarkable story is Juan Diego, who, like the Virgin herself, has several names and titles. His indigenous name was Cuhauhtlatoatzin, which translates as "The Eagle that Speaks." The eagle was a central symbol of the founding of the Aztec civilization. Juan Diego was also known to the local people as *"El Peregrino,"* the Pilgrim, who always walked alone, presumably, to worship and pray on Tepeyac hill. The testimony of indigenous witnesses taken down a century after his death confirmed an oral tradition that held Juan Diego to be a "holy man."

Much of the uncertainty about the historical details of Juan Diego's life stems from inconsistencies in the Church narratives themselves. During the colonial period, for example, the Franciscans, as part of their evangelization efforts, presented what were termed "Guadalupan plays" to indigenous audiences. Written in Nahuatl but supervised by the priests, much of the story was taken directly from the early accounts of the miracle. Emphasis was placed on the Virgin's loving care for the Indians; but the details of Juan Diego's life varied — his example clearly employed for purposes of moral instruction. The customary depiction of Juan Diego portrays him as a widower; but in these early Franciscan dramas, his wife, Maria Luisa, appears as an active participant. One might say that part of the tradition is casualness about historical fact.

As with the Virgin, the story of Juan Diego is perhaps best conveyed by imagery, and there is a rich symbolism in the iconography of Juan Diego himself that evolved over the centuries. One of the most recent and most popular depictions of Juan Diego encountering the Virgin comes from a Mexican calendar in the 1940s. We will later examine this evolving imagery.

A lesser character in the story, but also a highly symbolic one, is Juan Bernardino, Juan Diego's uncle. It is his beloved uncle's life-threatening illness that causes Juan Diego to delay obeying the Virgin's instructions, and even to attempt to avoid encountering her. In the Nahua culture, an "uncle" was an important representative of continuity in that uncles were among the "huehuetatoli," the wise men who maintained the oral tradition. To lose an uncle to risk the loss of the tradition and possibly one's identity.

Another central character, one about whom we have more historical evidence, is Juan de Zumarraga, the first Archbishop of Mexico. He is the prelate to whom Juan Diego delivers, first, the Virgin's request for a temple to be built at Tepeyac, and then the roses and the miraculous image on the *tilma*. Zumarraga becomes, therefore, the first Mexican religious leader to recognize the miracle and, in compliance with the Virgin's wishes, to then construct the *ermita* on Tepeyac hill.

Here we begin to confront some disagreements among scholars. There are insufficient records to determine with any exactitude Archbishop Zumarraga's reactions to these events, or exactly what role he played. We must rely on Church tradition passed on to us, itself based on an earlier indigenous oral tradition. What is known of Zumarraga with some certainty, however, is interesting and pertinent. Known for his sympathy to the Indians, he was, nonetheless, a former inquisitor, and expressed considerable skepticism about miracles. In one of the "Guadalupan dramas" written in Nahuatl, Bishop Zumarraga welcomes Juan Diego as "an honest man," but then exclaims: "You Indians always believe what you dream!" The bishop felt that the Church had no further need of miracles beyond those of the Gospels, and that to seek or desire them was more a matter of pride than faith. If this were the case, Zumarraga was hardly credulous, and would have been understandably resistant to Juan Diego's story and request.

Beyond those related directly to the miracle story, there are remarkable historical figures who later confirmed and, perhaps, enhanced it.

The first account of the apparitions to Juan Diego was presumably written by an extraordinary figure, Don Antonio Valeriano, an Aztec noble from the lineage of Moctezuma, who was the governor of the Nahuas in Mexico City in the late sixteenth century. Valeriano was educated by the Franciscans, including the illustrious Friar Sahagun, and, as an outstanding scholar and Latinist, he was the first Indian graduate of the Franciscan college. It was the testimony of later Mexican scholars that Valeriano wrote his *Relaction,* relating the Guadalupe story, as early as 1540, though others date it later, in 1557.

Another remarkable figure who played an important role in relating the Guadalupe events was an Oratorian priest, Father Manuel Sanchez, an accomplished scholar also known for his devout poverty and humility. In 1648, he wrote the first published account of the miracle at Tepeyac. An authority on St. Augustine and a former chaplain at the San Jeronimo convent (where Sor Juana would reside a century later), Father Sanchez devoted much of his life to his final work, the full title of which was *Imagen de la Virgen Maria, Madre de Dios de Guadalupe, Milagrosamente*

Aparecido en la ciudad de Mexico. Sanchez based his work on indigenous sources, and it was endorsed by later scholars such as Laso de Vega.

Father Luis Laso de la Vega, the vicar of the Guadalupe Church, was himself the author of the best-known account of the miraculous events. In 1649, he wrote a history in Nahuatl translated as "Being a Great Miracle," but better known by its opening line *Nican Mopohua* — "here is the account." Though some scholars challenge details and even the authorship — and, indeed, the event itself — the *Nican Mopohua* is considered the most complete record and is the most frequently cited.

The accounts given by Fathers Sanchez and Laso de la Vega were then further substantiated by three of the most renowned Mexican scholars of their era.

Luis Becerra Tanco was called the "Demosthenes of the Mexican language," referring to his eloquence in Nahuatl. A Creole who knew several languages, he was also a professor of mathematics. He testified to the account's authenticity before an official Church inquiry into the apparition in 1666. As many of the original documents had been lost in fires and floods, Becerra Tanco rested his belief in the details of the miracle on the indigenous oral tradition as well as their images and songs. He also lamented the previous Spanish indifference to the indigenous sources.

Francisco de Florencia was also a renowned scholar and priest. A Jesuit, he was the rector of their Colegio del Espiritu Santo in Puebla. He wrote his *Estrella del Norte* (Star of the North) in 1688, which also testified to the authenticity of the earlier accounts.

Perhaps an even more accomplished figure was Carlos Siguenza y Gongora (1645-1700), a priest who was renowned as an historian, mathematician, and astronomer. In 1687, he testified that while there was no certainty as to the origins of the Guadalupe story, he had personal possession of early indigenous documents verifying the accounts, particularly the papers of an Indian noble, Don Fernando de Alva (Ixtlicxochitl). In 1680, Siguenza y Gongora composed a long poem, *Primavera Indiana* ("Indian Spring"), in tribute to Our Lady of Guadalupe.

Another figure who was a major contributor to the propagation of the Guadalupe story was Miguel Cabrera, one of Mexico's greatest painters. Born in 1695 in Oaxaca to mulatto parents, Cabrera became one of the celebrated figures of his day. He was the official painter for the Archbishop of Mexico, and most of his work was religious in character. His portrait of Sor Juana de la Cruz remains the most familiar, and other works of his are among the treasures of the National Art Museum in Mexico City.

In 1751, Cabrera and other artists were among those who examined the *tilma* during an official inspection. While these and later inquiries led to several disputes among the examiners, there was general agreement as to the apparently miraculous elements in the image, particularly its remarkable preservation over the centuries despite the climate and its frequent exposure. Though noting some distortions in perspective, such as the minor disproportion of the hands, Cabrera remarked on the excellence of the drawing. He gave its precise measurements, describing it as what would be a nearly life-size rendering of a young woman of "fourteen or fifteen." The *tilma* itself was composed of delicate palm threads — *ayate* in Spanish. Perhaps most significantly, he observed that the image was composed of several different media. The face and hands were in oil while other parts were in tempera and gouache. This would suggest that whatever the source of the original image — Becerra Tanco suggested that the painter was "the sun" working in a "celestial workshop" — there had been some retouching to the *tilma*'s image.

Cabrera eventually made three copies of the *tilma* — one for himself, another for the bishop, and a third that was sent to Rome as a gift for Pope Benedict XIV. In 1756 Cabrera then wrote his *Maravilla americana* (American Marvel), a verifying account of the miracle based on the 1666 official Church inquiries.

For all of the many documents deposited over the centuries, the controversies regarding the historical character of the events, or the miraculous nature of the *tilma*, remain. One might assume a high degree of skepticism among secularists, particularly those inclined, as C. S. Lewis observed, to maintain an automatic rejection of anything deemed "miraculous" as their own form of dogma. However, the major arguments emerged within the Church itself. There has always been an understandable concern that reported "miracles" could actually be incursions of magic and superstition, which, in the long run, would weaken faith and doctrine. The Lateran Council, in this spirit, established penalties for false reports of miracles.

As early as 1556, the first serious dispute broke out and involved Bishop Montufar of Mexico City, who ordered an inquiry into the Guadalupe miracle. The bishop later became an advocate of the devotion and began construction on the major church. Many influential Franciscans, however, fearful that this was a return of idolatry, vehemently opposed the veneration of the image, claiming that it had been painted by an Indian. The bishop's inquiry did elicit testimony from other more supportive clergy who described the beneficial effects of the devotion, particularly on the Spanish.

It was much later, 1794, and in Madrid, that what is called the "anti-apparitionist" view was formulated. Juan Bautista Munoz, a scholar by royal appointment, presented a report to the Royal History Academy questioning the historical authenticity of the Mexican Guadalupe events. This was, he claimed, based on his examination, primarily, of Mexican documents. This skeptical point of view has also been expressed in Mexico at times. In his extensive 1996 study, Father Stafford Poole expressed similar doubts as to the credibility of the traditional account, based on historical evidence.

While no documentation is available to resolve the many disputes about facts and dates, it does seem that the indigenous accounts are generally consistent. The historian James Lockhart notes that expressions of hope that the Virgin Mary would intercede for them were among the most commonly expressed sentiments of the first Nahua converts. Furthermore, the Nahua Annals of Chimalpopca Galicia, covering the years 1546-1625, mention the miracle as having occurred, but in the year 1556, when it was accompanied by a comet. Similarly, another indigenous writer, Chimalpahin — whose full name is worth recording: Don Domingo Francisco de Anton Munon Chimalpahin Quauhtlehumitzin — also confirmed the Guadalupe miracle, but, again, as occurring in 1556.

Earlier Spanish and Creole chroniclers attributed much of the original story to the now-lost documents of Father Juan Gonzales, Archbishop Zumarraga's interpreter, who directly interviewed Juan Diego. Father Gonzales was considered such an honest and devout witness that he was once proposed for canonization.

In that so many unimpeachable and extraordinary figures — such as Sanchez, Becerra Tanco, Florencia, and Siguenza y Gongora — all testified to the existence of original Nahuatl writings, it seems reasonable to conclude that such records once existed. Inconsistencies in the reports, even of a serious nature, would be predictable, particularly after a long lapse of time. In any case, there is no basis or reason to question the integrity of any of these authors. We might be appropriately humbled to recall that Americans still dispute the facts concerning the assassination of President Kennedy, even though it took place in front of thousands, and extensive evidence and testimony was presented within months of the event.

The indigenous oral tradition seems credible on its own terms. A priest associated with the *ermita,* Father Jeronimo de Valladolid, noted that the indigenous did not rely on writing to tell their true history as much as they did on images — symbols, including colors — and, most importantly, the long-term effects of these stories on living human beings.

As to the continuing controversies, what can we learn from them? Perhaps little more than that such disputes are endless, and, sadly, pride of authorship and defensiveness do not seem to be removed by the presence of clerical collars any more than they are by advanced degrees.

First, let's recognize that there is simply no way to fully extricate this kind of "miracle story" from folk religion, myth, and legend. To try to do so is to risk diminishing its meaning; for as Father Yves Congar has pointed out, the popular mythic elements can actually add to the ultimate meaning, including its moral dimension.

Further, in sorting out the written "message," there is the inherent and insurmountable problem of language. On one hand, some scholars feel that the language employed in the traditional account tends to verify its antiquity. The Nahuatl in the *Nican Mopohua* is often cited as graceful and idiomatic, which would suggest an earlier model than the seventeenth century. Others have pointed out that the use of the words *Nican tlaca* or *nitlaca* for "we people here" suggests a native document from before 1600, by which time *macehuall* had became a more typical term for indigenous people. However, as we noted earlier, while some Spanish words, such as *anima* ("soul"), were readily adaptable to Nahuatl, the indigenous name for Guadalupe, that is, *Totlaconantzin* ("our precious mother"), implied equality with *Totlacotatzin* ("our precious father"), and thus presents a potential theological problem for Trinitarian Catholics. What was ultimately to be shared had to go beyond names and words.

Then there is the controversy referred to as the "substitutionist assumption," that is, the contention that Guadalupe simply replaced an indigenous deity. This theory seems dependent on the now largely discredited "Black Legend," which portrays the Indians as utterly desolate and passive. An examination of the actual process of the integration of beliefs, including sacred images, which created Mexican Catholic culture would suggest that no mere "substitution" was feasible.

A more substantial dispute has been sustained more by national pride than by theological concerns. Laso de la Vega's original document — the *Nican Mopohua* — is described as being in "excellent Nahuatl"; but, in it, the Virgin is given the Spanish name of Guadalupe, and the story has quite evident parallels with earlier Spanish devotions. Is this Mexican story, then, merely a Spanish imposition?

The Virgin of Guadalupe in Extramaduras has had devotees since probably the thirteenth century, which are centered in the area of Spain from which Cortes, Alvarado, and Pizarro all originated. It is believed that the image of Our Lady of Extramaduras was given to San Leandro by Gregory the Great at the time of the Moorish conquest. It was hidden and later discovered by a poor herdsman called Gil Cordero, whose son then made a miraculous recovery. Some clear comparisons can be drawn between these Guadalupan stories as well as those derived from other Spanish devotions.

There is also another interesting parallel. An image of the Virgin of Remedios was brought to New Spain by one of Cortes's soldiers and placed at the Great Pyramid in Tenochtitlan. It was presumably lost on the *noche triste* (the "sad night") in 1520 when the Spaniards were nearly massacred. It was later discovered by an Indian named Juan de Tovar ("One Eagle"). The image, though repeatedly lost, kept returning to the same location, where a chapel was subsequently built. Again, we can discern a pattern in the story. The similarity of all of these devotions should not be surprising in that they are all drawn from and affirm a common tradition. However, this neither affirms nor negates the historical details, the meaning, or, for that matter, the supernatural aspect of the Tepeyac story.

It also seems clear, as many scholars suggest, that the devotion to Guadalupe was, in part, promulgated by Creole aspirations and rivalry with Spain. This would explain why the devotion did not attract extensive support until the seventeenth century. Yet, again, whatever merit there is in this argument, it suggests not fraud or contrivance but simply historical development. Much later, Mexican liberation theologians were seemingly content to accept the story, even if mythical, because of its value in engendering the Mexican spirit of resistance to foreign domination. But neither the self-interest of eighteenth-century Creoles nor our twentieth-century political perspectives invalidate the role of the Virgin of Guadalupe as a unifying and integrating force throughout all of the historical periods since her appearance.

In the 1990s a heated dispute broke out at the basilica itself when its abbot expressed the opinion that the historical existence of Juan Diego couldn't be proven. This was taken as a form of apostasy, and led, eventually, to the abbot's resignation. It was perhaps a careless use of language, or a misquote, but what the abbot was presumably expressing is what any scholar would affirm. There is no "historical evidence" of people or events that meet modern standards without extensive documentation corroborated by more than one identifiable source. One might note that there is far more "historical evidence" of Juan Diego's existence by these standards than there is of Moses or any of the biblical prophets.

In the end, the Guadalupe story is more about a saint than an object. Juan Diego is far more than simply an intermediary carrying a cloak. It seems regrettable that, in trying to present physical evidence as to the extraordinary character of a garment — which would not in itself constitute a clear spiritual message — the true miracle, the transformation that Juan Diego instigated and represents, tends to be lost.

It is a truly miraculous event when a Macehual Indian in the sixteenth century becomes a messenger of divine revelation and when a Mexican bishop kneels, not before but *with* him, in a shared devotion to their common Mother.

How relevant is historical evidence and research?

It depends upon what meaning we place on the Guadalupe story and how it relates to our Catholic faith. We are now talking about the nature of belief. The theological questions concerning the nature of the miracle and the image have been explored for more than three hundred years. The image on the *tilma* has at times been deemed a "natural prodigy" created miraculously by the sun; an act of the Holy Spirit nearly comparable to the Incarnation; a product of the legendary workshop of St. Luke, patron saint of painters; and, ultimately, an act of the Divine Creator. These are beautiful metaphors, not explanations. If we could explain it, it wouldn't be a miracle.

When Jesus said, repeatedly, "your faith has healed you," he was referring to something far beyond "evidence." There can be no single interpretation or refutation, no reductionism that can affirm or deny our faith. In the end, our belief will come out of the whole of our lives and how we live and love over time.

In that spirit, let us give the last word to Juan de Zumarraga, the first Archbishop of Mexico, and, reportedly, the first witness to the miracle that would ultimately create a people and a nation.

Juan de Zumarraga: *"What [God] asks and wants are miraculous lives. Christians who are humble, patient, and charitable, because the perfect life of a Christian is a continuous miracle on earth."*

"Reading Guadalupe"

I would suggest that the most beneficial way for us modern Catholics to understand the Guadalupe events is not by way of contention over ancient documents but, following the indigenous, to attempt to fully absorb the story visually.

To "read" the story of Juan Diego's miraculous encounter with the Virgin of Guadalupe in this way, we must adjust our eyes. We are not reading "history," for little of the historical data can be verified. We must penetrate the meaning of the story with eyes of faith, considering, above all, what it meant to Catholic Mexico and, therefore, what it may be saying to us. To do so, I suggest that we must interpret the story, as did the indigenous and most of the Creoles and *mestizos* of New Spain, through its rich and sometimes complex imagery.

The original image on the *tilma* has been called a "sacred hieroglyph" — an icon transmitting a message to be contemplated. In itself, the image constitutes a momentous encounter between the indigenous tradition and Spanish Catholicism. To fully analyze the iconography — the symbolic details of the original image as well as the later changes or additions — lies beyond our ability and our purpose, but let's review the most basic features:

The Virgin is depicted, almost life-size, standing, encircled by rays as if emerging from the sun, looking down serenely with her hands clasped as if in prayer. The later more elaborate depictions in paintings and engravings show that she is gazing at Juan Diego. She appears young and has the features of a *mestiza* (though at times her seventeenth-century devotees claimed that she is a *criolla*). She is, therefore, frequently referred to as "the dark one" (*La Morena*, or sometimes in the diminutive *La Morenita*, "the little dark one"). Garbed primarily in royal blue and an earthy pink, she wears a traditional Indian tunic and a mantle adorned with stars. A widely accepted interpretation of the position of her belt is that it is an indication of pregnancy.

She also wears, in some versions, a crown of rays representing either the apostles or the tribes of Israel. The sun producing the solar rays symbolizes Christ, and the moon beneath her feet can be interpreted as signifying John the Baptist, who "waned" before Christ. These solar features were highly significant in that they represented rebirth to the Indians. The images surrounding and supporting the original image include angels, "angel-musicians," clouds, and flowers. The traditional indigenous religious symbols of songs and flowers are thus integral to the story the image tells.

This image of the Virgin of Guadalupe was carefully preserved and copied throughout the centuries, and, while there is continuity, there was also development and alterations in subsequent renditions of the image. There are aspects, such as the emergence from the sun, that point to the Woman of the Apocalypse in the Revelation of St. John, though the Guadalupan image has an angel with eagle wings at her feet, not a dragon. Over time, further symbolic elements were added that suggest other traditional images: the female figure in the Song of Solomon, the Immaculate Conception, as well as the Coronation and Assumption of the Virgin. The figure of the Archangel Michael was frequently incorporated into the expanding iconography, depicted as the Virgin's escort and the protector of her devotees. Saints were also added, including Joachim and Anna, Anthony of Padua, and Bernard of Clairvaux. As the devotion spread to Europe — particularly Italy — Mexico City and the terrain in the background became Europeanized, as did the appearance of the people depicted.

Additional symbols, such as a globe indicating her domain and the Mexican Coat of Arms, were added in the seventeenth and eighteenth centuries, reflecting the Virgin's new status as Patroness of the Anahuac, then Mexico City, New Spain, and finally North America. It is significant to note that in a painting depicting the Virgin as Patroness of New Spain, an interracial grouping is depicted with figures clearly indigenous, *mestizo* and black, commoners and royals — all displaying a new and equal dignity.

Broadly based, the Guadalupan art that emerged featured polished high art as well as folk and popular forms. In addition to paintings and murals by the most noted artists of the age, there were sculptures in stone, wood, and ivory for churches, shrines, and home altars. Eventually, the Virgin of Guadalupe was depicted in Talavera ceramics, and elaborate embroidery, some for religious garments, displaying the Virgin as well as medallions depicting miracles attributed to her.

These many visualizations were not merely for the instruction of illiterates or a replacement for books. Iconography speaks its own language. The miracle is not only depicted, but experienced as an epiphany, the emergence of a supernatural light of understanding. These images, not the later narrative descriptions, provide the heart of the tradition. When Father Manuel Sanchez ordered the first image to be engraved in 1648, he referred to the "imprint" left by the Virgin, and the 1685 pictures in Father Becerra Tanco's "Joy of Mexico" were faithful reproductions of the definitive imagery.

The "Old Basilica" opened in 1709 with a display of these storytelling images. The "first vision" is that of the Virgin telling Juan Diego that "I am your mother" as well as his initial sense of unworthiness, and is conveyed in posture and gesture. The "second vision" occurs when Juan Diego is attempting to avoid encountering the Virgin and her intercession. The "third vision" is the gift of the miraculous roses, and the "fourth" is the revelation of the image on Juan Diego's cloak. There was subsequently a depiction of a "fifth vision" in which the Virgin appears to the ailing uncle, Juan Bernardino, and promises him her healing.

The words of the *Nican Mopohua* and the later interpretations over the centuries, including countless books and sermons, are important and invaluable, but the essential "story" is told in pictures.

The changing images of Juan Diego tell their own story. The first probably appeared around 1653 and were the basis of the famous Miguel Cabrera and Juan Correa portrayals a century later. Cabrera attested that his work presented a "true likeness" of Juan Diego, as did Francisco Garden regarding his later 1777 painting. Both artists had inspected the *tilma* and were devoted to the tradition.

The portrayals of Juan Diego became widespread in the eighteenth century, and some of the most familiar images come from that time. One of the early anomalies in some accounts is that Juan Diego is sometimes described as a "boy" or "lad." This may have reflected the paternalism of the Creoles or perhaps the Virgin's use of the diminutive "Juanito." In any case, the traditional depiction of Juan Diego was that he was a wise elder and a widower. He most often appeared as a dark-skinned, bearded figure, sometimes dressed as a pilgrim or in native garb. Some versions show him as a *pelado,* that is, an Indian with a bald or tonsured head indicative of baptism. The Indians were not a hirsute people, but long hair and beards symbolized wisdom and strength to the Spanish, and so at times Juan Diego appears somewhat Europeanized.

Throughout the nineteenth century, there was relatively little change in Juan Diego's image, and by the end of the century, his depiction, including statues, began to appear near or on altars. Also by the end of the century all races, including blacks, were among those included in the iconography of the miracle, as in the 1913 mural by Valerio Prieto. Juan Diego, like his Mother, was increasingly able to draw all people to him.

The imagery in twentieth-century works retains the traditional elements of flowers and songbirds, but, importantly, Juan Diego is now clearly indigenous, as depicted in Father Santiago Madrid's 1999 painting. Most of the contemporary artwork tends to be of a popular nature — the traditional *ex-votos* (votive offerings) and *retablos* (religious pictures, often on wood), *milagros* (popular pictorial accounts of miracles), as well as a remarkable ceramic piece by the noted creator of "Trees of Life," Tiburcio Soteno.

An excellent collection of Guadalupan artwork, including some remarkable *milagros,* can be found in the Museum of the Basilica of Our Lady of Guadalupe.

Some Characteristics of Mexican Spirituality

We have attempted in this book to convey the rich inheritance of the Mexican Catholic culture. The vivid images and even the music may offer for many of us the best means of understanding this tradition, but let's briefly explore some of its distinct characteristics.

Mexican spirituality reveals itself by outward signs.
To understand the theology of Mexican Catholicism, one must focus on concrete manifestations rather than texts. Devotional prayers, processions, images, and objects are more prominent than concepts. In part, this relates to the indigenous heritage. Osvaldo Pardo and other contemporary scholars have recognized the fundamentally aesthetic character of Nahua religion, as did the earliest observers, such as Fathers Sahagun and Duran.

Mexican spirituality is ritualistic.
While ritual can be abused and emptied of content, the power of repetition and gesture, evident in all the world religions, has been weakened by a modern emphasis on the "personal" aspect of faith and salvation. The ability to affirm one's own religious experience is strengthened by these shared litanies and formalities.

Mexican spirituality is iconic.
The images are an important medium of worship, yet inevitably at times are objects of worship themselves. The Church patiently guides worshipers toward inner as well as outer manifestations, while providing the most influential and beloved of all the icons: the Virgin of Guadalupe.

Mexican spirituality is primordial.
While this aspect of Mexican spirituality is also drawn primarily from its indigenous sources, it doesn't mean that it is merely syncretistic or "primitive." The pre-Hispanic spiritual "seeds" provide an important sense of

continuity; but they also reclaim basic elements of religion that our self-conscious present-day viewpoint often neglects, such as ritual dance, decoration, and sacred dress. Anthropology, as Pope Benedict has noted, thus provides one of the most fruitful conjunctions with religious thought. Religion has always retained a strong element of instinctive behavior and cannot be reduced to a system of concepts or customs. This is the danger of the modern reductive interpretations. Our biblical religion is, in this sense, not just two thousand years old, but more than ten thousand. More than most, Mexican Catholic culture reveals its deepest roots.

The Mexican Catholic lives in a sacred world.
Mexican Catholicism lives in and outside of church. There is, for many, a continuous sense of the presence of God, even in the most mundane aspects of life. There is, therefore, often a thin line between this awareness and the celebration of ordinary events. The sacred and the profane are often thoroughly intertwined.

Mexican spirituality is experiential and relational.
Mexicans shape and test their faith through the experience of family and work. Prayer is highly personal. It is said that Mexicans "talk to God and His Mother" and they do so directly and intimately. The saints, esteemed as "family members," are often part of the conversation. Kinship plays a uniquely strong role, particularly the practice of *compadrazago* or "god-parenting."

Mexican spirituality is marked by a strong feminine temperament.
There are, of course, masculine and feminine aspects of all cultures in terms of "spirit" or psychological disposition. A masculine character is more evident in the European orientation toward power and goal-directed linearity. The Mexican Catholic temperament, on the other hand, is more nurturing and consoling than objectively critical. The centrality of the figure of the Virgin of Guadalupe, and other Marian devotions, is evidence of this inclination. God is found in intimate "feelings" — *sentimientos* — but this does not mean a lack of intelligence or critical acumen. It stems from a "maternal" emphasis on the healing power of love.

Mexican spirituality is popular and egalitarian.
The Mexican *fiestas*, especially the feast days of the saints, offer a highly communal form of spirituality as well as hospitality to others. The many popular devotions, some of which we will address further, cross lines of class and education that parish life alone might not. In no other aspect of Mexican life will one find a more genuine equality than in church.

The foundation of Mexican spirituality resides in the lives of the saints.
Devotion to the saints is an essential aspect of Mexican spirituality in that it provides concrete models rather than systems of abstract "values" or postulates of morality.

Mexican spirituality draws heavily on Beauty.
Beauty in this regard includes not only the celebrated and ornate places of worship, but poetry, song, dance, and bold architecture. Far from mere decoration, Beauty is a manifestation of the Divine. It is one of the most valuable gifts that Mexicans offer us.

Mexican spirituality is a journey in time.
Sometimes this is also a literal passage as migrants. This story of a migrant or pilgrim people resonates with all the stories and metaphors of the Bible. Journeys transform people and over time can provide a new identity. Spaniards and the various indigenous peoples in time became "Mexican" through extensive journeys that finally converged. There are inner as well as outer explorations that have produced their lasting imagery, songs, and the mythic as well as historical accounts of Mexican origins and trials. None of us, Mexicans or Americans, knows the end of our present pilgrimage.

Popular and Folk Religion

Much of Mexican Catholic life is a vigorous form of "popular religion," that is, a mixture of folk customs and Catholic practices. In that aspects are still imbued with remnants of indigenous belief in magic and superstition, some may find this folk Catholicism unpalatable, even embarrass-

ing. I have seen churches in remote rural districts with interiors decorated with images cut from popular magazines, and it is common to
confront artificial-looking wigged manikins of Jesus in glass cases. The
price the Church has paid for accommodating these quasi-religious beliefs, understandably rooted in the desperation of the poor, has probably
been some degree of alienation among the more affluent and better educated. In any case, a "popular" religion is always in need of some form of
mediation, and rituals must be reinvigorated by thoughtful reflection and
discernment. Mexican seminaries are turning out well-grounded priests
and theologians to meet these needs.

Some Mexicans are defecting to either offshoots of American evan-
gelicalism or New Age spirituality, both of which appear to offer a
greater individualism and, perhaps, for some, an escape from the confines of Mexican society. Many Mexicans resent these *sectas* as intrusive
and alien; but we should recognize that, while at times divisive, some of
the evangelicals and other groups have made worthy efforts to overcome
the endemic problems of alcoholism and spousal abuse.

Despite a growing diversity, there remain strong common denomi-
nators in Mexican Catholic culture that transcend class and education.
These include family ties, national identity, and cultural pride, but also a
sense of mystery about life that stubbornly resists the lures of materialism. Some theologians, Mexicans and others, affirm specific forms of
Mestizo theology related to *mestizaje* culture. Indeed, Mexican spirituality
has been shaped, to some extent, by a conscious resistance to assimilation. It is not our prerogative to assess these efforts. Again, we are looking for bridges, not barricades. Clearly, though, any theology that posited
a wholly separate religious identity for any ethnic or national group
would not be truly Catholic. Our shared task is to stimulate a greater degree of unity and understanding.

The relationship between belief and tradition, as Father Yves Congar
has observed, demonstrates the vital and creative role of the laity in shap-
ing a *sensus fidelium* ("sense of the faithful") out of common daily experience, particularly a shared suffering. The celebration of the *fiesta* in this
respect can be seen as having a prophetic role in that it reveals a
communality that defies the individualistic "spirit of the age." Similarly,
the figure of the Virgin of Guadalupe is seen as possessing revelatory

power beyond the normal categories of interpretation. The image of Guadalupe is not merely a "cryptogram" to be interpreted through symbols, but, as Octavio Paz sensed, a manifestation of "the Other," timeless and sacred, a healing power unlimited by interpretation.

The key to Mexican popular religion is undoubtedly the shared suffering of a long and painful history; but this is a participation in the suffering of Christ that extends beyond historical circumstances. Injustices must be redressed, but the meaning of suffering is that of the Cross, and the healing to be found only in the Resurrected Christ. The crucified and risen Christ is no more a Mexican or an American than he was simply a first-century Jew. He is all of us, and more. Only when suffering, including poverty and rejection, are perceived as a commonality, including a shared struggle, does the *fiesta* become prophetic and point to a life beyond death.

The Mexicans engaged in their journey to *El Norte* across the border have been viewed by some as "Galileans," that is, a rejected people, but one conveying a message of salvation, or as Monsignor Virgilio Elizondo put it, "outsiders with a sacred mission." This mission is further and best defined by the appellation "Galilean." The apostles were poor and marginalized, and even spoke with pronounced accents, but they were not "zealots" in a historically determined conflict. As Jesus explicitly commanded, they were missionaries to the ends of the earth — that is, to everyone.

In our time we have often been attracted to concepts of "new-ness," but history suggests that the most inspiring concepts that will arise out of our shared journey into the unknown will not be forms of an innovative or politicized theology. I'm convinced that the most original thinking within the Church will not come from the social analysis of intellectuals, but will grow out of popular devotions based on the direct experience of common people.

Bridges, Not Walls

Where Will the Journey Take Us?

I n that this has been a more personal journey than an analytical one, I have not attempted to directly address the serious social and economic problems facing Mexico, nor have I offered an assessment of the present state of the Mexican Church. Recognizing the problems of poverty and injustice is the obligation of every Christian, but I have no solutions to propose other than those found in the Gospels. Without a spiritual foundation, I don't believe that these problems, in Mexico or elsewhere, can be fully understood. Obviously, there are defects in the Church, and even, at times, scandals; but we should hardly be surprised or downhearted at this. Even Jesus himself lost one out of twelve.

Much of what I've offered in these reflections comes from personal experience during the years I've spent in Mexico; but, even here, I've proceeded cautiously. There is a quip heard among journalists that if you spend a couple of months in a country, you can write a book; a year or more, an article, and after many years, a few paragraphs. The Catholic Church is so old and large — two thousand years and counting, encompassing a fifth of the world's population — that almost anything you say about Catholics, positive or negative, probably has some truth in it.

When I asked for the opinion of a Mexican priest as to the state of the Mexican Church, he gave me a reply I've heard many times before: "Which Church? Which Mexico?" It is important to recognize the diversity in Mexico as well as the changes taking place. I recognize that I have only scratched the surface.

My first impressions of the Mexican Catholic Church, as I admitted at the outset, were almost wholly negative. A half century ago, I had the perspective of a young American — idealistic, egalitarian, and impatient. I was typical of my generation of university graduates, wholly indifferent to religion, which I considered an anachronism from a benighted past. Science and politics, I was sure, would empower us to create a new and better world. God was, at best, an onlooker, perhaps even a culpable one.

During that first journey into Mexico, I was impressed by the beauty of many of the mission churches, which we were filming for American TV. But the ritual devotion in one Sonoran town, centering on one's ability to lift a balsa wood statue of Christ, struck me as lamentably superstitious, and undoubtedly explained why Mexico was so backward. One of Father Kino's missions was still in use in the mountains of the Sierra Madre, but, for me, it was only a curious historical relic. I was far more impressed, that is to say, appalled, by the abject condition of the rural poor. The Catholic Church, I concluded, was merely a prop for an exploitive and unjust society.

There was some truth in all of my early observations. Yet it was the contradictions that stayed with me. What was the possible connection between poverty and beauty, corruption and sanctity? It took me decades to sort out these questions, and I needed help to do so. Over the years, I've been blessed with Mexican associates — some sought, others accidental, and some who became friends. I once spent time with an old priest in a *pueblito* in Michoacan where he had served for decades as town doctor and lawyer as well as pastor. He enjoyed telling me jokes in what for me was incomprehensible Spanish, but my visit provided a glimpse of the life and burdens of a priest in traditional rural Mexico.

As a journalist, I've conversed with numerous Mexican Catholics, lay and clergy, including a young indigenous seminarian and aging priests near retirement. I interviewed a prominent leader of the Liberation Theology movement as well as representatives of Opus Dei and the Legionaries of Christ. I've had Mexican friends who loved the Church and others who openly disdained it. I've listened to the passionate opinions of cab drivers and waiters as well as politicians. Finally, decades after my first encounter and severe conclusions, I became, in a sense, part of the story. I have participated — now as a Catholic myself — in masses in cathedrals and churches throughout the vastly contrasting regions of Mexico.

I broke down the wall and became part of the scene that I have tried to describe. Inside, one gets a different perspective.

My range of experience, though over a lifetime, only provides a snapshot in a nano-second of God's time. The contradictions, injustices, and obfuscations are all still there. The larger picture, my portrait of Catholic Mexico, however, is finally one of faith and beauty — the beauty of an abiding faith, a faith in God's revealed Beauty.

I have spoken of building bridges, not walls, between Americans and Mexicans. Where do we begin? Which part of our shared faith will provide the most solid foundation?

Pope Benedict has remarked that we Catholics will ultimately be judged by two aspects of our communal life: the saints and art. I believe that this is true; and it is significant to first note what is not on his short list — power, wealth, and politics. I further believe that Mexico's Catholic culture is closely related to these two criteria — saints and art. The saints are intimate friends, not just in Church, but in the ordinary lives of Mexicans. The saints teach us not only how to love God, but how God loves us. It is sometimes difficult to see this until life is stripped to its bare bones.

The saints are carriers of grace, humility, gratitude, and forgiveness. What's more, they aren't antique figures from the past. They exist now, and are everywhere. There are probably more saints alive today than all those listed in the voluminous lives of the saints, but they will never be known. Their anonymity is integral to their sanctity. The recognized saints provide only a glimpse of God's own artwork.

Beauty, as I've emphasized throughout, is central to Mexican culture, and not just in the remarkable art, architecture, and decoration so evident everywhere, but in the small things in ordinary life. I've suggested that the "Theology of Beauty" may provide the best understanding of Mexican Catholicism, and this is a gift to all of us. Beauty, and our gratitude for it, is a vital response to the modern crisis of belief, and is essential to our faith.

Saints are witnesses to God's love and art is human labor perfected as our gift to God. The mutual devotions and shared work that this suggests can provide the building material for our bridges. But we must first ask ourselves, do we really want to risk building bridges? Traffic flowing both ways brings change, and change can bring fear and resentment.

We must, therefore, be prepared to also build upon our shared wounds and the recognition of the suffering of others. This will be difficult for us Americans. Our culture is built upon success and often sees suffering as a form of failure, or at least weakness. The Mexican attitude, in contrast, too often embraces suffering in a fatalistic and passive way. Is there bridge-building material here?

We must know that we don't know. We must begin where we will end — in the Mystery of the Cross and in His Cry that mysteriously affirms God's love. Octavio Paz only told us what we already knew: We are alone, and not alone. We have been given eyes to see and hands with which to reach out. If we must, we will build in the thin air of contradiction and impossibility. It's been done before. Faith and humility will be our cement.

Let's begin.

Appendix One

Major Religious Sites

M exico is spiritually rich with churches, monasteries, and convents — some still active, others converted into museums, many with fine displays of religious art. There are also numerous public buildings the exteriors of which are often topped by stone crosses that reveal their religious origins.

What follows is a highly selective list of some of the outstanding religious sites in locations most likely to be visited by travelers.

Mexico City

The historical district — *centro historico* — was part of the Aztec city of Tenochtitlan and then the location of Cortes's headquarters. Now the seat of the government of the Federal District, it once contained countless religious buildings, most of which were confiscated over time by the various revolutionary regimes. The churches recommended below are all in walking distance within the district.

At the center of the city, and, in a sense, Mexico, is the Metropolitan Cathedral, located on the *zocalo,* the main plaza. Built over decades, from

1573 into the 1700s, it is dedicated to the Assumption of the Virgin Mary. Due to its location on what was once a lakebed, the building is in a constant state of restoration. It has three magnificent naves, splendid wooden choir stalls, and several baroque chapels. Behind the main altar is the magnificent *Altar de las Reyes* (Altar of Kings). The clock towers bear the figures of faith, hope, and charity. The adjacent building, the *Sagrario Metropolitana,* serves as a parish church.

Many of the interiors of the churches in the historic district are examples of the elaborate *churrigueresque* style, the distinctive Mexican Baroque, including the small and narrow but remarkable *La Ensenanza.* It is in an expropriated monastery at Donceles 102-104 that was once the location of the Supreme Court. Also worth visiting are the *Capilla de las animas* (Chapel of the Souls) behind the Cathedral on Calle Guatemala, and *Regina Coeli,* a jewel of the *churrigueresque* style, on Regina at Bolivar. At various times these historic sites are closed for repairs.

The Plaza Santa Domingo, several blocks from the *zocalo,* contains the church of the same name built in 1736 by the Dominicans. Above the entrance is a frieze of St. Dominic and St. Francis clasping hands. There is also an unusual chapel dedicated to *el Senor del rebozo,* the Lord of the colorful shawls that decorate it. Another outstanding church in walking distance from the *zocalo* is the *Profesa* on the corner of Madero and Isabel la Catolica. Built by the Jesuits, it was preserved by the Oratorians after the Jesuit expulsion. The artwork is outstanding and there are guided tours in Spanish on Saturdays. Toward the Alameda on Madero is the impressive Church of San Francisco and, next door, the small but equally impressive Church of San Felipe de Jesus. Further from the *zocalo* on Isabel la Catolica is the imposing exterior of the Church of San Agustin, confiscated by the government, and now only a shell. Also worth seeing is the exterior of the Church of San Bernardo with its entrance side-panel of the Virgin of Guadalupe. It is located on Carranza and 20th de noviembre.

Also in the central district is the convent in which Sor Juana lived and died. It is now the University of the Claustro de Sor Juana, a private secular college. The church of San Geronimo on its grounds is now an "extemplo," that is, deconsecrated, but in the atrium is the engraved communal crypt of the nuns including the remains of Sor Juana. It can be visited at certain hours. The entrance is at Izazaga 92 between Isabel la Catolica and 5th de febrero.

The once-celebrated center of Catholic learning, the Colegio de San Ildefonso, was turned into the National Preparatory School and is now a museum. It is primarily of architectural interest, but contains some famous Orozco murals. It is at Justo Sierra 16.

There are some beautiful churches and chapels in other parts of Mexico City as well. The Church of Santiago, a sixteenth-century structure made of volcanic rock, is on the *Plaza de las tres culturas.* This was the site of the last battle between the Spaniards and Aztecs. It was also the location of the 1968 massacre of several hundred protesting students by government agents. I would also recommend visits to the Church of San Jacinto in San Angel, San Juan de Bautista in Coyoacan, and the Convent of San Bernardino de Siena in Xochimilco, the exterior of which has some remarkable Indian sculpture.

The major pilgrimage site in Mexico City is, of course, the Basilica of Our Lady of Guadalupe. I recommend acquiring a separate and complete guide as, in addition to the image (the *tilma*), the "old" Basilica, and the museum, there are many other associated features not to be missed.

I would also highly recommend visits to the National Museum of Art and the Franz Mayer Museum, both of which contain splendid works of religious art and artifacts. The Museum of Anthropology in Chapultepec Park is world-famous and justifiably so. It provides a historical perspective on all the indigenous cultures.

Day Trips from Mexico City

Tepotzolan is a short distance north of Mexico City on the road to Queretaro — not to be confused with Tepoztlan, which has some nice churches but is now more of a New Age spiritual center.

Tepotzolan was one of the most important centers of religious education in New Spain. It was turned into a public monument in 1933 and further restored in the early Sixties. It is now the location of the *Museo Nacional del Virreinato* (National Viceregal Museum), which has a remarkable collection of religious art from the colonial period. The stunning

Church of San Francisco Javier and the beautiful *Capilla Domestica* are now part of the museum. During the Christmas season, traditional Nativity plays *(pastorelas)* are performed here. A visit to this museum is highly recommended.

Puebla is one of Mexico's largest cities, well known for its many churches, and its cathedral is considered second only to that of Mexico City. Built in 1649, it has the tallest bell towers in Mexico. Also of interest is the Church of Santo Domingo, originally part of a monastery built in 1611. The Capilla del Rosario with its abundance of gold leaf is considered a treasure of the Indian-influenced *barroco indigena*. The Jesuit Church of Campania once contained the remains of a remarkable figure, *la china poblana* — reputedly once a Chinese princess and considered by the citizens of Puebla to have been a holy woman.

Now a museum, the Ex-Convento de Santa Monica is of historical interest in that it was a clandestine convent from the 1850s to 1934 when the nuns were discovered by government spies. One can see the crypt, chapel, and choir stalls. The church next door, appropriately, contains an image of Our Lord of Wonders *(Maravillas)*. The Ex-Convento de Santa Rosa was the location of a less fortunate group of nuns. Confiscated by the revolutionary government, the structure was turned into barracks. It is now the Museum of Popular Arts *(Museo del arte popular)*. Finally, the Biblioteca Palafoxiana, the extensive book collection of the noted bishop and viceroy Juan Palafox y Mendoza, can be seen as part of the House of Culture *(Casa de Cultura)*.

Cholula, a short drive from Puebla, was a "holy city" for the indigenous. It is the site of the Church of Our Lady of the Remedies *(Nuestra Senora de los Remedios)* built on the top of a massive pyramid related to the mythic figure of Quetzalcoatl. The location offers a view of the volcano Popocatepetl. The Church of Tonantzintla, which has an ornate "Indian baroque" interior, is nearby. Also in the area is the Church of San Francisco Acatepec with an elaborate façade.

Further north, twenty-five miles from Puebla, stands **Tlaxcala**, the location of the Ocotlan Sanctuary, built in 1541 following a vision of the Virgin Mary.

Both Cholula and Tlaxcala are of particular historical interest in that they were on Cortes's route into the Valley of Mexico.

Taxco, the "silver town," popular with visitors, lies in the opposite direction from Mexico City. It is the location of the Church of Santa Prisca y San Sebastian de Maria, built in the years 1529-1552, notable for its frescoes, including a depiction of St. Felipe de Jesus, the first Mexican saint, martyred in the Philippines.

The Northwest

Guadalajara is Mexico's second-largest city, celebrated as the place of origin of mariachis and tequila. On October 12, the city holds its *fiesta* of Our Lady of Zapopan, which features a large procession from the cathedral to the Basilica of Zapopan. This eighteenth-century basilica is the religious center of the city and the icon of the Virgin of Zapopan is displayed in other churches for months prior to the fiesta. The Virgin of Zapopan is also a figure of particular devotion to the Huichol Indians.

The cathedral, constructed in the decades from 1561 to the 1700s, is eclectic in style but impressive. Other notable churches in Guadalajara include the Santa Maria de Gracia and San Augustin.

Central Mexico

The city of **Morelia** boasts the "most beautiful cathedral" in Mexico. Also of interest is the Church of San Francisco and the ornate Church of San Diego. The Jesuit Iglesia de la Compania de Jesus is now a library. The nearby Sanctuary of Our Lady of Guadalupe is naturally the scene of considerable devotion on December 12.

The town of **Patzquaro** and the **Island of Janitzio** are well known for their celebrations of *Los dias de los muertos* (the Days of the Dead) on November 1-2. This is now a religious event heavily impacted by tourism, and accommodations are sometimes difficult to find without advance reservations.

The basilica is notable for its statue of the *Virgen de la salud* ("Virgin of Good Health") and the Templo del Senor Santiago Tupataro celebrates the feast day of St. James on July 25. Patzquaro's plaza has a fountain with a figure of Bishop Vasco de Quiroga, the beloved "Tata Vasco," who did so much to develop the arts and crafts of the region. The Templo de la Compania de Jesus was Don Vasco's first cathedral.

Queretero in the State of Guanajuato is a large modern city and international business center. It was the location of several important historical events, including much of the planning of the 1810 revolt and, later, the execution of Maximilian. It has several lovely churches, including the Church and Ex-Convent of Santa Clara, which contains some striking Baroque *retablos* as altarpieces, and the Church and Ex-Convent of Santa Rosa de Viterbo. The Ex-Convent of San Augustin is now the Museum of Art.

The Jesuits were not the only religious order to contribute to the art and architecture of Mexico. The Franciscans inspired the creation of many magnificent churches, and in the Sierra Gorda mountains near Queretaro are five remarkably beautiful Franciscan missions from the eighteenth century. This is a side trip well worth taking.

San Miguel de Allende is a UNESCO world heritage site, and has preserved much of its eighteenth-century character, making it popular with visitors from around the world. Its most unusual church, *La Parroquia* or "parish" church, is on the Jardin, the main plaza. A local man without formal training, who based his imaginative design on postcards of European cathedrals, reconstructed it. There are several other churches worth visiting, all in walking distance from the Jardin, and there is also the nearby Sanctuary of Atotonilco, established in 1740 by Fr. Luis Felipe Neri Alfaro, and known for its interior of indigenous artwork.

Guanajuato, once the silver capital of New Spain, is one of Mexico's most unusual and attractive cities. The city is built on several hills, and the huge mining tunnels have been converted into underground passages for vehicles so that the streets are pleasantly uncongested. There are several very handsome churches, including the Compania and the Church of San Diego, built by the Franciscans in 1633, and reconstructed after a flood in the eighteenth century. The opulent Church of San Cayetano in nearby La Valenciana is best visited in the afternoon when the sunlight strikes the brilliant gold carvings.

Guanajuato was the birthplace of Diego Rivera, and his family home is now a modest museum. Another historical monument is the large "Granary" *(Alhondiga de granaditas)* on a hilltop where the insurgents overwhelmed the Spanish defenders in 1810, and where, later, the severed heads of Hidalgo, Allende, and others were displayed on the corner spikes. It is now a regional museum. The tallest point in town is *El Pipila,* a monument to a miner turned revolutionary hero. It is reached by a tram and offers a view of the whole area.

Also in the State of Guanajuato is the sanctuary of Christ of the Mountain (Cristo de la Montana) on a mountaintop near Silao at the geographical center of Mexico. The original sanctuary was destroyed during the Cristeros war, and, once restored, now has a museum dedicated to the Cristeros.

San Luis Potosi, a mile high, is the largest and most industrially developed of the former "silver cities" mined by the Spanish. The Plazuela del Carmen, the major square, was originally the site of an extensive Carmelite monastery, and is the location of the church, the Templo del Carmen. Across from the Alameda, the city park, is the magnificent Church of San Jose, which contains a miracle-working statue and many *retablos* attesting to the cures that have taken place. On the Plaza de los Fundadores is the Loreto Chapel with a remarkable Baroque façade. The nearby El Sagrado Corazon was a Jesuit church before the expulsion.

Zacatecas, west of San Luis Potosi, is the most remote of the "silver cities." It sits beneath a tall mountain and has preserved much of its charm by concealing its phone and power lines. There is a cathedral and two churches of note, San Augustin and Santo Domingo.

In the nearby town of **Guadalupe**, on the edge of Zacatecas, there is an active Franciscan monastery as well as a former convent, now a museum (Museo Virreinal de Guadalupe), which contains several outstanding artworks by the celebrated Mexican painters of religious themes, Cabrera, Villalpando, and Correa. Also of interest is the nineteenth-century Capilla de Napoles. The museum contains numerous paintings depicting the life of St. Francis.

The South

The south of Mexico, particularly the State of Tabasco, lost many of their most ancient and beautiful churches during the reign of atheist despots such as Garrido Canabal. More fortunate were the Mayan temples made of massive stones that have resisted the disruptions of Mexico's history.

Merida, only two miles from the famous Chichen Itza ruins, is the city considered the "Gateway to the Yucatan." Its cathedral is the oldest on the continent, built in the years 1561-98. It contains a remarkable statue called the "Christ of the Blisters," which bears the blister-like scars from being struck first by lightning and then finally scorched by anti-religious revolutionaries. The present statue is a replica.

Oaxaca, a favorite spot for travelers, boasts more than twenty churches, many in the distinctive Oaxacan Baroque style. Oaxacans are known to enthusiastically celebrate all of the religious holidays, and their major *fiesta* is that of the Virgin of Soledad on December 18. During Christmas, there is an unusual event called the "Night of the Radishes," featuring a display of sculptures all made from radishes. The Basilica de la Soledad was built in 1690 on a spot where, according to tradition, a burro stopped and refused to move following an appearance of the Virgin Mary. The basilica has a museum containing the lovely vestments, embellished by pearls, which adorn the figure of the Virgin of la Soledad.

Oaxaca's cathedral, built during a two-hundred-year period between 1553 and 1773, has a celebrated Baroque façade, but its interior was plundered by revolutionaries. The Church of San Domingo, built by the Dominicans in the 1550s, however, has a remarkable interior featuring a ceiling depicting the genealogy of St. Dominic. The oldest of the churches in Oaxaca is San Juan de Dios, an adobe structure near the public market, and frequented by vendors.

Chiapas

The hill town of **San Cristobal de Las Casas**, founded in 1528, is often the favorite of travelers in Mexico due to its unspoiled charm and usually pleasant weather. The Museo Templo y Convento Santa Domingo is the best known of the churches, and includes a museum. The Church of San Cristobal, perched high on a hill, is the scene of an annual pilgrimage during the *fiesta* of San Cristobal, July 22 through 25. At the top of the many steps to the church is a *mirador,* a lookout point offering a view of the city. Also highly recommended is a visit to Sna Jolobil (the house of weavers), a weavers' collective that offers a wide variety of their beautiful traditional textiles.

The mestizo townspeople, called *coletos,* run most of the businesses, and there are numerous small hotels and good restaurants. On the outskirts of town are several communities, such as Colonia Palestina, composed of Evangelical converts who were expelled from their native villages.

The indigenous population is sizable in Chiapas and consists of several groups speaking distinct languages, such as Tzotzil, Tzeltal, Zoque, Chol, and Tojolabal. Since the brief period of violence in the 1990s, the area has been relatively calm, though the issue of ethnic autonomy is still largely unresolved.

Two of the towns in the area most visited by travelers are San Juan de Chamula and Zinancantan, which offer striking contrasts as to their religious practices. The "Catholicism" practiced in Chamula remains, in effect, primarily Mayan. The statues inside the church are given the names of saints, but for the worshipers clearly represent various Mayan deities. There is no central altar, and women sit on the straw-covered floor — littered, curiously, with Pepsi Cola bottles — and offer "cures" effected by chicken blood. The Chamulan leaders that head the religious processions often stagger from the effects of *pox* (pronounced "posh"), their traditional alcoholic drink, which produces an ecstatic state integral to the ceremony.

In contrast, the nearby town of Zinancantan has a church adorned with both Catholic and indigenous symbols yet led by a priest who celebrates a traditional Mass. The main industry of the town is flower cultivation, and the atmosphere is distinctly different from Chamula.

In the *altos,* the surrounding mountains, there are numerous villages, such as San Andres Larrainzar, which have wholly indigenous populations. Some are led by women *alcaldes* (mayors) who have achieved their high status through their highly skilled weaving. Visitors to any of the indigenous towns should be cautious and respect the customs of the local people, who frequently object to photographs and also may solicit fees from tourists. The inhabitants of a number of these towns do not speak Spanish, and visitors are advised to hire an established tour guide.

The famous ruins of Palenque are a half-day's drive from San Cristobal.

Appendix Two

Fiestas and Popular Devotions

The *fiesta* and other forms of popular devotion are integral to Mexican life. As in other countries, the major celebrations are during Holy Week *(Semana Santa)* including Easter *(Pascua)* and Christmas *(La Navidad)*. There is also the Day of the Dead *(Dia de los muertos)* and other *fiestas* unique to Mexico such as *El Senor de la Conquista* (the "Lord of the Conquest"). There are also unusual devotional figures, such as *Mano Poderosa* (the "Powerful Hand"), depicted literally in some folk art, and the *Cinco Personas,* the Holy Family plus St. Anne and St. Zechariah. There are also processions of the *Senor de la Columna* (the "Lord of the Column"), which depicts Jesus bound to a column during the flagellation.

There are numerous pilgrimage sites and sanctuaries, such as San Juan de los Lagos in Michoacan, and Nuestro Senor del Rayo in Jalisco. It would be best to consult local Church authorities regarding participation in these events.

There are reportedly more than seventeen hundred separate sites or sanctuaries devoted to the Virgin Mary in Mexico. The numerous devotions include that of Our Lady of Guadalupe, but also, among others, *Remedios* ("Remedies"), *Dolores* ("Sorrows"), *Merced* ("Mercy"), and *Refugio*

("Refuge"). This last was the focus of a major devotion in the nineteenth century. Her image was derived from a Greek icon of the "merciful Virgin" who offered refuge to sinners. Her gilded mantle bore symbols of the names of the Holy Family (HIS — Jesus, M — Mary, IPH — Joseph). These Marian sites are concrete manifestations of both the ancient Mediterranean focus on the Virgin as a figure of unconditional mercy and indigenous spiritual themes.

Among the devotions brought from Spain is that of *El Santo Nino de Atocha* ("The Holy Child Jesus of Atocha"). This is a fifteenth-century Spanish votive figure from Atocha in Andalusia near Madrid. Jesus is depicted as an ordinary child who brings water and bread to the Christian prisoners of the Moors. An image of the Virgin of Atocha was brought to Plateros in the mining country of Zacatecas during a time of harsh exploitation, and this also became a devotion of travelers going to and from New Mexico.

Also among the lesser-known Spanish devotions is that of *San Ramon Nonato* (Raymond Nonnatus), whose name derives from his cesarean birth. He was the Spanish cardinal of Aragon who in 1218 founded the order of Mercedarios (Mercedarians). He is the patron saint of women giving birth and of endangered infants.

Semana Santa: Holy Week in Mexico

Here are some of my impressions of Holy Week in San Miguel de Allende:

Palm Sunday (Domingo de Ramos)

Palm Sunday began with two long processions from the opposite sides of town to the central church. In one procession, a young man portraying Jesus, was riding a burro, and in the other, a statue of Jesus was borne by singers, surrounded by dancers, many of them indigenous. Thousands of the faithful crowded into the central plaza, overflowing the church. The statue of Christ was carried toward the altar as everyone cheered, and waved palm branches and crosses sold by numerous *vendedores* along the way, some of them children. The cheering, almost the chant of a sports crowd, concluded with cries of *"Viva Cristo Rey!"* There were so many people jammed into the church that the priests had to squeeze their way among us to offer communion, as no one could move, much less form a line. The solemnities to come couldn't suppress the continuous victorious chant of "Honor and glory to Christ!"

Holy Week, incomparably complex and many-layered, offers something more than we can easily absorb or understand.

The statue of Christ, carried into the church on Palm Sunday, remained at the side altar for Monday Mass. A children's choir was accompanied by a brass band, playing the traditional music heard also at the Passion play performances held during the week. A very old priest spoke at great length — simple words, yet eloquent.

On Wednesday, there was another remarkable procession at the end of the day, a few hundred people this time, including a band, statues, and many women carrying symbolic objects, such as flowers, birds, and food. This is the *fiesta* of "the Lord of the Blows" *(golpes),* an integral part of the Passion. The people performed the Stations of the Cross, which are marked not only on the walls of the churches but on various public buildings. Again, it was an extraordinary blend of piety, tourism, carnival, passion, and indifference — all in one.

At the weekday noon masses, people were displaying the older forms of piety, kneeling at length and approaching the altar on their knees — an old Mexican tradition, yet it was the Mexican tourists who had to be admonished by the priest to keep quiet.

Holy Thursday

The Holy Thursday service was more than two-and-a-half hours long. Three priests washed the feet of young men dressed as apostles. This was after three processions to the altar presenting the gifts of different sanctifying oils and before a very long sermon by one of the young priests. There were so many people that, again, the priests had to move among us to give communion — this time in both species, dipping the host in the wine. Then, to conclude, another procession ended at a side altar — a beautiful fountain with flowers and a decorated space, which represented

Christ's tomb. And outside, there was so much drumming, music, and noise that it sounded like Carnival.

Good Friday (Viernes Santo)

The side chapel contains the funeral bier of Jesus, and a stream of people came by, some briefly kneeling, some simply making signs of the cross. Outside, the plaza was even more crowded with a large gathering of tourists. Everyone, of whatever nationality, seemed to have a tiny camera. At about noon there was a reenactment of the condemnation of Jesus (a bloodied statue) with fully costumed centurions, a Pontius Pilate who shouted his lines, and a rough-looking Barabbas. The carefully enunciated Spanish naturally sounds much like Latin and the ancient church and crowds of poor people provided a biblical ambience.

At the conclusion of the "trial," there was a procession with additional statues and centurions on horseback. Within the hour, another procession arrived, again with statues of Jesus, Mary, and Joseph. The stone statue of Jesus carrying the cross, a centurion next to him, was particularly powerful and was followed by the children's choir singing the regional liturgical music. The two processions more or less converged, and there was a prayer ceremony in front of the church. The priest could not be heard from the center of the crowded plaza as a carnival mood prevailed, respectful but noisy.

The final and the largest procession of the week then took place at the end of the day with well over six hundred participants, including the singing children and a male choir. The streets were packed, probably twenty to twenty-five thousand people within a few blocks, yet the crowds were remarkably respectful, considering that the procession started late, stopped at times for as much as ten minutes, and took well over an hour. The sun set on a holy and remarkable day.

Holy Saturday

A quiet day of reflection.

Easter Sunday (Pascua)

A beautiful day and a conclusion to a remarkable week. The early morning weather was warm, but the plaza was virtually empty as were most of the streets, still blocked off from the past processions. The few people on the street gave me warm greetings.

I went to the eight A.M. mass at the parish church. As the mass began, I was suddenly so caught up in a spirit of joy that I held on so that it wouldn't sweep me away. Afterwards, during the morning, I strolled to three other churches where masses were in progress. I passed by all three masses when the Alleluia was being sung and thought that this is what life was meant to be — an endless Alleluia sung everywhere.

Good Friday and Easter are, in a sense, one single event in that they exist beyond time and, thus, simultaneously. Easter "follows" Good Friday only in our sequential concept of time.

It is as if one saw Jesus on the cross through one of those early kaleidoscopes that could create a single image by spinning many. The Crucified and Risen Christ would become an overlapping one — a single image of Jesus dying and rising. Our Buddhist friends would see this as the reflection of a greater reality and so, I think, would our saints. It's a concept that can challenge and puzzle us, but if we grasp the image, it might change our lives.

Jesus lives to die again and rise again. It has been a blessed week, both a beginning and an end, one and the same.

Day of the Dead (*Dia de los Muertos*, November 1 and 2)

Following Easter and Christmas, the religious celebration most attended by visitors, and promoted by the Mexican tourist industry, is the Day of the Dead — actually "days" — on November 1 and 2. These are, in fact, the traditional All Saints and All Souls Days commemorated in the churches. There is, however, an almost desperate effort on the part of civic authorities, particularly in the Federal District, to secularize these holy days into a Mexican version of Halloween. This recognition of the inevitability of death is advertised, literally, as a raucous "celebration of life," with empty slogans such as, "Remembering the dead inspires more life!" What the advertising is meant to inspire is more revenue for restaurants and bars. The fundamental contradiction in Mexican contemporary culture — the tension between its Catholic foundations and its commercialism — is nowhere more apparent than during this time.

Nonetheless, the religious roots of the tradition remain strong among most Mexicans, and there are masses and candlelight vigils celebrating the "days." The cemeteries — and not just the nightclubs — are filled with people remembering and honoring loved ones. The slogans deceive no one. One can present a brave face that looks straight at death; but without faith, it is as vacuous as the hollow candy skulls.

The *Día de los muertos* tradition stems from an integration of pre-Hispanic rites with Catholic beliefs. The dead were often buried in tombs in or near their homes in earlier times. Recognizing that life continues on some mysterious level, family and friends memorialize their dead by creating *ofrendas,* elaborate "altars" composed of flowers, food and drink, photos, personal items, and religious images. Most of these "altars" are either in homes or at gravesites, and the cemeteries are filled with people truly celebrating the lives of the beloved dead. Other "altars," some quite large, are constructed in public places, some as communal tributes to various groups of people, such as officials, artists, or police officers.

The indigenous belief was that the souls of the dead return to their burial places once a year as a form of communion with the living. If buried in cemeteries, the dead are sometimes guided back to their homes by paths of flower petals. The souls of deceased children return at midnight on October 31; adults on November 1. The objects in the *ofrenda* include food, drink, and symbols of what the deceased enjoyed in life. The spirits are believed to consume the essence of the offerings, and the family then shares the food and drink afterwards.

There is a great deal of traditional art, much of it ingenious and humorous, related to the Day of the Dead, including *catrinas,* the adorned skeletons of women, and sugar skulls bearing a person's name. *Pan de muertos* is special bread baked for the occasion, and marigolds are the traditional flowers that decorate the "altars" and graves.

In many of the contemporary promotional efforts, there is an emphasis on the indigenous origins of the tradition, thus separating the event from its equally Catholic roots. This leads to some distortion of the indigenous concepts as well. The original rites were neither a tribute to nor a defiance of death but an ancient ritual of regeneration in which the dead were seen as "seeds" for new life to come, a belief compatible with Catholic faith (1 Cor. 15:35-45).

The efforts to commercialize what is essentially a deeply religious event may also reflect the different concepts of death that emerge from the intense urbanization taking place in Mexico City. The urban dweller with little or no communal life, and even with diminishing family contacts, tends to experience death as an isolated and meaningless personal tragedy.

Human nature, however, doesn't change. Now combined with Halloween and photo-snapping tourism, there is a party atmosphere throughout the two days of *Dia de los muertos;* but if one observes carefully, there is genuine prayer as well as mourning beneath the veneer.

Holy Innocents (December 28)

A key to understanding the deepest roots of traditional Mexican Catholicism is found, I believe, in the attitude toward suffering. Though inevitable, it is seen as a Christ-like offering to God.

In the past, the Feast of the Holy Innocents was related to another tradition, that of the *Nina Muerta* — literally "the dead little girl." While it is now seldom seen, I think it is worth examination in that it illustrates this still-underlying attitude.

The death of a child, under any circumstances, is one of the greatest tragedies that human beings suffer. In Mexico, the death rate, not just of infants but of children under the age of seven, was quite high as late as the 1930s, and remains much higher than in the United States. In response to this tragedy, an unusual devotion appeared, centered on deceased children, especially little girls.

The practice, common as late as the 1950s, was to dress the dead child and then take photos of her or him often in the arms of the mother. A little girl was dressed to represent the Immaculate Conception while a little boy was often dressed as St. Joseph. They wore paper booties, and the photos or, more rarely, paintings showed displays of flowers, particularly lilies. The subsequent funeral procession was also primarily composed of children, the boys in white and the girls dressed as angels.

A collection of these photos can be seen in a special edition of *Artes de Mexico,* and they are heartbreaking. The seemingly passive acceptance of the usually poor mother makes the image even harder to bear.

The child that dies after baptism is still deemed an *angelito,* a pure soul who goes directly to heaven. The child dying before baptism goes to purgatory, but has a less certain role because it has not been given a (baptismal) name that can be invoked. Godparents play an important role in all of the ceremonies and assist financially.

Children in Mexico once wrote letters to the Virgin, petitioning her to care for their souls. The letters were then burned on the Feast of the Assumption so that, in keeping with primarily indigenous beliefs, the message could rise to heaven.

We must remember that until modern times, children, especially in poor countries, were treated as and expected to act like adults; and yet they were to remain pure and innocent.

The recognition of the suffering caused by the death of children has, of course, deep biblical roots:

> In Ramah is heard the sound of moaning,
> of bitter weeping!
> Rachel mourns her children,
> She refuses to be consoled
> Because her children are no more.
>
> (Jeremiah 31:15)

The Holy Innocents in the Gospels, the children slaughtered by Herod in his vain attempt to prevent the coming of the Messiah, were the first martyrs, that is, the first to die for Christ. As the prayer of the Mass of the Holy Innocents declares:

> The Holy Innocents offered you praise
> by the death they suffered for Christ.

This cult of the *Nina Muerta* was also directly related to the concept of the Immaculate Conception and the ideal of virgin purity.

The response of a contemporary Mexican poet is, however, more reflective of contemporary feelings: *"There is nothing to celebrate in this sleep."* The noted author Albert Camus explained his resistance to Christian faith by his refusal to worship a God who allowed the death of innocent children.

This is an understandable and all-too-human response. Few of us, facing the loss of our own child, could honestly feel differently. The American response to the death of children from any cause is, "It must never happen again!" And yet it does.

The tragedy of the death of a child makes the concept of the child's funeral as a "coronation" or celebration provocative and, for some, offensive. It is also somewhat puzzling to conceive of the deceased child — the *angelito* or little angel — becoming a mediator in our lives.

This is challenging to us as American Catholics because our culture has no equivalent. It also points to the paradox of our contemporary spirituality: The more we try to protect ourselves and our children against the threat of suffering and death, the more vulnerable we seem to become.

Notwithstanding the pain and discomfort these images inflict on us, I believe that, in essence, the *Nina Muerta* is a deeply Christian devotion. The poor grieving mothers who posed for what are clearly imitations of the *Pieta* did not have theological concepts to guide them, nor were they commemorating an event in the Scriptures. What they sensed was the power of the Incarnation — and its price. "The Word was made flesh" and the human body at any stage is subject to pain and death. In the final analysis, what these mothers "imitated," even more than the example of Christ, perhaps, was that of his Mother, who also knew what it meant to lose a child.

Nacimiento (La Navidad) — Christmas in Mexico

Christmas — the Christ Mass — celebrates the *nacimiento*, that is, the birth of Christ. Unlike Easter, the most universal Christian holiday, Christmas in Mexico is unique — delightfully so — and quite characteristically Mexican. I think that this, in part, is due to the Mexican desire to retain their identity through traditional devotions while, at the same time, experiencing the possibility of the new and unexpected. What holiday celebrates both renewal and the birth of the new more fully than Christmas?

The festive colorful devotional art related to Christmas has a special charm. Extraordinary in its craftsmanship, this popular art is the culmination of a long and rich tradition, yet displays unique and personal stylistic elements.

St. Francis created the traditional depiction of the Christmas story in the thirteenth century. Reportedly, it included not only the manger scene and carols, but live animals. The Franciscan friars then adapted these Nativity plays in ways with which the indigenous could identify, offering the maternal figure of Mary as well as incorporating elements of a traditional agricultural festival. Father Motolinia wrote of the Indian enthusiasm for these events. Songs and flowers were also incorporated, both important elements in Indian ritual life. The poinsettia — *noche buena* in Spanish, the flower of the "good night" or Christmas Eve — originated as the *cuetlaxochil,* the Aztec "flower of purity."

By the seventeenth century, the carols, called *tocotins* by the Indians, were an established musical form, and Sor Juana composed at least one. During this time, the European images of Christ as a child were appearing in finely wrought Mexican and Guatemalan silver statuettes with a high degree of craftsmanship and art. During the nineteenth century, a growing awareness of Mexican identity led these artisans to imagine the manger as a typical Mexican locale with distinctly Mexican figures.

Apparently, it was the Augustinians who introduced the *posada* tradition — the procession that re-creates the Holy Family seeking shelter at an inn, a *posada.* Over time, I've trailed several of these processions through the streets, mixing with throngs of candle-bearing, singing participants, as well as live burros and sheep. The custom is to stop and receive gifts and the hospitality of friends and neighbors, and many shops are highly decorated for the occasion. One of the most delightful *posadas* I have witnessed was that from an orphanage, with children as the Holy Family. Mary, riding on a burro, was perhaps twelve, and obviously chosen for her composure, while Joseph, complete with sombrero and penciled moustache, was probably the same age but a foot shorter.

Retablos, Milagros, and *Ex-votos*

The *retablo* — the word is a contraction of *retra-tabla,* "behind the altar" — is actually a form of *ex-voto* that is a propitious offering for atonement or of thanks. The *retablo* is a painting, usually on wood, depicting the actions of a particular holy figure, often a miraculous intervention or cure. A *milagro* is a smaller work or object that is also a form of thanks for a miracle and is pinned to, or placed by, a statue or altar. An *ex-voto* relates to a vow or *voto* connected with petitional prayer.

This has been described as "curative art" and is often the work of ordinary people, many living in poverty and isolation, which nonetheless expresses the relationship between faith and beauty. It is a popular form that may have a magical appeal but is, nonetheless, genuinely religious art. As with all of the various devotions in Mexican Catholic culture, these objects relate to the redemption that we receive through Christ's Resurrection.

Some additional dates to remember in Mexico:

January 17 — Blessings of the Animals
February 2 — Candelaria (Candlemass)
First Friday in March — Our Lord of the Conquest
May 3 — Santa Cruz (Holy Cross)
June 29 — Santos Pedro y Pablo (Peter and Paul)
September 29 — San Miguel (St. Michael the Archangel)
October 4 — San Francisco (St. Francis)
November 21 — Christ the King (Cristo rey)
December 7 — San Juan Diego
December 12 — Our Lady of Guadalupe

Acknowledgments

A s is evident from the frequent citations, I am deeply indebted to Octavio Paz, whose work, poetic and critical, has inspired me as it has countless others for decades.

I have also incurred debts to many historians, anthropologists, and other scholars whose knowledge proved to be invaluable as well as accessible to a non-specialist. I have strived to accurately report their assessments even when they differed from mine. They include, most particularly, Jan Bazant, Marjorie Becker, Louis Dupre, Umberto Eco, J. H. Elliott, James Lockhart, Jean Meyer, Oswaldo Nardo, Jaroslav Pelikan, Teofilo Ruiz, and George Tavard.

Much of the chapter on Jesuit spirituality and the arts draws on the insights of Alfonso Alfaro, Director of the Research Institute of Mexican Art, whose article "The Burning Bush: Aesthetics and Mysticism" can be found in *Artes de Mexico,* issue number 70, 2004. A thorough examination of Jesuit accomplishments in New Spain can be found in two editions of *Artes de Mexico.*

Carl Anderson and Msgr. Eduardo Chavez wisely chose a devotional approach to Our Lady of Guadalupe in their popular study. While I have attempted to address some of the broader historical questions, I have gained much from their work. I also learned much from the insights of Paul Badde, Msgr. Virgilio Elizondo, and Jose Luis Guerrero as well as from the more critical but meticulous scholarship of Fr. Stafford Poole. I trust that all our views converge in faith and charity.

My personal guides for many years have been Pope John Paul II, Jacques Maritain, Henri de Lubac, Chiara Lubich, and Rene Girard. I hope that this work reflects at least some of their faith and acumen. I have also been blessed by spiritual directors who, over the years, became friends as well as teachers: Fr. Denis Meehan, Fr. Ralph Weishaar, Fr. Patrick Boyle, and Fr. Anthony Scannell. I owe them all much more than can be expressed.

I wish to thank many friends and colleagues for their support and valuable insights, including Gil Bailie, Carlos Bajo, Cecilia Gonzalez-Andrieu, George Moore, Martha Elena Rodriguez, and Leah Buturain Schneider.

My colleagues at the Windhover Forum — Michael Feeley, Sister Margaret Devlin, Lino Lauro, Gabriel Meyer, Leah Buturain Schneider, and Fr. Alexei Smith — have provided friendship as well as encouragement, as have my interfaith "spiritual brothers," Jim Carolla, Rabbi Scott Shapiro, and Paul Wolff.

My daughters, Teresa and Bethe, provided not only their love and support but, at times, food and shelter; and my thanks to Larry and Rick and my grandsons, Alex and Ben, for so generously sharing their time and space. A special thanks to Bethe for locating many of the book's splendid images.

The late Murray Goodman played an important role in introducing me to Mexico. His wife, Beatriz Contreras, son Michael, and I share many memories of this dear friend. To his and my *companeros* around the table in the plaza in Coyoacan — especially Pepe, Luis, and Lourdes — *gracias a todos*. My years in San Miguel de Allende have been especially enriched by the friendship of Federico Cervantes and Ildika Lakatos and Jim and Blanca Giampaoli. My old friends Mardi and Eugenio Cordero are also woven into my life and share memories of some delightful times in Vera Cruz.

My thanks to Sandra DeGroot, Bill Eerdmans, and all those at Eerdmans Publishing for making hard work a pleasure.

Once again, I am deeply indebted to my friend and editor Gabriel Meyer who has done much to shape the form and deepen the content of this book.

Benevolently gracing all of us has been Our Lady of Guadalupe who, I pray, will continue to draw us closer together. *Gracias a nuestra senora, madre de todos.*

Select Bibliography

Anderson, Carl, and Msgr. Eduardo Chavez. *Our Lady of Guadalupe.* New York: Doubleday, 2009.

Badde, Paul. *Maria of Guadalupe.* Ft. Collins: Ignatius, 2008. (English.)

Badde, Paul. *La Morenita.* Mexico DF: Buena Prensa, 2004. (Spanish.)

Bazant, Jan. *A Concise History of Mexico.* New York: Cambridge University Press, 1977.

Becker, Marjorie. *Setting the Virgin on Fire.* Berkeley: University of California Press, 1996.

Benedict XVI. *Jesus of Nazareth.* New York: Doubleday, 2007.

Bruno, Friar. *St. John of the Cross.* Whitefish, MT: Kessinger, 2003.

Casarella, Peter, and George Schuer, SJ, editors. *The Thoughts of Louis Dupre: Christianity and the Culture of Modernity.* Grand Rapids: Eerdmans, 1988.

Congar, Yves, O.P. *The Meaning of Tradition.* Ft. Collins: Ignatius, 2004.

Dulles, John W. F. *Yesterday in Mexico, 1919-1936.* Austin: University of Texas, 1961.

Eco, Umberto. *Art and Beauty in the Middle Ages.* New Haven: Yale University Press, 1986.

Elizondo, Msgr. Virgilio. *Guadalupe: Mother of the New Creation.* Maryknoll, NY: Orbis Books, 1997.

Elliott, John H. *Imperial Spain, 1469-1716*. New Haven: Yale University Press, 1989.

Elliott, John H. *Spain: Its World, 1500-1700*. New Haven: Yale University Press, 1989.

Fox, Vicente. *Revolution of Hope*. New York: Penguin, 2007.

Greene, Graham. *The Power and the Glory.* New York: Penguin Classics, 2003.

Greene, Graham. *The Lawless Roads*. New York: Penguin Classics, 2006.

Guerrero, Jose Luis. *Flor y canto del nacimiento de mexico*. Mexico DF: Ciudad de Mexico, 1990. (Spanish.)

Henry, Robert S. *The Story of the Mexican American War*. Indianapolis: Bobbs-Merrill, 1950.

John Paul II. *Redemptoris Mater* (encyclical). San Francisco: Ignatius, 1988.

Kasl, Ronda, editor. *Sacred Spain* (catalogue). Indianapolis Museum of Art. New Haven and London: Yale University Press, 2009.

Krauze, Enrique. *Mexico: Biography of Power.* New York: Harper-Collins, 1998.

Lasch, Christopher. *The Culture of Narcissism*. New York: W. W. Norton, 1979.

Le Clezio, J. M. G. *The Mexican Dream*. Chicago: University of Chicago Press, 1993.

Lewis, Oscar. *Tlepotzlan: Village in Mexico*. New York: Holt, Rinehart and Winston, 1960.

Lockhart, James. *The Nahuas after the Spanish Conquest*. Stanford: Stanford University Press, 1992.

Matovina, Timothy, and Gerald Pozo, editors. *Presente! U.S. Latino Catholics from Colonial Origins to the Present*. Maryknoll, NY: Orbis Books, 2000.

Meyer, Jean. *La Cristada*. 3 volumes. 1975-78. (Spanish.)

Meyer, Jean. *Tierra de cristeros*. University of Guadalajara, 2002. (Spanish.)

Meyer, Michael C., and William H. Beezley, editors. *Oxford History of Mexico*. New York: Oxford University Press, 2000.

Museo, Franz Mayer. *Retablos y Exvotos*. Mexico DF: Artes de Mexico, 2000.

Navone, John, SJ. *Toward a Theology of Beauty.* Collegeville: Liturgical Press, 1996.

Parsons, Elsie Clews. *Mitla: Town of Souls*. Chicago: University of Chicago Press, 1936.

Paz, Octavio. *Collected Poetry.* New York: New Directions, 1991.

Paz, Octavio. *Labyrinth of Solitude.* New York: Grove Press, 1961.

Paz, Octavio. *Sor Juana: Traps of Faith*. Cambridge, MA: Harvard University Press, 1990.

Peers, E. Allison. *Studies of the Spanish Mystics*. 2 volumes. London: Sheldon Press, 1930.

Pelikan, Jaroslav. *The Christian Tradition: A History of the Development of Doctrine*. Volume 3: *The Growth of Medieval Theology*. New Haven: Yale University Press, 1973-90.

Perez, Arturo, editor. *Asi Es: Stories of Hispanic Spirituality*. Collegeville: Liturgical Press, 1994.

Poole, Stafford, C.M. *Our Lady of Guadalupe: The Origins and Sources of a Mexican National Symbol, 1531-1797*. Tucson: University of Arizona Press, 1995.

Prescott, William H. *The History of the Conquest of Mexico and the History of the Conquest of Peru*. New York: Random House, 1979.

Restall, Matthew. *Seven Myths of the Spanish Conquest*. New York: Oxford University Press, 2003.

Ricoeur, Paul. *Memory, History and Forgetting*. Chicago: University of Chicago Press, 2004.

Riding, Alan. *Distant Neighbors: A Portrait of the Mexicans*. New York: Vintage/Anchor, 1987.

Rieff, Philip. *The Triumph of the Therapeutic: The Uses of Faith after Freud*. Chicago: University of Chicago Press, 1966.

Rodriguez, Richard. *Days of Obligation: An Argument with My Mexican Father*. New York: Viking, 1992.

Ruiz, Teofilo. "Spanish Society, 1400-1600." In *Social History of Europe*. Upper Saddle River, NJ: Pearson Education, 2002.

Ruiz, Teofilo. "The Other 1492: Ferdinand, Isabella and the Making of an Empire." Course 899. The Teaching Company.

Tavard, George H. *Juana Ines de la Cruz and the Theology of Beauty: The First Mexican Theology*. Notre Dame: University of Notre Dame Press, 1991.

St. Teresa of Avila, anthologies:
  The Soul's Passion for God, edited by Keith Beasley-Topliffe. Nashville: Upper Room Books, 1997.
  Ecstasy and Common Sense, edited by Tessa Bielecki. Boston: Shambhala, 1996.

Toor, Francis. *Treasury of Mexican Folkways*. New York: Crown, 1947.

Trueblood, Alan. *Sor Juana Anthology*. Cambridge, MA: Harvard University Press, 1990.

Unamuno, Miguel de. *The Tragic Sense of Life*. New York: Cosimo Classics, 2005.

Walsh, William Thomas. *St. Teresa of Avila*. Charlotte, NC: TAN Books, 2009.

The *Artes de Mexico* publication is without question one of the most outstanding — and beautiful — journals published anywhere. Among the issues that I found invaluable, all of which are bilingual, were *The Day of the Dead, Visions of Guadalupe, Jesuits and Art, Jesuits and Education, Nacimiento, La Nina Muerta, Queretero,* and *San Miguel de Allende.*

Like many other visually impaired persons, I am grateful to those organizations which provide valuable works in audio editions, including the National Library for the Blind, the Now You Know Catholic studies, The Mars Hill audio journal, The Great Courses, the Teaching Company, the Rev. Raymond Brown biblical studies on Welcome Recordings, and, most particularly, the Gil Bailie lectures on religion and culture made possible by the Cornerstone Forum.

Index